Additional Praise for Lyn Di Iorio Sandín's *Killing Spanish*:

"Lyn Di Iorio Sandín's *Killing Spanish* ventures remarkably into uncharted territory, appreciably widening the available scope for studying US Caribbean/Latino literary texts. Drawing on psychoanalytically nuanced literary criticism and contemporary cultural studies, the author identifies allegory as the trope par excellence for scrutinizing the fragmented identities that parade the pages of the novels she examines and in so doing illustrates the value of attending to rhetorical and aesthetic features as critical tools capable of unleashing the cultural and political meaning of Latino literature. She investigates the role of Spanish as a site in relation to which her writers construct notions of family, national origins, and cultural roots, while considering the possible rapport between the allegorical realism of the Latino fiction writers covered in her study and the magical realism of the major Latin American figures one might regard as their literary ancestors. Clearly written and sensitively argued, this study provides a fresh inquiry into the distinct behavior of US Caribbean/Latino literary texts. On the whole we have here a scholarly intervention that, in steering clear of the overused explanatory conventions to which Latino texts are habitually subjected, constitutes an invigorating contribution to the field."

—Silvio Torres-Saillant, Director of the Latino-Latin
American Studies Program, Syracuse University

KILLING SPANISH

LITERARY ESSAYS ON AMBIVALENT U.S. LATINO/A IDENTITY

LYN DI IORIO SANDÍN

First published in 2004 by
PALGRAVE MACMILLAN™
175 Fifth Avenue, New York, N.Y. 10010 and
Houndmills, Basingstoke, Hampshire, England RG21 6XS
Companies and representatives throughout the world

PALGRAVE MACMILLAN is the global academic imprint of the Palgrave Macmillan division of St. Martin's Press, LLC and of Palgrave Macmillan Ltd. Macmillan® is a registered trademark in the United States, United Kingdom and other countries. Palgrave is a registered trademark in the European Union and other countries.

ISBN 1–4039–6394–0 hardback

Library of Congress Cataloging-in-Publication Data

Sandín, Lyn Di Iorio, 1964–
    Killing Spanish : literary essays on ambivalent U.S. Latino/a identity / Lyn Di Iorio Sandín.
        p. cm.
    Includes bibliographical references and index.
    ISBN 1–4039–6394–0
    1. American literature—Hispanic American authors—History and criticism. 2. Hispanic Americans—Intellectual life. 3. Assimilation (Sociology) in literature. 4. Hispanic Americans in literature. 5. Group identity in literature. 6. Ambivalence in literature. 7. Minorities in literature. 8. Ethnicity in literature. I. Title.

PS153.H56.S36 2004
860.9'868—dc22   2004040120

A catalogue record for this book is available from the British Library.

Design by Newgen Imaging Systems (P) Ltd., Chennai, India.

First edition: November 2004
10   9   8   7   6   5   4   3   2   1

Printed in the United States of America.

For Mami and Enrique.
And for Daddy who is still with me in many ways.

Contents

ACKNOWLEDGMENTS

I am grateful to many people who contributed in a variety of ways to this book. The following friends and colleagues read and commented on parts of it at different stages in its composition: Juan Flores, Rose Glickman, Laura Hinton, Geraldine Murphy, Genaro Padilla, José David Saldívar, and Silvio Torres-Saillant. Dorothy Wang was enthusiastic about the project from the beginning. When the book was reaching its conclusion, Fred Reynolds, then chair of the English department at the City College of New York, helped me obtain a small but crucial research stipend. Carla Cappetti's incisive, then unpublished, article "The Beast in the Garden: History and Nature in *Their Eyes Were Watching God*" helped me clarify my ideas about the speaking donkey in Loida Maritza Pérez's novel, discussed in chapter four. Elizabeth Mazzola read the whole manuscript at one point. Without her coruscating yet subtle wit, which dispelled my occasional doubts, and her insightful commentary, I would not have been able to finish the project. My greatest debt of all goes to Richard Pérez who not only read the manuscript countless times but who on many occasions became my eyes and hands at the library thereby freeing me up to write at points in the process when time was of the essence.

Not only did the late Edward Rivera read and comment on two chapters, his ghost also impelled the writing of chapter five and still haunts my work. Two City College of New York Eisner fellowships and one Center for Puerto Rican Studies award released me from some teaching duties so I could write. Félix Matos Rodríguez at the CUNY Center for Puerto Rican Studies located at Hunter College (the Centro) set up a special forum where an all-Latino/a audience responded to my ideas about U.S. Latino allegory. Xavier Totti published an early version of chapter five in *The Centro Journal* (Spring 2002, Volume XIV, No. 1).

A chance encounter at a gallery in Old San Juan in May 2003 led to my discovery of the work of Manuel Neri. A photograph of his beautiful painting *Indios Verdes No. 4* graces the cover of *Killing Spanish*. I am thankful for the artist's permission to reproduce a work whose mood helps set the tone for my book. Kathy Roe's insights into Edward Rivera aided in the shaping of the memoir portion of chapter five. David Unger helped me make speedy contact with Marina Tristán. I am grateful to Ms. Tristán and Nicolás Kanellos, both at Arte Público Press in Houston, Texas, for so quickly granting permission to reproduce Miguel Piñero's "A Lower East Side Poem." Jorge Matos at the Centro came to the rescue at the last minute with a vital research tidbit. Aida Lugo and the library staff at the Centro de Estudios Avanzados de Purerto Rico y el Caribe, in Old San Juan, Puerto Rico, helped me locate vital newspaper articles for chapter three on Rosario Ferré.

All the students who have taken my U.S. Latino and Caribbean literature classes at CCNY have influenced me through their enthusiastic engagement with many texts that are still considered marginal by American literature scholars. Former graduate students Ruth Fuglistaller, Rod Jackman, Nailah Moonsamy, and Leigh Shulman stood out for their feedback on some of the ideas in the book as did former undergraduate Elaine Chanza for her research efforts.

My editor Amanda Johnson's wonderfully buoyant attitude and incredible efficiency, and Laura Morrison's painstaking attention to detail, made the editorial process pleasurable; the production staff at Palgrave and Newgen labored tirelessly to turn the book into a finished product. I was delighted to work with all of them.

Finally, I would like to thank my family. My mother Esther Di Iorio Sandín has always inspired me with her faith in me and her fierce will to overcome the most difficult circumstances. Ina Martínez pointed out her strong emotional investment in my work, noting that in many ways it has been fed by "family energy." The book would have been a different product without Enrique Martínez. He carried out some significant research and was a sounding board for many ideas. Above all he nourished me with his deep love and spiritual comradery.

CHAPTER ONE
INTRODUCTION: TOWARD A TYPOLOGY OF U.S. LATINO/A LITERATURE

The protagonists of contemporary U.S. Latino/a fiction are caught in a bind.[1] On the one hand, they face the pressures of assimilation into mainstream American culture. On the other, they are profoundly enmeshed in families closely tied to their communities of origin. Due to the proximity of the places of provenance—Cuba, the Dominican Republic, Puerto Rico, Mexico—to New York, Miami, and Los Angeles, the settings for the novels examined in this book, and the persistent use of Spanish both as pure and hybrid marker, families are idealized by protagonists as close to the Latin American or Caribbean "source." To resolve the predicament, the protagonists in the fictions I examine project desires that are unacceptable in the U.S. mainstream onto their dark doubles—mothers, sisters, wives, sometimes even fathers and brothers—alternate, allegorized, versions of the self. Madness and death are most often the fates of these doubles: this is how the seven U.S. Latino and Latina writers I examine deal with aspects of the self that are entrenched in a rather more communitarian, undifferentiated way of being in the world.

Doubles (Mad, Black, and Dead)

This book is not an exhaustive study of all contemporary U.S. Latino/a fiction. However, the typology I describe also applies to texts by other U.S. Latino and Latina writers.[2] Although the authors chose English as their language of creative expression, they are all, in different ways, bound to Spanish, be it broken or pure, and bound to a memory or an awareness—sometimes more powerfully to a denial— of the lands of origin. The Puerto Rican Rosario Ferré, the Cuban American Cristina García, the Dominican American Loida Maritza Pérez, the Nuyorican Edward Rivera, and the Chicana Yxta Maya Murray ascribe "dangerous" or unassimilable traits of U.S. Latino/a identity to characters (male and female) who, due to madness, or a violent anger, are better able to both deploy and resist features of U.S. Latino/a identity than their counterparts, the sane protagonists, who behave following more normative standards. In texts by these writers the double is often a dead mother, or is methonymically related to a dead mother, sacrificed by the text for her unassimilable qualities. It is the conventional realist protagonists, however, whose ambivalence generates the doubles that act against them or against the established order. In much the same way, according to Angus Fletcher's still definitive study of allegory, the Renaissance allegorical hero generated subcharacters, doubles who opposed, or sided with, him in his struggle.[3] The abundance of textual doubles characterizes both medieval, and contemporary U.S. Latino/a, allegory. Although I may not be the first critic to notice that many contemporary U.S. Latino/a texts are allegorical, this book is the first in-depth study of the phenomenon.[4]

In the work of two other writers, the dynamic varies. In the short stories of the Dominican American Junot Díaz, persistent triangulation of characters dominates the stories as much as doubling. Díaz's double character is sometimes a sensitive male who must be sacrificed for the ambivalent triumph of a self-destructive machismo. At other times this sensitive male is the protagonist. When the suffering and/or mad mother appears in these stories, she is quite different from the madwoman in the work of the women writers and of Rivera: In Díaz's stories she is a woman whom suffering has frozen into almost total passivity and affective withdrawal. In Piri Thomas's seminal autobiography, *Down These Mean Streets*, when the black Cuban father denies the son, and the white Puerto Rican mother accept him, the doubles of both parents and of Piri himself proliferate in the text, culminating in the disappearance of a father double that signals Piri's ultimate ambivalence around issues of fatherhood and race. In the works of both of these chroniclers of street masculinity, the father's disappearance from the text is more heavily symbolic than the mother's. Although these fathers are not dead bodies in the stories, their absences affect the street allegories in the same way that the dead mothers haunt the other novels.

Significantly, the sacrificed double is often a black or mixed race character. The angry women in three of the novels by women writers—*The Aguero Sisters, Sweet Diamond Dust*, and *Geographies of Home*—are all madwomen of mixed race. They are ultimately expelled from their narratives, either through murder, suicide, or a simple act of renunciation by families who see them as contaminated. *The Agüero Sisters* starts and ends with the murder of the mother by the father; Gloria, the mulatta, burns down the plantation house in *Sweet Diamond Dust*, leading us to believe that she too will die in the ensuing conflagration. In *Geographies of Home* the mad sister, who hates being black, rapes the sister who is comfortable with her blackness, an act of such violence that the "good" mother of the two women is forced to reject the mad daughter she had previously tried to protect, in some way expelling the angry aspect of the self. In *Down These Mean Streets* the ominous disappearance of a character standing in for the black father signals Piri's ultimate inability to come to terms with his blackness.

As Marta Caminero Santangelo has noted in *The Madwoman Can't Speak* (1998), the paradigm of the angry madwoman may no longer be valid for feminist literature.[5] Caminero Santangelo deftly shows that madness is the result of the refusal to recognize boundaries between the self and the other. Mad characters so driven to the erasure of difference are self-destructive, often rejected by the texts that create them, and ultimately poor models for a feminism emphasizing agency.[6] Caminero Santangelo asserts that the classic model of the madwoman as a feminist symbol is outmoded. For example, in *The Madwoman in the Attic* (1979) Sandra Gilbert and Susan Gubar had proposed the madwoman as a representation of the suppressed and repressed creativity of nineteenth-century British women writers. Caminero Santangelo notes that the madwoman's madness prevents her from constructive participation in the world, and thus outweighs the expressive value of her anger. However, I'm not sure that there ever was a madwoman in literature whose posture was not ambivalent, mobilizing at once both the strength and vulnerability repressed by patriarchal mores. I am not suggesting, however, that madness is an uncomplicated sign of resistance in U.S. Latino/a texts. Rather, I am fascinated by the way the madness, and its concomitant violence, are always linked with past origins, an identification which must be given up so that characters can assimilate to the new American reality.

The persistence of the figure of the murdered character, the madwoman, or the double, in the work of these seven writers with very different nationalist identifications points to an ambivalence about (a past) Caribbean or Latin American origin as well as (a present) unassimilable U.S. Latino/a identity. Because thus far U.S. Latino/a literary criticism has been mostly nationalist in orientation—divided into studies of Puerto Rican or *boricua*, Chicano, Cuban American, and Dominican American writers, this study aims to challenge those boundaries demonstrating that even if U.S. Latinos cannot often admit to the common habitudes that transcend national origin, our fictions betray them. The murdered or "disappeared" or mad characters in these fictions then become symbolical revenants, ghosts who persist in returning to the U.S. Latino/a narrative in story after—allegorical—story.

Americanized Protagonists

What is the relationship between the educated, upwardly mobile Latino/a narrator/protagonist and the community from which she/he hails? The idea of the minority strongly rooted in the history and social activity of the community of origin is one of the elements used to distinguish minority literature by important theorists and writers such as the French philosophers Gilles Deleuze and Felix Guattari; postcolonial critics such as David Lloyd and Abdul JanMohammed, and Gayatri Spivak; African American literary stars such as Toni Morrison and bell hooks; and Latino critics espousing interminority and transborder criticism. For example, Chicano critic Jose David Saldívar provocatively postulates a "dialectics of Our America," linking the literary representations of subjugated peoples in Latin America with U.S. minorities. The Dominican critic Silvio Torres-Saillant navigates between his trans-Caribbean poetics and his identification with the Dominican community in New York. Puerto Rican sociologist and cultural critic Juan Flores, who often incorporates literary commentary into his analyses, and literary historian Lisa Sánchez González have also emphasized the divide between an island Puerto Rican literature written by a largely bourgeois intelligentsia and the Nuyorican or *boricua* tradition, which reveals (and often revels in) working-class identity. However, the only comprehensive study of U.S. Latino/a Caribbean literature, by William Luis (1997), is historical rather than theoretical in nature and tends to isolate the traditions of each group (Cuban, Dominican, Puerto Rican), rather than find points of commonality.

Critics such as Eliana Ortega and Nancy Saporta Sternbach postulate a notion of inter-Latina writing rooted specifically in feminist and working-class consciousness.

At the beginning of the introduction to the anthology, *Breaking Boundaries*, Ortega and Saporta Sternbach quote six excerpts of verse by Chicana, Dominican and Puerto Rican woman poets to describe the work of the Latina writer as expressive of "a paradigm of self-affirmation . . . self-perception and a self-definition that stems from her rootedness in her heritage and in her historical circumstances."[7] Inextricable bonds to a community that has suffered a recent history of uprootedness and economic upheaval combines with a feminist sensibility to characterize Latina writers. However, Ortega's and Saporta Sternbach's characterization seems to fit the poets and critics in their anthology much better than the female or male writers in this book. This divergence is overdetermined by the fictional form of the books I examine as well as the thematized rift between upwardly mobile characters and the families/communities they come from. In their fictions, Díaz, Ferré, García, Pérez, Rivera, Murray, and Thomas all create protagonists who are driven by "the nostalgia for lost origins" and yet are sobered by the awareness that complete identification with lost origins can also legitimize the mainstream, individualist master narrative.[8]

Killing Spanish

U.S. Latino/a Caribbean Studies critics often highlight the differences between Latinos born and raised in the United States and islanders, observing that U.S. Latino/a writers do not have the same concerns and obsessions as their counterparts in the homes of origin.[9] Frequently U.S. Latino/a writers do not read or speak the language of origin, and more often than not islanders and Latin Americans are disdainful and critical of them for that reason. The vilification of the Nuyorican for speaking broken Spanish is a now ancient theme in and out of Puerto Rican and Nuyorican literature, at least as old as Pedro Juan Soto's 1956 powerful short story collection *spiks*. The Nuyorican response is *ressentiment*, a rejection of this rejection. Note, for example, the island Puerto Rican Ana Lydia Vega's parody of the broken Spanish and supposedly vulgar behavior of a Nuyorican in the 1981 story "Pollito Chicken," and the New York Puerto Rican writer Nicholasa Mohr's angry critique of that story as "incorrect and ludicrous" in an eloquent 1987 *testimonio* style essay.[10] The island side: a fear of losing the plenitude of Spanish to the constant depredations of English. New York Puerto Ricans, on the other hand, understand that what motivated the diaspora had an economic and racialized cause—the so-called industrialization of the island in the 1940s, which led to the exodus of a largely poor and mixed race population to New York. With this context in mind, Rosario Ferré, for example, is most often classified as an island Puerto Rican and/or Caribbean and/or Latin American writer. My study of much of her prodigious output is meant to highlight her transformation from a writer favoring Spanish and her island/Latin American identity to a U.S. Latina writer who mainstreams her work in English, a feat that requires "killing Spanish," a richly ambiguous project.

The phrase "killing Spanish" is also a direct deliberate, translation of a common Puerto Rican idiom "matando el español," which refers to what islanders believe happens to Spanish when Nuyoricans or Dominican Yorks of a working-class background forget, hybridize, and reconstitute language fragments. Fragmentary and hybridized Spanish, or the use of Spanglish, are more common in mainland based

Latino/a poetry.[11] In the fictional works examined here there is an instructive gendered disjunction—most of the women writers do not experiment much with Spanglish and, indeed, hardly use Spanish at all, Pérez's text being the most remarkable of all for the absence of Spanish. Rivera experiments with the rhythms of broken Spanish, Spanglish, and linguistic echolalia in a way that is unique among U.S. Latino/a writers. Díaz, and to a lesser extent Thomas and Murray, also experiment innovatively with fragmented Spanish.[12] Rivera's humorous echolalia sometimes consists of the repetition of a phrase or word from one language into another, with a slight but purposeful difference. Deliberately literal translations are replete with irony and mimicry. Thus when Rivera's narrator refers to "some wild herb called 'good grass'" at the beginning of the quasiautobiographical *Family Installments*, he is showing how U.S. Latino/as make sense of their dual cultural and linguistic situation by literally translating a Spanish word without actually naming it:

> To calm her down, Papá Santos would give her a concoction of boiled milk with ginger and some wild herb called "good grass," and soothe her with words while she drank it.[13]

"Good grass" is a literal translation of the Spanish word for wild mint—*yerbabuena*—but it is also a reference to the slang term in American English for marijuana. This type of echolalia permeates Rivera's work and—I can say from my perspective as friend and colleague of the late writer—was also a characteristic tick of his speech. What is left of the original word is the young narrator's tongue-in-cheek translation cum definition. The writer obviously knows the original word, but to put it into the text would be to give the reader an excess of information that veers away from the narrator-protagonists own tenuous and uniquely fluid relationship to his background and to the Spanish language. Rivera stays true to his experience and offers up his own wonderfully worked over fragment.

Díaz's mixture of Spanish with English without italics—so that an unwitting reader might mistake the Spanish for English or for mistakes—and without quotation marks when using dialogue were so downright revolutionary when his stories were published in 1996 that almost every book written by a U.S. Latino/a writer since has copied one or both of these stylistic devices, which reflect the incorporation of the varied rhythms of code-switching characteristic of mainland (and island) Latinos. Above all, the refusal to italicize is an attempt to show that Spanish words are not used to indicate and highlight difference among U.S. Latino/as, who are constantly switching back and forth between the two languages. The use of italics—which I myself find difficult to avoid—disrupts the constantly changing, peformative, relationship between English and Spanish. Significantly, Díaz repeatedly credits Rivera and Piri Thomas as two of his principal U.S. Latino literary influences, and one would assume that their irreverent incorporation of broken Spanish rhythms into their texts had a great deal to do with their influence over the younger writer.[14]

Allegory

The disjunctions within U.S. Latino/a Caribbean literary discourse, and between it and the particular Latin American literary discourses that may be designated their "origins," I have chosen to call allegory precisely because allegory is a trope that emphasizes division and fragmentation. The most basic definition of allegory describes it as either the construction, or interpretation, of a work of literature in which a more concrete sense refers to an "other," abstract level of meaning.[15] Whereas allegory always points to a level of interpretation, symbolism tends toward concreteness, figural representations that seem to stand by themselves. Because of the apparent didacticism of allegory, it was thus devalued by the English Romantic poets in particular.[16] Unlike the symbol it was seen as inorganic, a ruptured tropological vehicle. Twentieth-century critics, especially Walter Benjamin and Paul de Man, have restored respect for allegory on the grounds that the ruptures it represents are more accurate delineations of the fractured modern condition than the totalizing idealizations of the symbol.[17]

De Man regards the rupture that allegory uncovers as productive, an improvement on the view of Frantz Fanon, for example, for whom allegory represents the "second phase" of a literary evolution that starts with assimilation and culminates in a national literature. This intermediary stage, between assimilation and casting off of literary shackles, that would presumably engender a "new" literature often produces allegorical works, says Fanon, because in the second phase "the native is disturbed; he decides to remember what he is."[18] Allegory represents rupture for Fanon, then, because it implies—through remembering—temporal divergence from the origin, a position from which the native intellectual then looks back and laments the loss of the unity of childhood. Allegory for Fanon marks an "exterior" relationship with the native writer's community. His analysis ascribes the structure of allegory in native literature to a split in the native psyche itself. There are two levels in the figure when it occurs in native literature because the native writer, in acquiring a colonial education, has diverged from his people. He is divided from what he was, just as the two levels in the trope of allegory are divided. In the progression represented by a national literature the two levels have merged into a unity.

However, in a discussion of U.S. Latino/a Caribbean literature, indeed in a discussion of any literature written by minorities in the United States, we cannot ever aspire to the totalizing perfection represented by Fanon's third stage and, indeed, in postcolonial criticism, writers such as Homi Bhabha have rejected holistic notions of an unadulterated literature by positing the idea of mimicry. Bhabha's famous description of colonial mimicry as "the desire for a reformed, recognizable Other, *as a subject of a difference that is almost the same, but not quite*" [original italics] emphasizes that mimicry is not just a defensive strategy but a mode of resistance, albeit unconscious.[19] Allegory, like mimicry, is about repetition with a difference. But mimicry, unlike the trope of allegory, does not account properly for temporality. In some ways mimicry is a more potent device because it is actually less specific than allegory. What accounts for difference in allegory is the passage of time. As de Man puts it in his argument for the superior flexibility of allegory in relation to symbol:

> Whereas the symbol postulates the possibility of an identity or identification, allegory designates primarily a distance in relation to its own origin, and, renouncing the nostalgia and the desire to coincide, it establishes its language in the void of this temporal difference.[20]

Allegory, as a "rhetoric of temporality" explains the existence of the differences and decontextualizations of practices—such as magic, and religious beliefs—represented as naturalized in *The Agüero Sisters* and *Geographies of Home*. In both these texts magic is represented as a contradictory practice: on the one hand, a way of gaining access to the original homeland, on the other, a tie to the past that is of questionable use for the new American reality. Perhaps Benjamin's notion that allegory is the only literary form capable of expressing the fragmented experience of modern reality is most pertinent here: "In the field of allegorical intuition the image is a fragment, a rune . . . The false appearance of totality is extinguished."[21] For Benjamin allegory is more relevant as a representational vehicle than classical symbolism because it undermines the idea of permanence and beauty contained in *static* symbolic representations of nature. It is for this reason that Benjamin stresses the notion of melancholy in his book on baroque, allegorical German drama (or *trauerspiel*)—a melancholy arising from scenes of ruins and decayed vegetation—which undermines nostalgia for a holistic, ideal past, an imaginary place where life was always better than it is in the present. Instead of these idealized memories, what allegory puts into relief is the impossibility of recapturing the past. This melancholy realization recaptures the past only in static, lifeless fragments:

> If the object becomes allegorical under the gaze of melancholy, if melancholy causes life to flow out of it and it remains behind dead, but eternally secure, then it is exposed to the allegorist, it is unconditionally in his power. That is to say it is now quite incapable of emanating any meaning or significance of its own; such significance as it has, it acquires from the allegorist.[22]

The most interesting aspect of this notion of allegory, then, is that the allegorist reassembles the fragments—of a past that can never really be accurately reproduced or represented—into his own version. Jenny Sharpe clearly demonstrates that Benjamin's interpretation of the past is always contingent on the present: "In other words, our ability to read the past is contingent upon a present that transforms it into an image we can recognize."[23] Thus Benjamin's notion of allegory undercuts "the idea of a past waiting to be recovered," the idea that discrete events in chronological time are "parts of a totality."[24]

This challenge to the notion of the past as an unbroken series of events leading to the present is clearly relevant to U.S. Latino/a Caribbean literature in which the recent dislocations from a Spanish Caribbean home of origin are constantly remembered, lived, reinvented. This repositioning of a fragmentary past is thematized particularly in *The Agüero Sisters*, *Geographies of Home*, and in Rosario Ferré's first novel written in Spanish, *Maldito amor* (translated into English as *Sweet Diamond Dust*). A mother murdered by the father and known only through family members' different recountings of the past in *The Agüero Sisters*; the resolution of a family crisis accomplished by a mother's momentary connection to her past in the Dominican Republic through the "magic" ritual of plucking feathers from a chicken in *Geographies of Home*; the reinvention of the history of the family patriarch who is rememorialized as a Spanish founder of a plantation line, but revealed to have been a mulatto fieldhand from a nearby farm in *Sweet Diamond Dust*: these are some of the ways in which the U.S. Latino/a writers I am addressing choose to reinscribe the notion of the origin as well as to constantly question and subvert the possibility of ever grasping hold of it. While *Family Installments* begins with a representation of a Puerto Rico in which ubiquitous poverty, madness, and sexism encouraged the family to immigrate, *Drown* dichotomizes the differences between the origin and Latino/a America less rigidly. Díaz's monstrous double Ysrael whose face was eaten by a pig—a defacement that richly characterizes the nature of poverty in the Dominican *campo*—nonetheless has ambitious plans to immigrate to the States and remake himself. The street allegories of *Down These Mean Streets* and *Locas*, however, are remarkable for the lack of nostalgia about, and even memory of, the place of origin. These texts differ from the other books in major ways. The protagonists Piri, in the Thomas book, and Lucía and Cecilia in the Murray novel, grew up in the United States but have no memory of the homeland. It is the parents who carry the memories, but characters who take to the street feel more of an investment in their street families than in their blood relations. In these narratives, the street satisfies the longing for territory. The characters replace the homeland with the street, thus erasing the desire for a magical (or any) recovery of the place of origin. In these allegories, the protagonists find at least a temporary plenitude in street identity, a feeling at once of being new and being home. But life on the street involves so much fronting and masking that anxiety consumes the characters. Piri ends up physically leaving the mean streets, Cecilia becomes a maid, and Lucía embraces the violent lifestyle of the gang at the cost of psychological fragmentation.

In 1987 Aijaz Ahmad deftly refuted Frederic Jameson's well-known sweeping generalization in 1986 that all so-called Third World literature is "necessarily allegorical." Ahmad noted that it is impossible to group all so-called Third World literatures in the same category, as if the histories and nations of Africa, Latin America, and China were all the same.[25] He also observed that allegories have indeed been written by modern or contemporary American writers, like *Gravity's Rainbow*, by Thomas Pynchon and Ralph Ellison's *Invisible Man*. Still, the fact that Ellison is African American is deeply significant, since the allegorical tendency that marks U.S. Latino/a literature shapes American minority literature in general. However, proximity to the land of origin, with all that it implies in terms of the widespread use—and hybridization—of Spanish, accentuates the allegorical relationship for U.S. Latino/a witers. I am convinced that if Fanon's stages apply to American minority writers, U.S. Latinos are planted firmly near the start of this allegorical stage.

Jameson's discussion of "canonical" and "non-canonical" forms of literature, and his delegation of Third World literature to the latter category seems insufficient now in the first decade of the new millennium. But the 1986 article is still influential, powerfully contrasting the determinants of the Western canonical novel and the so-called "third-world text." Jameson believes that Third World texts are "national allegories" in which the individual story is always the story of the nation and that such stories are perforce "alien" to Western readers brought up on a different literary diet.[26] The Western novel, as the product of "capitalist culture," is characterized by "a radical split between the private and the public, between the poetic and the political, between what we have come to think of as the domain of sexuality and the unconscious and that of the public world of classes, of the economic, and of secular political power: in other words, Freud versus Marx."[27] This distinction is insightful, as Patrick McGee has pointed out in a revisting of the Jameson/Ahmad debate, because Jameson's use of the term allegory is "useful in describing the relation to language one finds in third-world and other oppositional literatures."[28]

Magical Realism and Archetypes

The particular allegorical nature of Latin American literature is more pertinent to the discourse in this book and underlines a more focused difference than Jameson's generalized distinction between the "canonical" Western novel and the "non-canonical" Third World text. The link between Latin American and U.S. Latino/a Caribbean literatures that I wish to highlight is magical realism. Alejo Carpentier, the precursor and "father" of the Latin American school of magical realism, coined the term *lo real maravilloso*—or the marvelous real—in 1949 to designate a way of life of which the magical was an everyday aspect. Carpentier, who knew André Breton and had actively participated in the European Surrealist movement, declared the marvelous real a more successful aesthetic style than Surrealism because the former was a manifestation of "American" ontology whereas the latter relied on a forced manipulation of reality. The precious ingredient that obtained in the Latin American marvelous real was a faith glaringly absent for Carpentier in Surrealist game-playing: Surrealists did not believe in the fantastical games they concocted to release the unconscious, unlike the Haitian practitioners of Voudoun who inspired Carpentier to write his seminal novel about the Haitian revolution, *The Kingdom of this World* (1949).[29]

Additionally, Carpentier, stressed the organic relationship between the fantastical phenomena he was depicting in his fiction and the American *terrain* itself. For him magical/religious practices such as Voudoun were the result of a kind of symbiosis between the Haitian land and its people.[30] I cite Carpentier, however, to show how the "double identity" I see in U.S. Latino/a Caribbean literature has a source in Carpentier's deeply riven and exoticizing attitude to the "other," non-European, American reality:

> Because of the virginity of the land, our upbringing, our ontology, the Faustian pre-sence of the Indian and the black man, the revelation constituted by its recent discovery, its fecund racial mixing [*mestizaje*], America is far from using up its wealth of mythologies.[31]

Although Carpentier considered himself "American," and thus distinct from his European cronies in Paris, he was looking with his European eye when he identified American and Caribbean Otherness as arising from the "Faustian presence of the Indian and the black man." In this vision, virgin land and the faith of darkskinned peoples can help rejuvenate a skeptical, rationalist, world-weary, European outlook. In Carpentier's masterpiece of short fiction, "Viaje a la semilla" ("Journey Back to the Source"), the universe of reason and paper documents identified with forward moving time is undermined by a kind of Santería hex that obstructs this forward motion and allows the protagonist—a plantation owner—the relief of identifying with his slaves and animal mascots and of travelling back in time to his childhood and the undifferentiated "source" of all being.

In a psychoanalytical reading of Carpentier's literary approach, Antonio Benítez Rojo has shown, in fact, that Carpentier felt a split identity in which Europeanness, his own, and Cuban culture's aligned itself along the axis of the father, whereas Afro-Caribbean identity for him was essentialized along maternal and archetypal lines. This, of course, also fits in with an "archetypal" quality of U.S. Latino/a Caribbean literature that I am pinpointing.[32] Identification with the animal or racialized Other can bring healing and/or danger in Carpentier's work, a prescription that this Latin American and Caribbean father of letters bequeathed to U.S. Latino/a Caribbean literature.

The split identification is apparent in Carpentier's essay where he locates the source of *lo real maravilloso* in the narratives written by the conquistadors:

> [The Latin American] . . . opens up Bernal Díaz del Castillo's great chronicle and finds himself befor the only honest-to-goodness book of chivalry that has ever been written.[33]

And:

> The marvelous real is found at every stage in the lives of men who inscribed dates in the history of the continent and who left the names that we still carry: from those who searched for the fountain of eternal youth and the golden city of Manoa to certain early rebels or modern heroes of mythological fame from our wars of independece, such as Colonel Juana de Azurduy.[34]

Although Carpentier recognized Indian and African traits as the basis for *lo real maravilloso* and invented a new mode for Caribbean and Latin American literary expression, his vision was profoundly primitivistic. In his narrative, the privileged perspective is still the White European *father* figure's, whose stepping on American terra firma is memorialized as the conquest of a world marvelous because it is both "new" and because it is profoundly Other. In fact Carpentier's declaration of the superiority of American "marvelous" reality over the European brand of Surrealism is based on a misreading. When he extols Bernal Díaz del Castillo's narrative as a first example of the marvelous real, he fails to point out that Díaz del Castillo himself had co-opted the fantastical elements of the European tales of chivalry as a way of describing the European encounter with the Americas.[35] This dualistic allegorical vision characterizes *lo real maravilloso*, what we now call magical realism.

Many critics have observed the tendency of allegory to create a "Manichean" dualism of characters who fall either on one side or the other of a binary construction.[36] When authors divide characters into two antithetical aspects—or doubles—they tend also to double the plot, doubled stories, one for each half. This aspect suggests a magical relationship between the two levels on which the plots are told. That is, "magical causation" rather than the probability inherent in realism tends to govern allegories: magic happens because symbolic or archetypal characters are in conflict, generating parallel plots by means of nonrational, magical events rather than the verisimilitude of Aristotelian probablilty.[37]

The marked archetypalism in U.S. Latino/a Caribbean literature—in particular the focus on the conflict between maternal and paternal traits—is accompanied by a strong emphasis on the almost naturalistic realism that Angus Fletcher says distinguishes a universalizing allegory.[38] The magical irrupts in U.S. Latino/a Caribbean texts not as full-fledged magical realism that dominates the text with an atmosphere of strangeness, but as an archetypal, often vestigial sign of the maternal. This happens because U.S. Latino/as equate mothers with the Mother/land, that virgin, faustian territory Carpentier venerated, which is also a repository of sacred power and magic. This allegorical element leads to a supreme ambivalence about the magical in the U.S. Latino/a Caribbean text. Dreaded and desired, when it finally appears, the magical is cloaked in ambiguity and failure. There are only a few moments of magic in *The Agüero Sisters* and a single symbolic major magical occurrence in *Geographies of Home*. But generally these books are written in the mode of contemporary American realism, as are all the novels by Rosario Ferré. However the tension between the realism on the one hand and the archetypal characters and doubles, as well as the moments of the magical, on the other hand, underlines the allegorical tendency in the U.S. Latino/a Caribbean text.[39] Unlike the magical realist texts, which may be their literary ancestors, the dominant U.S. Latino/a Caribbean literary mode displays a kind of war of the archetypes, pitting struggling individuals against Latino/a families whose values and practices are often entrenched in an outmoded, yet often idealized and yearned for, way of being.

In the context of contemporary American literature, U.S. Latino/a Caribbean literature does not yet comprise a large body of work, specifically compared to African American literature. Nonetheless, I hold that the dominating allegorical tendency of these texts gives them a definite, unique identity. These are some seminal U.S. Latino/a Caribbean works that exemplify the allegorical tendency: *A Perfect Silence* (Alba Ambert), *Drown* (Junot Díaz), *Dreaming in Cuban* (Cristina García), *The Agüero Sisters* (Cristina García), *Family Installments* (Edward Rivera), *The House on the Lagoon* (Rosario Ferré), *When I Was Puerto Rican* (Esmeralda Santiago), *In the Time of the Butterflies* (Julia Álvarez), *Our House in the Last World* (Oscar Hijuelos), *The Mambo Kings Play Songs of Love* (Hijuelos), *Geographies of Home* (Loida Maritza Pérez), *Silent Dancing* (Judith Ortiz Cofer). In the case of the actual titles of *Dreaming in Cuban* and *When I Was Puerto Rican*, the past is identified with essential Being (being Cuban, Puerto Rican). Among these writers, most of whom are women, there is a tendency to create allegories in which the place of origin (which is mostly the same for authors and characters) dominates the text both symbolically and in terms of the action. However, the "allegorists of the street," discussed in chapter six, downplay the weighty influence of the origin. Hence the use of the present tense with such imperative signification in the title of *Down These Mean Streets*, and its present-day successor, *Drown*. Thomas's perspective in his memoir is definitely backward looking at a past that cannot mesh with the present. The island past is never allegorized because the narrator never lived it. The title is a reminder that the violent reality that formed Thomas is still with us, even though he was lucky enough to escape its worst consequences. Díaz's title can be read as the narrator's self-sentencing in the title story (I drown) or as an example of resistant aggression (drown!). Rather than allegorically memorializing a frozen past in the temporal split, the younger writer's title simultaneously reflects the present tense in Thomas's book and title (D[]own), and emphasizes the persistently bleak material conditions for many working class U.S. Latinos, despite the almost thirty years that separates their works.

U.S. Latino/a Allegorical Realism

If magical realism was a style of literature practiced by Alejo Carpentier and Gabriel Garcia Márquez, U.S. Latino/a writers are forging a type of allegorical realism in which the magical intrudes powerfully but infrequently into the text. It is both invoked and yet feared by a U.S. Latino/a literary discouse that prefers a gritty, realist, surface. In works of García Márquez and Carpentier the strange, the "magical," is never far away since the writer's origin is still geographically accessible. In the U.S. Latino/a text the home of origin is distant indeed, geographically and psychically. Thus the magical becomes a substitution for the reality of the origin, and an almost spectacular violence accompanies these displaced appearances.

The significance of this literary mode is not just that it transcends polarities (primitivist/modern, irrational/rational, native/assimilated), but that it marks a new relationship with the "magical" ruins of the origin that U.S. Latinos and non-Latinos alike find workable. In texts like *The Agüero Sisters* or *Geographies of Home*, U.S. Latinos practice Santería or Dominican Vodún episodically, with ambivalence, through mediation, and with a degree of unfamiliarity, for they often come to these practices second or third hand. In the U.S. Latino/a texts where the magical irrupts infrequently, it seems fragmentary. Sometimes a ritual is performed and fails, as in Pérez's novel, or there are many consultations with ambiguous results and uncanny repercussions as in García's *The Agüero Sisters*. Sometimes, however, it just a word that invokes the whole underground structure of magic, as in the mention of Eshú in Díaz's story, "Fiesta 1980."[40] The character's mother in that story throws candy out the window to feed the Orisha, invoking protection for the family car trip and keeping Eshú, the voracious aspect of Eleguá, the Afro-Caribbean god of the crossroads, away from the festivities. We don't hear about this powerful figure again in any of the Díaz stories.

The Allegorists of the Street

Miguel Piñero, Piri Thomas, Junot Díaz, and Yxta Maya Murray leave the lands of origin behind, to demarcate a new territory, the "mean" Latino street. If the originary mother is killed off in the books by Ferré, García, Rivera, and Pérez to facilitate assimilation, in the street allegories the community symbolized by the Latino family is completely replaced by the street family—"my boys" in the fictions by Díaz and Thomas, the "clika" in Murray's *Locas*.

These authors, however, have a bleaker outlook on assimilation into mainstream society. In their flashbacks or direct dramatization of life inside an apartment or house in New York or in the islands, Ferré, García and Pérez trace a difficult but not impossible process of assimilation that demands a sacrifice in order to succeed. The street subject renounces assimilation and then takes up as mask the stereotyped image used to marginalize the denizens of the street as poor, racialized, uneducated, inassimilable. Piri Thomas calls his mask "cara palo," a wooden face, a hardened façade that presumes to mastery over the street. However, the mask of mastery is also a mourning mask. What is mourned is the street subject's incapacity to attain either originary or mainstream American identity. What is striking about the street literature is its intensity. The Latino street is declared as the space of both a frightening ambivalence and an exhilarating creative energy:

> So here I am, look at me
> I stand proud as you can see
> pleased to be from the Lower East
> a street fighting man
> a problem of this land . . .
> this concrete tomb is my home
> to belong to survive you gotta be strong[41]

Miguel Piñero's "A Lower East Side Poem" is a classic of U.S. Latino/a street literature, beloved among Nuyoricans and Dominican Yorks in particular because this speaker's declaration of pride in a New York Latino identity has nothing to do with the islands of origin, which are rejected outright ("I don't want to be buried in Puerto Rico" he says in the next stanza). The speaker does not belong on the island. But as "A problem of this land," he knows he is excluded from a normative American identity. Street literature resolves the dilemma of not belonging to the island or of fitting into the white/black U.S. racial binary by embracing the violence of day to day existence on the mean street. The speaker in Piñero's poem is "proud" to be a "street fighting man." He lives by a warrior ethos of his own making that entails a death wish. The proximity to death that is a constant for those who live in the "concrete tomb" turns the unhomely street into the new Latino home.

To sum up, this book proposes that allegory is the trope par excellence for the fragmented identity of U.S. Latino/a Caribbean subjects, Dominicans and Puerto Ricans, constantly traveling back and forth—literally and metaphorically—the short distances between the U.S. mainland and the island; as well as Cuban Americans whose group exile, still recent, has generated a literature of nostalgia. Allegory is also relevant to the study of certain works by other U.S. Latino/a writers who are not linked to the Caribbean, such as Yxta Maya Murray (a Chicana). U.S. Latino/a allegories generate the following characteristics. (1) Archetypal characters representing universal traits, rather than those forged out of a tradition of literary individualism. Hence the obsession in U.S. Latino/a literature with stories of mothers and fathers (be they in fictional or quasi-fictional narratives) whose binary relationship may cause a proliferation of double characters in these books. (2) "Double" plots generated from this binary opposition between mothers and fathers or other archetypal figures or characters born in, or closely linked to, the island of origin. (3) Protagonists, born or raised in the United States, who are torn between the archetypal qualities of the allegorized or double characters and the present difficult, seductive U.S. reality. (4) A character (often a woman representing the origin or racial identity) dies or disappears so that the protagonist can assimilate. (5) The influence or presence of magical moments, significant because they too are like the return of the repressed, allegorized past, but that are put into question by never dominating the realist mode of the U.S. Latino/a Caribbean text. (6) A kind of "contagion," symbolized by madness, miscegenation, or both as the result of the "divisiveness" of the allegorical mode both in Christian allegories, discussed by Angus Fletcher, and in U.S. Latino/a Caribbean literature. Contagion is the sign that there has been a fall from unity. In Christian allegory it is the fall from God symbolized by the battle between sin and redemption. In U.S. Latino/a Caribbean literature, separation from an idealized island of origin shatters the unity; reflected in either madness or miscegenation or both. Miscegenation is, of course, a theme of Caribbean literature in general, arising from plantation history, but García, Ferré, and Pérez show how fragmented and submerged black subjectivity is within a more general representation of U.S. Latino/a Caribbean identity. (7) When the Latino/a subject moves from the house to the open range of the street, (s)he hides the mimetic relationship with the parental figures, renouncing both originary and mainstream identity in favor of the melancholy mask of mastery over the street, the new Latino home. (8) Language contagion: archetypalism evident in many of the texts—where fathers take on traits of the colonizer and mothers represent the "native" element of Latino/a culture in the language. English may take over the narration in a patriarchal and colonizing manner, but some Latino/a writers (notably Rivera, Díaz, Murray, and Thomas) freely "contaminate" English—and challenge Spanish purists—with an echolalic, subversive Spanish. Thus the disturbing significance of the dead bodies of Latinas; and the madness of Latinos and Latinas; in these contemporary texts is strangely subverted by the killing of the Spanish language itself.

In chapter two on Cristina García, commenting on her first two published books, I argue that the prevalence of character doubles in her second book, *The Agüero Sisters* (1997), is a byproduct of allegory, a metonymic effect of the novel's basic metaphor: the murder of the mixed race mother by the father. This mad and murdered mother figure represents—and also forecloses direct confrontation with—a feared/desired Afro-Cuban identity. In chapter three "Killing Spanish: Rosario Ferré's Transition from *autora puertorriqueña* to U.S. Latina Writer," I propose that Ferré, one of the few Latino/a writers to have written significant works in both Spanish and English, emerges as a writer in English by sacrificing "Spanish" through the death of the mother in her book, *Eccentric Neighborhoods* (1998). Chapter four, " 'That Animals Might Speak': Doubles and the Uncanny in Loida Maritza Pérez's *Geographies of Home*," shows that this Dominican American writer's 1999 novel offers the most vehement inscription of the tendencies of contemporary U.S. Latino/a literature: the representation of the origin as a raped and raping mother, and a critique of magical realism as a viable resistance vehicle for U.S. Latinas.

Chapter five, "Latino Rage: The Life and Work of Edward Rivera," has a different focus from the other essays in the book, for it is a memoir cum literary criticism. Ferreting out an aspect of the fragmented Latino/a psyche, I demonstrate how the protagonist of Rivera's novel, *Family Installments* (1982), rages against his inbred humility by projecting both his fury and his passivity onto other characters. I expose the relationship between these often hallucinatory doubles and the author's own real-life demons. Because of Rivera's echolalic fixation on language, in this chapter I elaborate on the ghostly effects of fragmented Spanish.

The "street" writers disavow nostalgia for lost origins by expanding the spatial contours of the house/family figuration. This is the subject of chapter six, "Melancholic Allegorists of the Street: Piri Thomas, Junot Díaz, and Yxta Maya Murray." *Down These Mean Streets* (1967) is the first of these books to focus on the street as home, challenging U.S. Latino/a family romances with its "dirty" realism. In Junot Díaz's celebrated stories, a doubled male character is sometimes sacrificed, a sophisticated rewriting of the woman-as-origin figure. I examine *Locas* (1997) by Chicana writer Yxta Maya Murray here, as she is the only Latina to write about the street. Ambivalent masking is as crucial to street identity for Murray, as it is for Díaz and Thomas. And, as in the work by most of the U.S. Latino/a Caribbean writers in *Killing Spanish*, at the root of Murray's allegory there is a dead mother. I refer to the condition David Eng and other theorists term "racial melancholia" to analyze the intensely creative and self-destructive energies brought together by the ambivalent U.S. Latino street mask and to show how the street allegorists complicate theories of identity that tend to fetishize and generalize both whiteness and originary identity as lost objects.

In its focus on loss, mourning, dead bodies, and ghostly matters my book shares much with certain recent studies by theorists in the fields of sociology, psychoanalytical literary criticism, and cultural studies. U.S. Latino/a literary studies, on the other hand, is dominated by works that focus on the cultural and historical specificities of Chicano/a, Cuban American, Dominican American, Nuyorican, and Puerto Rican literary representations. My purpose in writing *Killing Spanish* is to explore a distinctly literary phenomenon that I identified in a great number of mostly fictional works by U.S. Latino/a writers with varying historical, geographical, and political relationships to the United States. I show here through close textual readings how allegory elucidates U.S. Latino/a literature, interrogating and reencoding its bodies, doubles, and masked identities. My ultimate aim is to garner a wider audience for a compelling body of literary works and to open a discussion of the destructive and productive ambivalences that attend contemporary literary representations of U.S. Latino/a identity.

CHAPTER TWO

WHEN PAPI KILLED MAMI: ALLEGORY'S
MAGICAL FRAGMENTS IN CRISTINA GARCÍA'S
THE AGÜERO SISTERS

My examination of Cristina García's second book, *The Agüero Sisters* (1997)—about the investigation by two sisters of their father's murder of their mother in Cuba when they were children—centers on its allegorical tendency, which illuminates the larger issues of identity in this Cuban American writer's work and in contemporary U.S. Latino/a literature in general. In what she has called an "excavation" of her Cuban origins, García extracts and arranges diverse images and memories from a past history into a narrative process Walter Benjamin calls the "synthesis" of fragments, a quintessentially "allegorical way of looking at things."[1]

In the second part of this chapter I examine magical realism in García's narrative and compare it to its presumed "original," Caribbean magical realism, by way of José David Saldívar's provocative discussion of the links between works by Latin American and Caribbean authors and those by American minority writers also deploying magical realism. I argue that the sporadic, yet crucial, magical realism in García's novel is a byproduct of the allegorical structure of her book with a different function from that of Latin American or Caribbean magical realism. Arguably the source of the magical in García's work, the Latin American literary style that started with Cuban writer Alejo Carpentier's theory of *lo real maravilloso* often reflects a communitarian reality so powerful it has political as well as spiritual implications. In García's book, on the other hand, the magical always results from an alienated individual's repression or mystification of past events, and often through a projection of the beliefs and practices of Afro-Caribbean Santería onto misunderstood characters and situations.

Part One: Allegory in *The Agüero Sisters*

Cristina García emerged on the literary scene in 1992 with the phenomenal success of her first novel, *Dreaming in Cuban*, a book highly praised by critics and still enthusiastically consumed by the reading public. *Dreaming in Cuban* has a fairly simple premise: a contrast of the subjectivities of family members who stayed on the island at the outset of the Cuban Revolution with those who left for the United States. The novel is focalized through the perspectives of three generations of women: the grandmother, Celia, who remains in Cuba; Celia's daughter Felicia who also stays behind, eventually succumbing to madness; a second daughter Lourdes who flees revolutionary Cuba for the United States after she is raped by a Fidelista soldier; and Lourde's daughter, Pilar, who grows up as an American. Despite these different perspectives, however, *Dreaming in Cuban* is essentially a bildungsroman, narrating the coming into identity of Pilar, an aspiring painter who hates her mother's political conservatism and dreams of reunion with her Fidelista grandmother. The title *Dreaming in Cuban* then posits the problem of rupture with the origin and offers a remedy, "dreaming"—a kind of rewriting—of the relationship with the origin.

Pilar's desire to meld with the origin is finally acknowledged toward the end of the novel when she acts upon her conviction that she and her mother must return to Cuba to see Abuela Celia whom Pilar has yearned for since she left the island when she was four years old (the same age as García herself). The "return" to Cuba in *Dreaming in Cuban* comprises barely one-eighth of the book's total narrative. This last section, entitled, appropriately enough, "The Languages Lost" is very perfunctorily drawn and does not resolve the deep questions regarding nostalgia for the origin and the inextricable relationship between past actions and present identity raised earlier in the book. Pilar and Lourdes are in Cuba for just a few weeks before they decide to leave, Pilar's yearnings and doubts miraculously and suddenly resolved:

> I've started dreaming in Spanish, which has never happened before. I wake up feeling different, like something inside me is changing, something chemical and irreversible. There's a magic here working its way through my veins. There's something about the vegetation, too, that I respond to instinctively—the stunning bougainvillea, the flamboyants and jacarandas, the orchids growing from the trunks of the mysterious ceiba trees . . . I'm afraid to lose all this . . . But sooner or later I'd have to return to New York. I know now it's where I belong—not instead of here, but more than here.[2]

The contradictions here are characteristic of an ambivalent U.S. Latina identity. On the one hand, Pilar's fascination with the origin compels her to exotify and mystify Cuba in phrases that could have been culled from a tourist brochure: "stunning bougainvillea," "mysterious Ceiba trees," "ringside view of the sea." However, on the other side of the exotic lies the homely. Instead of standing outside and observing its witchery, Pilar gives into the desire to merge with it, to "dream . . . in Spanish," so that the "magic" of the origin will occasion a "chemical and irreversible" change.

The nature of this change, the nature of this magic, is not thoroughly investigated in this first book. Almost as soon as she gets to the island, Pilar decides that she belongs "more" to New York than to Cuba, a realization that the focalization of Pilar's Americanized voice in the narrative never puts into question. *Dreaming in Cuban* traces an uncomplicated binary relationship between past and present, origin and new place but never moves toward a definition of identity that gets beyond the internalization of exoticized images of Cuba, of a Cuba seen though Pilar's Americanized eyes. Like Pilar, the narrative is nervous about staying too long with the origin, as if too much focus on Cuba will indeed provoke an unpredictable "chemical" change. In fact, not only does Pilar easily succumb to "Americanness" by the end of the narrative, the one character that offers a more complex representation of the Cuban past, Abuela Celia, is killed off by suicide. *Dreaming in Cuban*, in fact, fits quite comfortably Fanon's negative conception of allegory since what Fanon critiqued was a nostalgia that—despite its tendency to despair over the rift between past and present—also tended to embrace the deracinated present. However, *Dreaming in Cuban* shows that a huge price is paid for the acquisition of a Latina identity that is qualitatively, because quantitatively, "more" American than Latin American. The narrative pays in terms of renunciation—the deaths of some major characters such as Abuela Celia, by suicide, and her daughter Felicia, through madness and a mysterious Santería-inflected decline. As Gilbert and Gubar showed, this is one way in which female characters relinquish a hard won authority and self-esteem that has come at too great a cost.[3] The narrative also pays in the construction—for the Cuban American Pilar–of a relationship to Cuba that locates her in the same terrain as a curious tourist. *Dreaming in Cuban* traces the two lines of an allegorical narrative but nervously snips the umbilical cord connecting the two levels at the end of the story, afraid of the strange beast that might birth itself.

García's "excavation" of the past in *The Agüero Sisters*, however, shows aesthetic mastery of her treatment of the theme of the relationship between past Cuban and present Cuban American identity in *Dreaming in Cuban*.[4] One of García's most felicitous moves in the second book is to make the relationship between origin and diverging identity one that is already inscribed in the origin itself. In this second book, which has not achieved the success of the first either in terms of critical praise or copies sold, the past relationship between the Agüero sisters' mother, Blanca, and their father, Ignacio, figuratively enacts the relationship between essential Cuban/Caribbean identity and assimilative/logocentric Cuban–American identity. The novel presents the relationship between the parents as an ideal union of the important components of U.S. Latino/a Caribbean identity, as well as brilliantly undermines such a totalizing notion of unity.

If, as Joel Fineman states in his article, "The Structure of Allegorical Desire," "allegory begins with structure, thinks itself through it, regardless of whether its literary realizations orient themselves perpendicularly or horizontally, that is, as primarily metaphoric or primarily metonymic" then in *The Agüero Sisters* the allegorical structure lies in the configuration of the family, and arranges itself on both metonymic and metaphoric axes, but is dominated by what Fineman calls "the metaphoric code."[5] On the metaphoric axis, the story of the sisters, told in present time, both discloses and is disclosed by the story of Ignacio Agüero's failed romance with his wife, Blanca. This is a narrative told not only in past tense and contrapuntally to the present time narration of the sisters' search, but which physically remains unavailable to the sisters until the end of the novel. The story manuscript is buried in Cuban soil waiting for the sisters, or rather one sister, Constancia the logos-bearer whom the story identifies with the father, to recover it. In this vertical structure, the surface, and horizontally expanding story—of the sisters' relationship to each other, their husbands, children, lovers and the shifting geographies they inhabit (Cuba, Miami, New York)—is subsumed by the power that the allegory endows upon the literally submerged narrative about the mother and father. On the horizontal, or metonymic, axis, the story functions most successfully as a search, specifically Constancia's search for the manuscript, an allegorical device that is ironized by García since Constancia, in fact, has no idea that she is searching for the manuscript.[6] The most important metonymic vehicle, then, in the present-time story is the instance of magical realism in which Constancia wakes up one morning with her mother Blanca Agüero's face pasted on her own.[7] The appearance of the face is metonymic evidence on the horizontal axis for the presence of Blanca Agüero in the story, a presence that both the past murder by the father and Constancia's own present denial has repressed.

Most of the other action that develops on the horizontal axis is mere embellishment, an effect of the novel's allegorical structure. These inessential stories include: Constancia's relationship with her second husband Heberto; his subsequent participation in a conservative Miami "brigade" that plans to invade Cuba (an obvious allusion, and parody, of the Bay of Pigs attack since Constancia and Heberto, in their early fifties in the novel's present-time narration are part of Miami's upper-middle-class conservative stratum); the stories of Constancia's children particularly her son's murder of his father, Constancia's first husband; the stories of Reina's many love affairs; and a first-person narrative by Reina's daughter Dulce. Although all these stories bear upon the theme of a hybridized Cuban American identity, they also function as pure metonymic elaboration and unfolding of the allegorical structure. Following Fletcher's encyclopedic study, *Allegory: The Theory of a Symbolic Mode*, I would characterize this multiplication of action on the metonymic level as evidence of allegorical "contagion," which dictates such occurrences as character doubling as well as the repetition on the metonymic level of actions that occur on the metaphoric level.[8] That is, the relationship between murdered mother and murdering father is the primary metaphor of the text, which is replicated in so many different ways in the story, overdetermining the allegorical structure.

What Fletcher calls the "doubling effect" may be seen, for example, in the representation of Constancia's consecutive marriages to the brothers Heberto and Gonzalo Cruz. While still living in Cuba, before emigrating to the United States, the young Constancia, the sister who most resembles the murdering father, Ignacio Agüero, marries Gonzalo Cruz but cannot stand his infidelities and abandonments and divorces him to marry his apparent polar opposite, the more reliable, if sexually uninspiring older brother, Heberto. But, in fact, the "difference" between the brothers reflects their sameness. That is, the brothers represent aspects of one character; they are doubles, a phenomenon that Fletcher notes is typical of allegorical texts.[9] Like Spenser, then, in Fletcher's reading, García too is "playing" with the illusion that man has a "unified, well-defined ego."[10]

Although Constancia sees Heberto, her second husband, as "different" from her first husband, his brother Gonzalo, the narrative reveals that they are the same, "congenitally."[11] That is, *in origin* they are both liars. What differentiates them is the process that obsesses this text and much U.S. Latino/a literature, in general, the process of divergence, of departure from the origin, a process that involves the passage of time: "Heberto's lies are innocent" in the present tense; Gonzalo's lies "were blatant" in the past.[12] It is the passage of time that has made the brothers opposites. In terms of the structure of allegory, however, Heberto *is* Gonzalo, a repeated, tamer version of Gonzalo, one which the dominating Constancia can live with. Significantly, the text kills both brothers off. Heberto dies of a heart attack in the failed invasion of Cuba, which itself refers to the Bay of Pigs invasion. And Gonzalo dies in a Miami hospital, suffocated with a pillow by Silvestre, the gay, deaf son whom he has never seen who then disappears from the hospital and from the text. Weak male characters? Definitely. All doubles? All the male characters of any importance in the book are either killed off like Ignacio Agüero, Heberto and Gonzalo Cruz and their father Arturo, or simply vanish from the text like Silvestre. So doubling seems to replicate in miniature the general overriding allegorical structure of the book, which has its focus on the re/membered relationship between Ignacio and Blanca Agüero, the origin for the Agüero sisters.

Heberto and Gonzalo Cruz, have their originary point too, a father whose eventual death in Miami becomes the occasion for the two brothers to both reminisce about him and to come together in an alliance that will culminate in Heberto's participation in Gonzalo's brigade invasion of Cuba and his death. The brothers recall many things. But the one memory the text records they have of their father is described in the following scene:

> They recalled, too, the night their father took them to a whorehouse . . . in Havana. Heberto and Gonzalo were only eleven and nine, but Papa made them watch him fuck an opulent mulatta with Oriental eyes . . . The heat that rose from their coupling nearly stifled the boys' breath.
> . . . Heberto . . . suspected his brother of corrupting Constancia, of humiliating her the same way their father had the slant-eyed whore.[13]

Time has leveled the intensely passionate love that Heberto had once felt for Constancia so that in the present time of the story his attitude toward her is much the same as his brother's was. Heberto is also dismayed at the new "confident" Constancia who has achieved material success selling cosmetics in New York.[14] On a conscious level Heberto comes to feel repelled by his wife because he suspects that his womanizing brother has treated her like a prostitute. But on a deeper level, the contagion that Heberto fears and that the text reproduces has to do with the origin itself. The scene that haunts him depicts a primal coupling. The pair in question are not man and wife. However, significantly, the whore is a mulatta like Constancia's mother Blanca.[15] The scene then is another example of the "parallel plots" that Fletcher says are so common to allegory.[16] The major plot in the book is about the rational, Westernized Ignacio Agüero's obsession with the witch-like, mysterious mulatta ironically and appropriately named Blanca because—never given the opportunity to narrate her story in either third or first person, unlike her fellow characters—she is a blank page onto which the other characters project their stories/memories.[17] The name is also appropriate because Blaca has very pale skin, which also serves to mask her mixed race origins, as well as the beliefs that presumably result from her racial identity. In the anecdote about the Cruz brothers' visit to the Havana brothel, the text mimics the major lines of the Ignacio/Blanca relationship. It is this traumatic moment in the brothers' lives that occasions a sort of split. If, as I have been arguing, Gonzalo and Heberto are really doubles, they experience a moment of splitting when they witness their father's abusive coupling with the prostitute. As a result, Gonzalo becomes a womanizer much like his father and Heberto represses his sexual urges so that he can barely stand the embraces of his future wife who both attracts and repulses him. She has already had intercourse with Gonzalo who, in exhibiting his father's machismo, comes to stand in for the father. In this sense Heberto's marriage to Constancia underlines his imitation of the paternal characteristics displayed by his brother. In *The Agüero Sisters*, unlike in *Dreaming in Cuban*, the past is unbearably present; sexual intercourse itself is a metaphor for the past.

However, because the doubled relationship of the Cruz brothers obviously echoes that of the Agüero sisters who are meant to carry some kind of archetypal vestige from each parent, I am also suggesting that Gonzalo and Heberto are doubles who, like Constancia and Reina, are each dominated by gendered, archetypal parental traits.[18] Gonzalo displays dominant and negative machista traits inherited from his father: lecherousness, unreliability, abusiveness, coarseness. Heberto is not just passive and feminized, compared to his double/brother. His traumatized reactions to sex locate him on the same level as the victimized mulatta who in turn echoes the role of Blanca, who was also abused—although not sexually—by her husband. The doubles proliferate metonymically; the patriarchal father's abuse of the mulatta (a racialized mother figure) takes on allegorical significance.

This literary economy is repeated in the relationship between the Agüero sisters and in each sister's relationship to the parents. The reverberations of the parents' story from past to present displays what Joel Fineman calls allegory's "structural effect."[19] Depth in the narrative is provided by the buried story because of its metaphorical power. As Fineman says:

> And so it is always the structure of metaphor that is projected onto the sequence of metonymy, not the other way around, which is why allegory is always a hierarchicizing mode, indicative of timeless order . . . This is why allegory is "the courtly figure," as Puttenham called it, an inherently political and therefore religious trope, not because it flatters tactfully, but because in deferring to structure it insinuates the power of structure, giving off what we can call the structural effect.[20]

The "hierarchicizing" in the narrative is brought about by the way the submerged story bears upon the present-time story offering a possible solution to the mystery (of why the father killed the mother). The fragments of the buried story emanate a "structural effect" promising not just narrative solutions, but sacred "political and therefore religious" ones as well.

What is this submerged story? In contrast to the present-time narrative—about Reina's life in Cuba then Miami, and Constancia's in Cuba, New York, and Miami—the submerged story is the narrative that Ignacio Agüero, a Cuban naturalist, writes shortly after he kills his wife and before he commits suicide. Significantly, he buries the confessional manuscript on the mother's land, near the old ranch that had belonged to his wife's family out in the Cuban countryside.

Even before we come to the beginning of Ignacio's narrative, *The Agüero Sisters* opposes an Edenic, mysterious, almost unimaginable originary land to the corruption that human enterprise and modes of knowing entail. Later in the book a similar binary divides magical and scientific ways of knowing, the poles separating Blanca and Ignacio Agüero and, later, their daughters Reina and Constancia. At the beginning of the book, an Edenic Cuba before Discovery is invoked:

> As naturalists, Ignacio and Blanca Agüero had traversed Cuba with a breadth and depth few others achieved over considerably smaller territories . . . Together they had spent years cataloguing the splendor of Cuba's flora and fauna . . .[21]

The impulse that gives rise to the desire to catalogue knowledge through Linnaeus's system of botanical classification and what Foucault calls a "dual theory of the sign," or the binary system, is a product of the enlightenment.[22] The answer to the question posed at the end of the quoted passage is that the very impulse that spurs the desire to know and catalogue the world also produces imperialistic impulses, the destructiveness that results from a misplaced desire to possess the object of knowledge. The use of natural history in the text elaborates the allegory because Ignacio's cataloguing of Cuban fauna metaphorizes his failed attempts to "know" his wife both psychologically, and even in the biblical sense as we will see. The text also depicts a complicity between the science of natural history practiced by the petit bourgeoisie and the imperialist machinery of the United States in Cuba.[23]

So in *The Agüero Sisters* the experts in the field of "tropical zoology," during the Platt Amendment period of U.S. rule after the Spanish-American war of 1898, are Americans such as Dr. Samuel Forrest of Harvard University who come to Cuba to teach *the study* of tropical zoology to Cubans.[24] Although the Cuban *guajiros* had prior knowledge of the "discoveries" toward which they point Dr. Forrest and Ignacio Agüero, it is the scientists who receive the credit. This happens, for example, with the discovery of the flame-red shrimp, named after Ignacio and his famous tutor: "Forrestia agueri."[25] For this episode, García might have had in mind as an exemplar of colonial tutelage, Bronislaw Malinowski's introduction to Fernando Ortiz's 1947 English-language version of *Cuban Counterpoint*, the book that established a world-wide reputation for the Cuban anthropologist and literary scholar. In the island-wide competition for who will be field assistant to the famous zoologist, it is Ignacio Agüero, of course, who succeeds. His answers about natural history reveal not just his mastery of Darwin's theory of evolution but a subtle understanding of power relations and hierarchy. When Forrest asks a rote interview question, Ignacio replies cunningly that his favorite member of the animal kingdom is the parasite, which response piques Forrest's interest in the seemingly bland Ignacio.[26] He further engage Forrest's attention with his own theory about the difference between animals and human beings: ". . . humans have developed a variety of receptacles and containers for their needs, and animals have not . . ."[27]

Ignacio's theory of human and animal difference resembles the notion of compartmentalization, a type of repressive strategy in which emotions and experiences are cut off from consciousness so that the sufferer is hardly aware of what he or she feels. Extreme examples of cases of compartmentalization are serial killers who repress reality to the extent that they forget what happened, what they did, who their victims were.[28] And Ignacio is a killer. We see this in the murder of Blanca recounted twice, once in the book's prologue—told by an omniscient narrator who does not focalize through any character's perspective—and in the ending, told in Ignacio's confessional manuscript. His first-person narrative is an attempt to explain why he killed his wife. What we gather, ultimately, is that the naturalist could never dissect, as skillfully as he did his specimens, his wife: "Analyzing people is infinitely more taxing than distinguishing among even the subtlest variations of subspecies," Ignacio tells his perplexed child Constancia.[29] And, focalized through Reina's memory, the text points to murder as the naturalist's solution to his marital difficulties: "Would her mother be . . . stuffed and inert like everything Papa killed?[30] The accomplished native scientist and imitator of Dr. Forrest has a better understanding of dead bodies that can be labeled than live ones that speak and behave in mysterious ways. And Ignacio here also stands in for Cubans who have internalized colonialist knowledge. Ignacio strives for the American scientist's authoritative position and seeks to replicate it in his paternalist hold over his wife.

Although Blanca and Ignacio have contrasting personalities, García complicates the binary opposition between them. For example, although Blanca is clearly aligned with the forces of Afro-Cuban Santería, she is, like Ignacio, a trained naturalist. However, in Ignacio's first-person account in the buried manuscript, Blanca's relationship with science is quite different from his own:

> When she worked with sulfur, for example, her normally green eyes took on a yellow-ish tinge. If an experiment called for phosphorus, she vibrated with its unearthly glow.[31]

We are back in the territory of the strange "chemical" change that I described *Dreaming in Cuban*'s protagonist Pilar as both experiencing and resisting at the start of this chapter. In García's first book, Pilar's lifelong yearning for the origin takes her back to Cuba, "the home" she left as a four year old. But, once there, she discovers, not so reluctantly, that she already has a home in New York, preferring to see Cuba through the eyes of a tourist. In the first book there were literally no survivors of an essential Cuban identity since its purest representative, the grandmother, committed suicide by drowning at the book's conclusion; the other characters were either killed off in the course of the narrative or, like the nephew Ivanito, sought asylum in the United States. García's canny move in *The Agüero Sisters* is to inscribe the divergence in identity in the origin itself and to do this by rendering the story of Ignacio's murder of his wife an allegory for the loss of an essential identity.

Although Ignacio and Blanca can each be seen to represent archetypal—and respectively masculine and feminine—qualities, it is likelier that, like the Cruz brothers, as well as Reina and Constancia, they are, rather, psychological doubles.[32] Significantly, Ignacio is the one who characterizes Blanca's actions and qualities for us, who in a sense speaks for her. Because of Ignacio's tendency to repress his desires, Blanca, in all her witchery, represents everything Ignacio must disavow. He projects his fears and desires onto her "blank" page. The differences between them do play out to some extent in the binary oppositions: magic/science, female/male, intuitive/rational, and even essentially Cuban/Americanized Cuban. But Ignacio's suicide, shortly after he murders his wife with a gunshot wound to the head while they are out on a research expedition, shows that Ignacio's psychological existence is dependent on Blanca's. It also seems that what in *Dreaming in Cuban* is dramatized as the Americanized Cuban's intolerance of an incomprehensible Latin American/ Caribbean identity in *The Agüero Sisters* is rendered subtler and more complex by identifying this split and rejection as already present in a quasi-colonized Cuba. This is allegorized in Ignacio, the white, Galician Cuban's attraction/repulsion for his beautiful mulatta wife, Blanca and the latter's identification with Afro-Cuban Santería.

Part Two: Magical Ruins

Cristina García used elements from Santería, the Cuban religion based on the syncretism between colonial Spanish Roman Catholicism and the Yoruba religion from Nigeria, in both *Dreaming in Cuban* and *The Agüero Sisters*. However, as García herself notes, it is really in *The Agüero Sisters* that Santería permeates the deepest fibers of the narrative, where the kind of "hierarchicizing" Fineman describes manifests itself.[33] In this equation, the figure of the murdered/silenced absent mother, Blanca Agüero, overlaps with the magical aspects of Afro-Cuban Santería; both othered categories reinforce each other. In particular, the narrative identifies Blanca Agüero with Oshún, the Yoruban Orisha who in Cuba is also syncretized with La Virgen de la Caridad del Cobre. However, the identification of Blanca Agüero with Oshún is as submerged, fragmented, and elided as is the figure of Blanca herself, a character who is constructed wholly through the memories of her daughters and the story told in the buried manuscript written by Ignacio Agüero. The identification with Oshún is suggested in two ways in the text: (1) in relation to Constancia's sense of unease about her mother and her attempt to find out the truth about the latter's death by consulting a Santero on her own in Miami; (2) by the way in which Blanca's "change" from passionate ardor to indifference toward her husband is dramatized in a remarkable scene with mythic overtones in which Blanca is bitten by an alien underwater creature while bathing in a river. Rivers are sacred to Oshún, as García notes by focalizing through Constancia: "In Cuba, Constancia had heard of Oshún, of the goddess's fondness for rivers and gold and honey."[34]

This subtle use of Santería in *The Agüero Sisters* is one that contrasts sharply with both real-life rituals of Santería as well as depictions such as, for example, Cuban filmmaker Sergio Giral's 1997 film *María Antonia*. In this film the eponymous heroine's plight in 1950s Cuba is that of being doubly bound by poverty and by the strict rules of what the movie reveals as an extremely patriarchal religion.[35] The Santería ceremonies García depicts seem decontextualized in comparison. Instead of representing rituals that take place in the context of a community of believers, García shows us Constancia's constant private consultations with a Santero named Oscar Piñango. In the Giral film, the heroine is usually surrounded by Santería believers, even in the highly charged scene at the end of that film in which she incites her new lover to murder her while she is performing a dance for Oshún. The film is sensationalist, especially in its insistence on exposing the naked body of María Antonia in the last scene. The kind of violence the movie depicts may be common among the working-class characters who attend the Santería ceremonies, but it is not typical of the ceremonies themselves.[36] What is authentic in Giral's representation, however, is the communal nature of the ceremonies. García, on the other hand, tends to isolate the aspects, or fragments, of Santería that are pertinent to her story. In *The Agüero Sisters* García has little interest in showing us a Constancia surrounded by a community of the faithful.[37] Instead, she demonstrates that the Santero's divinations correspond to Constancia's unconscious desire to understand her mother (and the mystery of her mother's death), which is the same desire that drives the allegory. When the Santero reads the pattern of cowry shells, he tells Constancia that she must travel to "where the curse was born . . . the grave was first dug."[38] She interprets this mysterious prophecy as an injunction to travel. But her literal desire to visit her land of origin corresponds to a willingness to rethink her erstwhile closed and judgmental attitude toward her mother.

The split in the Cuban American author's psyche manifests itself in the text through a recovery of fragments of the authentic Santería ceremonies that are then used to construct a text that allegorizes the very formation of Cuban American identity. What at first seems merely a metaphor the text will prove to be reality. "The curse" on the one hand is nothing more nor less than the incomprehension and alienation that is born/e between the rationalistic Ignacio and the intuitive, sprite-like Blanca. The "grave was first dug" is not just a metaphor for the death of the couples' relationship nor merely the signifier of literal death. It points to the impossibility of knowing. For it is not just Blanca's story that is silenced by Ignacio's retelling. Because Ignacio is so obsessed with Blanca, he tells her story better than he tells his own. His Blanca may be pure projection but it is this spectral figure who dominates the text rendering Ignacio himself nebulous, and generating allegorical subplots concerning the daughters and grandchildren that seem flat and superfluous. It is the body of history that must, but never can be, exhumed.

Allegory successfully conveys the only kind of knowledge that Constancia can glean about her mother. García's extraction of the moment in which the Santero performs the divination from the communal context of a typical Santería ceremony is illuminated by Walter Benjamin when he posits that "any person, any object, any relationship can mean absolutely anything else . . . In the field of allegorical intuition the image is a fragment, a rune."[39] Benjamin's theory of allegory refers to just such cultural situations as that of minority writers who recuperate fragments and try to constellate them into new meanings. The new meanings diverge both from the original context in that the fragments were part of a different picture as well as from their mere solitary existence as fragments. What García does then, seen from Benjamin's perspective, is not just take Santería rituals out of context and distort them out of ignorance and American bravado, but infuse them with a precarious, fragile, utterly contingent meaning.

As Patrick McGee notes in a discussion of allegorical tendencies in contemporary African literature "the meaning is not identical to the intention of the allegorist but reflecting his or her relation to the given historical context."[40] If this is true then the allegorical tendency accounts for what some may interpret as tentative, and inauthentic gestures that arise from García's disjunctive position as a U.S. Latina. What Benjamin's theory of allegory proposes, as Jenny Sharpe notes, is "a past that is unstable and contingent upon the present."[41] The writing of history never reaches a final version because the past is always changing with each new present. Seen from this vantage point, while they do not cease to be lonely events suffused with Constancia's dread of what she suspects but would rather not acknowledge, Constancia's visits to the Santero, a child of Oshún, throw light on the mysterious, magical Blanca whom Constancia has mostly forgotten. It is because of Constancia's visit with Oscar Piñango in the present-time narration that when we encounter the river scene, described in past narration by Ignacio, Blanca is identified with Oshún. However, Blanca's absence from the text itself generates Benjaminian ruins, fragments that the other characters and the reader invest with a supercharged, almost sacred, meaning. The river scene is one such fragmented and highly evocative moment. Here follows the scene, perhaps the most subtly drawn and complex in the entire novel, in which Ignacio describes the couple's ill-destined honeymoon sojourn on the Isle of Pines and what happened to Blanca in the river:

> One day, Blanca playfully coaxed me, fully dressed, into the river. When I was chest-high in the slow waters, she dove in beside me and tugged off my belt. Her boldness startled me, and I lost my footing. A force I could not fathom pulled me down and held me underwater. Just when I was certain I'd drown, I heard a child's voice imploring: Yield to the river! Yield to the river! Instead I broke free into the morning air.[42]

Blanca's seductive behavior recalls the river goddess Oshún's behavior with her lovers, Changó and Ogún, in the patakís.[43] Ignacio deliberately tells us she looks like a "river goddess" and puts into her mouth the words "I am the river." However, upon a second reading, and in the absence of any corroboration by the silenced Blanca and by her daughters' memories (they are both as yet unborn), much of what occurs can be seen to be either made up by Ignacio or as unconscious projection. This is especially true of the most mystical moment in the scene when Ignacio hears "a child's voice imploring: Yield to the river!" In many ways this scene seems to be about Ignacio's sexual limitations, and even impotence. He is plainly unused to his new wife's sexual appetite. It strikes him as "boldness," makes him lose "my footing," which for a repressed individual like Ignacio sounds as if it could mean premature ejaculation. "Just when I was certain I'd drown" is this repressed character's response to such sexual humiliation. Let us not forget Ignacio's psycholgical compartmentalization. The child's voice he hears is probably a projection of his own childish fear in this situation. He is literally afraid of drowning in the primal/sexual/amniotic fluids of the mother/goddess/sexual woman that Blanca becomes in the river, which in Santería as well as in many other mythological systems is a symbolic place of sexual union.

The couple's second attempt to make love is described by Ignacio as a kind of aggression on the part of Blanca, an aggression that *masculinizes* Blanca whom Ignacio, sounding strangely passive, describes as "kiss[ing] me with a hard ardor." Ignacio describes his orgasm in almost masochistic terms as a "surrender[] to a violent pleasure." The presence of violence is doubly emphasized by the "wound on [Blanca's] . . . left heel," which is, shall we say, the Benjaminian *ruin* signifying the first, perhaps last, sexual encounter between Blanca and Ignacio in the text. This rat's or snake's bite on the heel is so suggestive of the Biblical judgment God makes in the garden that "the bite" seems like coding for the repressed Ignacio's feelings about sex.[44] The wound marks this scene as a moment of sexual trauma, resonating in some ways with Arturo Cruz's abusive coupling with the mulatta, a scene I described earlier. And Heberto's own shock and ensuing association of Constancia with his father and the prostitute, through the metonymic agency of his brother Gonzalo, echoes Ignacio's behavior here.

What seems even more interesting to me than Ignacio's coding of his sexual immaturity and insufficiency in this scene, however, is this supposedly rational character's easy attribution of things he doesn't understand about his wife to the mythical structure of Santería. Ignacio is so afraid of his wife's sexuality that he is more capable of deifying it than of ascribing it to her desire. That is why ultimately he has to kill her. Because, for him, the man of science, it is too painful to live in an ignorant state than it is to ascribe the quintessentially "chemical" Blanca's sudden lack of sexual ardor after the honeymoon on the Isle of Pines to a lack of chemistry with her husband. Ignacio tells us that after the honeymoon, Blanca falls pregnant, which state seems to bring on madness, a condition, however, that Ignacio continues to attribute to the rat or snake bite in the river.[45] It is Ignacio's projections, really, that link Blanca to Santería but, in fact Ignacio manages to give his own beliefs an "objective" air by attributing the magic and irrationality to the silenced Blanca.

In his narrative, Ignacio writes that Blanca's madness and pregnancy succeed the river episode and again supplies details linking his wife's strange behavior to Santería. Five months after giving birth to Constancia, the daughter who will be spurned by her mother, and thereafter hate her, Blanca runs off. Five is the Santería number ascribed to Oshún. Oshún in Santería lore is the fire Orisha Changó's favorite lover, and vice versa. Blanca's next lover is described by both Ignacio and the lover's own daughter Reina (who remembers meeting this man only once in her life at her mother's graveside) as a large mulatto wearing the red and white bracelet of Changó on his wrist. "He had a broad, smooth face and eyes that suggested a touch of Oriental blood," writes Ignacio.[46] When Blanca Agüero returns to her husband's home two years after having run off with the mysterious Changó-identified stranger, the unreliable narrator, Ignacio, is again compelled to link the unexpected return of his wife with Santería cosmology.[47] She arrives "in the midst of a terrible thunderstorm." This detail implies that Changó the thunder Orisha may be angry with Blanca for abandoning her lover, a "son" of Changó. And Blanca is pregnant "as the Santera [Ignacio consulted] had prophesied."[48] It is Ignacio who sees Santería involved in this important event. It is also Ignacio who describes Blanca as beaten up and abused upon her arrival: "One eye was bruised shut, and her clothes were torn and dirty . . . She wore a single high-heeled shoe and a strand of onyx beads that fell past her massive stomach."[49] This description mixes elements of ritual identification ("onyx beads" given to protect a baby in Santería) with aspects of dress that make it look as if Blanca had just been raped or was some kind of wild bacchanal or whore. It's apparent, although never stated outright, that Ignacio links sex, something we have shown he doesn't understand well, to Santería, which is also mysterious to him.

Ignacio's desperate state of mind after Blanca's desertion leads him to visit a Santera for consolation: "When logic fails, when reason betrays, there is only the tenuous solace of magic, of ritual and lamentation."[50] Ignacio's visits to the Santera are similar to the visits his daughter Constancia will make many years later. Unlike those born into Santería who practice the rituals in the context of singing and dancing with other believers, Ignacio and Constancia are motivated by the "lamentation" of loss, which spurs their visits to practitioners who both these characters secretly regard as witch doctors. Ignacio and Constancia are similar in many ways. Constancia adores her father as a child and hates both her mother and her sister Reina whose natural sensuality the text links with the mother. Both Ignacio and Constancia hope their feelings of loss can be healed, but don't really believe this will happen.[51]

García's text invests less in faith in Afro-Caribbean religions than in the allusiveness of the religious symbolism that the text (or Ignacio) attaches to Blanca. In fact, what is so unique about García's fragmentary use of Santería is how—by merely hinting at a cosmological link between Blanca and the Orisha Oshún—the author allows the relationship between a goddess belonging to a system of belief that is only fragmentarily accessible to a middle-class white *Cubana* like Constancia to inform Constancia's sense about her lost mother better than any relative or family album. Seen in the context of Benjamin's theory of allegory, the magical realism in García's text then is quite different from its Latin American and Caribbean progenitors. This subtle distinction bears pondering. In *The Dialectics of Our America*, José David Saldívar reexamines the notion of an "'extended Caribbean,' a coastal and insular region stretching from southern Virginia to easternmost Brazil," a region "more responsive to the hemisphere's geographical and political crosscurrents than to narrow national ideologies."[52] Saldívar notices that certain African American and U.S. Latino/a writers incorporate techniques of magical realism in their writing and that this is proof of the continuity between Latin American and American minority writing.[53] Saldívar's penetrating discussion of Ntozake Shange's work provides excellent examples of this idea. Particularly informative is Saldívar's analysis of the influence Shange's visits to Cuba and Latin America have had on her work and her vision.[54] I have also noticed that most of Toni Morrison's novels, except for *The Bluest Eye*, contain moments of magical realism, such as the episodes of the swamp women and the night women in *Tar Baby*; Milkman's encounter with the mythical old women at the end of *Song of Solomon;* and, of course, the presence of the famous ghost in *Beloved*. However, by comparing an instance of magical realism in *The Agüero Sisters* to a famous precedent in Caribbean literature, I hope to show that magical realism, as far as U.S. Latino/a literature is concerned, takes a different shape from the Latin American variety. Saldívar has already offered a fine summary of the history of magical realism in *The Dialectics of Our America*, so I limit myself to revisiting the ideas of the first, and one of the most important, exponents of magical realism, the Cuban writer, Alejo Carpentier.[55]

Lo real maravilloso, Carpentier's vision of Caribbean reality, functions through a perception of a radical disjunction in the coexistence of two enormously different worldviews. In *The Kingdom of This World* (1949), the novel in which Carpentier first dramatized this theory, he dramatically manipulated a legend that arose from a historical incident that eventually led to the revolution which culminated in Haiti's independence in 1804. At his execution Mackandal, a reputed sorcerer who had led an underground resistance movement (1751–57), managed to writhe free of his bonds. Upon seeing this, the Haitian crowd rioted and, amid the subsequent disorder, the people did not see that Mackandal indeed had been executed. A legend had it that he turned himself into a bird to escape his captors. Carpentier represents the episode as dividing into two existent realities, one for the whites who see the troublesome rebel burn, one for the blacks who see their hero transform himself into a bird and fly away. *Lo real maravilloso* in this example, then, is the representation of a kind of dialectic between two possible visions of reality, one for the blacks who "see" the marvelous and who eventually are able to change their position in the "real" world because of their belief in what they see, and one for the whites who don't "see" the marvelous at all but whose vision is represented by a privileged narrator who sees all. Far from being simply another manifestation of the fantastic in literature, it was a kind of realism, an actual manifestation of a vision of the world and a way of life that accurately depicted Latin American, specifically Caribbean, reality.[56] Gabriel García Márquez, in his 1982 Nobel Prize speech, and Saldívar have also discussed magical realism as a groundbreaking version of social realism in which what seems magical, from a Western perspective, is actually a reflection of a destabilized Latin American reality.

Carpentier distinguished the marvelous real and regarded it as superior in comparison with European surrealism, a movement in which he had participated actively, claiming that the marvelous real was truly a manifestation of an "American" ontology whereas surrealism relied on artificial manipulations of reality and game-playing. The basic ingredient that Latin American reality contained, absent in European surrealism, was faith. Because of this faith what might seem marvelous or magical from a Western point of view was merely a part of the natural Caribbean, Latin American way of being.[57] Additionally, Carpentier, stressed the organic relationship between the fantastical phenomena he was later to depict in his fiction, notably in *The Kingdom of This World*, and the American *terrain* itself stating that magical/religious practices such as Voudoun, for example, were the result of a kind of symbiosis between the Haitian land and its people. Cristina García and Toni Morrison are writers whose use of the style is fragmentary, fitting the allegorical equation that Benjamin describes. Let us examine the episode I already briefly mentioned in which Constancia wakes up one fine morning in Miami, after having had bad dreams about plastic surgery, *wearing her mother's face*.[58]

García's utilizes the magical in this episode to illustrate Constancia's state of mind and show that she is repressing knowledge of her mother and about the past. It resembles the use of Santería to show Ignacio's and Constancia's ambivalent yet hopeful relationship to Cuban magical practices. In García's text, which was published fifty years after *The Kingdom of This World*, the disjunction in two worldviews is something that does not necessarily connect the private individual with the public arena. Mackandal's destiny—whether he burned at the stake, or escaped his fate by transmutation into another creature—is an urgent matter for both the slaves and the masters of Carpentier's Haiti. But García's postmodernist magical realism is so ambiguous that characters, narrator, and reader are left with doubts. In *The Kingdom of This World* the slaves believed what the narrator and the whites doubted.

There's nothing terribly shocking at first about the sudden appearance of Blanca's face on Constancia's. One of my students even thought the appearance of the face was the result of plastic surgery since Constancia has a dream about plastic surgery right before waking up with her new face. This misreading is understandable. García spends a considerable portion of the book detailing this character's cosmetics line called Cuerpo de Cuba, which features body products such as Muslos de Cuba, Cara de Cuba, and so forth. A looks-obsessed creature such as Constancia would have a nightmare about plastic surgery gone wrong. But of course, the nightmare, like all nightmares, bears another meaning.

The "whirring" sensation in Constancia's dream seems to come from the dream surgeons' activities. Their excision of "roots and useless nerves" is a figure for the kind of memory cleaning Constancia needs to do. The "operation" is bringing her closer to "the deafening white," which is not the memory, necessarily, of what happened between her parents but of the "white" act itself, the space that supersedes memory, "forgetfulness" as described in the excerpt of the Hart Crane poem quoted as one of the book's epigraphs. This is also the blank space of repression, which, of course, in the text is always cleverly covered over with each character's rationalizations and excuses. Just as Blanca herself is never allowed to be as bare as forgetfulness. She is always marked, written over, by her relations with the other characters. She is alternatively: Reina's beloved mother who took her on walks all over Havana; Constancia's detested mother who deserted her when she was born; Ignacio's beloved Oshún and mad, whorish wife. So, the superimposition of Blanca's face on Constancia's is literally the return of the repressed. If metaphorically Constancia has not been able to wipe her mother from consciousness that fact now becomes physical.

However, literarily, this magical realism is hard to notice. Constancia herself looks twice in the mirror to be sure. As readers, we have to mouth over the passage several times lest we make the same mistake as the student who thought Constancia had had a bad face job. What I am trying to say is that there is a kind of indeterminate quality to this magical realism. It might be something else that the author is recording here. Perhaps Constancia has Bell's Palsy, which forces the face into strange contortions? The effect of García's magical realism is quite minimal in comparison with Carpentier's. On the other hand, once we recognize that the magical realism in this scene has a kind of fragmentary or attenuated relationship to its Other, Latin American magical realism, we also have to acknowledge that it works very well in an entirely different way. From the beginning of the book, García depicts Constancia's hunger for magic and miracle, in particular her avid interest in a popular Miami show called *La Hora de los Milagros*, which comically reports miracles as mundane as a chicken flying backward into a pot to make a soup that will save its owner's life.[59] Constancia is divided between two worlds. Unlike Ti Nöel, the protagonist of *The Kingdom of This World* who believes in Mackandal's transformations because, as Carpentier puts it, they are part of his "land . . . upbringing . . . ontology."[60] She is no longer in a place where faith in the magical is easy because it is historically based. Like all subjects in this contemporary world who attempt to brew knowledge out of the slips and slivers of memory, she is still getting used to the idea that there is no origin to recover. She must simply learn how to balance fragments that are constantly forming themselves into new, never to be entirely resolved, and contingent, revisions and re/versions.

To sum up, *The Agüero Sisters* provides an exceptionally complex and unsentimental examination of the relationship between evolving U.S. Latina Caribbean identity and a Caribbean origin perceived as magical. The existence of character doubles (Ignacio and Blance, Reina and Constancia) and double plots shows how obsessively past relationships influence present reality as the characters seem compulsively drawn to repeat the past while remaining vulnerable to its long-standing effects. At the same time, the novel's moments of magical realism—in their scarcity and ambiguity (Blanca's metamorphosis into Oshún's handmaiden, for example, which I have shown to be Ignacio's projection)—demonstrate that the magical is as lost as the origin with which it is linked. Characters such as Ignacio and Constancia tend to mystify as magical situations or people they don't understand, especially the nature and actions of Blanca Agüero. Magical realism, when it appears momentarily, and fragmentarily, in Garcia's text, implies the psychological return of a reality the characters do not consciously recognize. The reinvention of the past and the projection of spiritual or magical aspects onto the present in García's text underlines the partnership of desire with great doubt, an uneasy avatar of the deep faith that Carpentier described as essential to the existence of *lo real maravilloso*.

CHAPTER THREE

KILLING "SPANISH": ROSARIO FERRÉ'S EVOLUTION FROM *autora puertorriqueña* TO U.S. LATINA WRITER

My approach to Rosario Ferré's work focuses on her use of the allegorical vehicle of the house, which, early on in her career, served to critique the nationalist, paternalistic narratives of Puerto Rico's early-twentieth-century literature. Much of the scholarship on Ferré's fiction underlines the existence of the female, black, mulatto, and "Other" voices in her work that the patriarchal narratives left out in their attempts to contain Puerto Rican literary identity.[1] I hold, however, that Ferré's use of the house trope changed markedly from the early feminist viewpoints of her fiction in Spanish, to the "translation" of Puerto Rican history and culture attempted in *The House on the Lagoon* (1995), her first novel in English to the quasi-autobiographical tendency of her second novel in English, *Eccentric Neighborhoods* (1999).[2] I also contend that *Sweet Diamond Dust* (1986, tr. 1988)—Ferré's novella, written in Spanish, about a plantation family undermined by those on its margins—and *The House on the Lagoon*, set up anti-patriarchalist narratives, which are histrionic and unconvincing because the "Other" voices Ferré has been so lauded for bringing in to interrupt the paternalist discourse are really doubles and projections of the subjectivities of her repressed and suppressed upper-middle-class women narrators. In *Eccentric Neighborhoods* the allegorical features—expressed in the house/nation trope and in character doubles—give way to a quasi-memoir, a narrative in which the protagonist, Ferré/Elvira, can focus on her individualist desires while recognizing that the price of her freedom is literally the dead body of her repressed, conservative mother. The daughter interprets the blood that pours out of the mother's mouth—when the corpse is turned over—as a sacrificial mark, a kind of ghostly protest, which underlines the price of the mother's self-repression while alive. The sacrifice of "Spanish" identity, in the person of the Puerto Rican mother in this book, ultimately marks Ferré's translation, from a novelist writing out of a uniquely politicized island background, to the more individuated territory of U.S. Latina writer.

Rosario Ferré's work presents a gratifying challenge to a critic of U.S. Latino/a literature. This is because Ferré is the only Latino/a Caribbean writer to date who has written many and significant works in both English and Spanish. Her books of short stories, *The Youngest Doll (Papeles de Pandora)* and *Sweet Diamond Dust (Maldito amor)* were part of a rich and important literary production in mid-1970s to 1980s

Puerto Rico in which Ferré and other island writers defined a point of rupture with the nationalist and paternalist stance that had overdetermined the course of Puerto Rican letters until then.[3] Her first novel in English, *The House on the Lagoon*, was a 1995 National Book Award Finalist. However, besides a short novel in Spanish, *La batalla de las vírgenes* (1993), her three novels in English and the short story collections in Spanish, Ferré has produced four important works of literary criticism in Spanish, several books of poetry and children's stories, as well as transcribed and composed an "autobiography" of her father, Luis A. Ferré, former governor of Puerto Rico and former leader of the Partido Nacional Puertorriqueño, or PNP, the political party that advocates statehood for Puerto Rico.[4] She has, in addition, herself translated her books of stories into English and has rewritten her English-language novels in Spanish.[5]

At first glance, then, Ferré's ambitious, impressive production in English and Spanish would seem to be part of the role she has carved out for herself as a fiction writer, poet, and critic—generally and impressively, a woman of letters.[6] However, since the publication so late in her literary career of the novels in English, Ferré has been hounded by critics and a public composed mostly of Puerto Ricans with *independentista* leanings who have accused her of betraying her roots in Spanish and on the island because of the temptations of reaching a wider English-speaking market.[7]

A comparison of Ferré's early works written in Spanish with the two recent novels in English does turn up strikingly different formal effects implying an extreme ideological divergence from the earlier to the later work. Ferré's early work challenged one of the most important metaphors of Puerto Rican literature, so strongly shaped and influenced by political nationalism, the metaphor of the "gran familia puertorriqueña" metonymically tied to the allegorical vehicle of the house.[8] As Juan Gelpí notes, Ferré, along with the island writers Manuel Ramos Otero, Magali García Ramis, and Ana Lydia Vega, rebelled against René Marqués, one of the patriarchs of Puerto Rican literature, who saw the island as "a house in ruins" after the arrival of the Americans in 1898.[9] In her early fiction Ferré undermined the notion that the American invasion threatened the purity of Puerto Rican culture, showing that this was a nationalist myth invented by a landed class whose hegemony in Puerto Rican society was indeed destroyed by the invasion but not for the reasons or to the detriment that the myth defined.

Mimetic Desire and Doubling in "When Women Love Men"

In Ferré's work the rift between individual desires—seen for Puerto Rican women specifically as the product of American feminism—and loyalty to a community still focused on a creolized but essentially "Spanish" code of values, gets played out in the dynamics of triangular relationships. In applying René Girard's ideas on mimetic desire to her work I have been particularly interested to note that doubling in her fiction frequently, although not always, pivots around racialization. For example, "When Women Love Men" is one of Ferré's most famous and oft-cited short stories. By Girard's standards it is "novelistic"—the author is extremely conscious of the dynamics of mimetic desire that motivate her characters: the white wife and black mistress of a wealthy island Puerto Rican man, Ambrosio, whose death unleashes an intensification of the women's interest in, and desire for, each other. These women are allegorical types—pitting black Puerto Rican versus Spanish origins—and mimetic doubles.

I am not the first critic to note how well a Girardian reading suits this story. Frances Aparicio makes the following comment on the roles of the white society-wife and the black prostitute in "When Women Love Men:"

> René Girard's model of triangular desire [ ] is effective in deciphering Ambrosio's role as a mediator between the desires of both women. By coming face to face with each other—that is, by dismantling the allegorical binaries that each represents—"their own true face" would finally come to *the surface*. What surface metaphorically and textually, I propose, are the racial, class, and gender constructs penned by the patriarchal writers such as Brau, Pedreira, and Blanco.[10]

Aparicio's reading emphasizes that the binary relationship between the black mistress and the white wife is allegorical, implying that the madonna/whore marianista dichotomy tends to displace itself along racial lines in Spanish Caribbean and Latin American literature. Aparicio goes on to point out, following Rafael Falcón, that in Latin American and Puerto Rican literature in particular, "the[deployment of black characters can function only in relation to a liberal project separate from black agency, authority, and authorship."[11]

Aparicio notes that Ambrosio, the white patriarch, is the mediator for the two women. But that is a simple reading of the complex dynamics of mimetic desire in the story. While Ambrosio is alive, the women desire what Ambrosio, as the mediator, desires—namely each other. Once they start to focus upon each other, mimetic desire changes the dynamics in the story and Ambrosio's role as mediator transforms accordingly. For once the women start to desire each other, they also become mediators for each other and Ambrosio becomes a redoubled object of desire. Then, after his death, he is a more distant, and for this reason, idealized mediator, since the women now desire each other as mediators *and* objects. As models or mediators for each other, Isabel Luberza and Isabel La Negra become doubles in my view. They become more like each other in desire due to double mediation.[12]

Ferré's deployment of black characters—Isabel la Negra in this instance—might also correspond to the kind of shadow-playing Toni Morrison claims is one of the keys to understanding the American literary imagination. In *Playing in the Dark* Morrison notes that nineteenth-century American literature (as well as contemporary literature written by nonblack authors deploying black characters)—in particular what she terms "American Romance,"—is characterized by the use of black characters upon whom the unacknowledged desires of the white characters are projected. What Morrison calls shadow-playing I would also term doubling. Isabel Luberza is shadow-playing with Isabel La Negra: the white wife needs the black mistress to preserve her own psychic safety and freedom.

What is questionable and controversial is the way Ferré wants to equalize the grounds between the black woman and the white woman, to say that they are shadow-playing with each other, that each desires the other in the same way.

A Morrisonian reading underscores how unequal their desires are in the Puerto Rican social hierarchy. Isabel Luberza shadow-plays with the idea of Isabel La Negra's sexual potency but that potency is itself the product of patriarchal Puerto Rican society. In desiring Isabel La Negra in this way, Isabel Luberza imitates Ambrosio's desire for Isabel La Negra's blackness as a kind of supplement or support to his paternalist subjectivity. In taking on this desire Isabel Luberza, the sesually repressed and suppressed white upper-class Latina, feels sexually liberated and freed. Whereas before she had been frigid and sexually neglected by her husband, now her desire for the black woman makes her feel more sexual—even though the women do not have real sexual contact. The experimental splicing of the two women's points of view in the story underlines the fact that they desire, and merge with, each other, ontologically. This of course reminds us of the fact that Girard calls mimetic desire "the ontological sickness."

Isabel La Negra, on the other hand, receives the short end of the stick, for what she desires in her double she cannot access as easily as Isabel can access a sense of freedom through imitating Ambrosio's desire for black women. The story shows that Isabel La Negra fetishizes Isabel Luberza just as much as Luberza fetishizes La Negra. But La Negra's lack—status and social privilege—cannot be filled as easily as Luberza's lack, sexual potency. The precise inequivalence is this: A rich white man can always acquire a beautiful black woman to fill his sense of lack, his sense of being distant from the cultural source, in this case Puerto Rico's Afrosyncretic culture. Isabel Luberza imitates and takes on her husband's desire for plenitude through sex. On the other hand, Isabel La Negra does not desire Isabel Luberza because of Ambrosio's desire for his wife (which was nil) but rather because Puerto Rican society at this particular moment in the early twentieth century will allow Ambrosio to have a white wife, not a black or mulatta spouse. Ferré writes the women as desiring each other equally in the arena of the erotic, but analysis reveals that Luberza cannot be the same type of erotic object for La Negra as La Negra is for Luberza if the original mediator is the patriarch. Even after he dies, and the women become mediators for each other, the dead patriarch's mediation takes on even more power—the power of ghost, God, Father of the culture.

As we shall see, doubling in Ferré's *Sweet Diamond Dust* follows a similar racialized dynamic that is the product of triangular desire. In *The House on the Lagoon*, however, the doubling and mimetic desire follows a gender pattern similar to that in *The Agüero Sisters*. In *Eccentric Neighborhoods*, however, Fletcher's allegorical typology is useful in tandem with the mimetic desire model because Elvira so clearly makes a choice between the aristocratic mother's conservative "Spanish" ideology, which in that book signifies being naturalized, and the father's rationalism, which is derived from his own family's nouveau riche association with American progressivism in neocolonial Puerto Rico.

Burning Down the Plantation House in Sweet Diamond Dust:
The Double Did It

In 1980 the distinguished Puerto Rican/Dominican writer, Jose Luis González, published an important collection of essays called *Puerto Rico: The Four-Storeyed Country*.[13] In the title essay González constructed a controversial Marxist historical model to explain the reason why, in total contradiction to Cuba where resistance to

American colonial intentions cut across class lines, there had been no resistance, among either the elite landed class or the peasantry in Puerto Rico, to the American invasion of the island in the 1898 Spanish-American war. González undermined the usual explanation of Puerto Rican culture as a product of Indian, Spanish, and African elements. He showed that, due to the unstable pattern of Spanish colonization in the first two centuries after the "discovery," the group that in his mind authentically comprise the first storey of Puerto Rican culture are black Puerto Ricans.[14]

González's paradigm continues to ring strangely in the ears of an island public used to the easy mythology of the even parts Spanish, Indian, and African theory. The "mixture" theory is commonplace in the hispanophone Caribbean, although in Puerto Rico and the Dominican Republic there has always, until recently, existed the tendency to minimize the importance of the African component. In *The Four-Storeyed Country* González downplays both the Spanish and Indian heritage, dismissing the Spaniards because they did not tend to become permanent residents of the island until the 1700s and noting that because of the genocide of the Indians throughout the Caribbean the influence of the latter is, of necessity, minuscule.[15] Puerto Rico would have followed the tendency of much of the rest of the Caribbean, he claims, becoming "a popular mestizo culture of a predominantly Afro-Antillean type."[16] The Spanish initiative, after the Haitian Revolution, to lactify the Spanish Caribbean by encouraging the immigration of numerous European settlers, precluded this. Notable among these settlers were large groups of Corsicans, Majorcans, and Catalans who, according to González, not only comprise the second solid storey of the house of Puerto Rican cultural identity but created, as well, "a virtual colonization."[17] They accomplished this by buying up the coffee farms in the islands mountainous interior "cordillera," setting themselves up as an enterprising bourgeoisie in direct competition with the owners of the coastal sugar plantations, who were of a mostly more "aristocratic" Spanish lineage.[18] González goes on to complicate his paradigm by arguing that the third storey of identity was instituted in 1898 by the American invasion itself, which brought to a crisis the extreme conflict between the landed classes and the peasantry, of all races. What for the landed classes constituted a disastrous loss of land, and financial and political power was for the peasantry a liberating moment. He goes on to clinch his model with the argument that the fourth storey of the cultural edifice began in the late 1940s with Operation Bootstrap, Governor Luis Muñoz Marín's intensive industrialization drive, which resulted in the largest wave of Puerto Rican immigration to New York. What González stresses throughout the essay is that the emphasis on the Spanish legacy—and thereby on the purity of the Spanish language as a signifier of resistance to the barbarous Americans—is a myth invented by the landed classes whose nostalgic stance looking back at the happy plantation past underlines a present where that once serene family is beset by lamentation, where the beautiful edifice is a house in ruins.

If the house in ruins represents "the crisis of the paternalist canon" as Gelpí argues and if the first storey, of these Puerto Rican literary houses, represents black identity, as González claims, then the burning down of the house by Gloria Camprubí, the mulatto "outsider" to the De la Valle family, in Ferré's novella *Sweet Diamond Dust*, must correspond to the razing of paternalist discourse by those on its margins. That is the way Ferré's novella has been read by Gelpí,[19] among others, and that is the way it lends itself to be read given its correspondence to González's paradigm. Ferré in *Sweet Diamond Dust* sets up a series of stories none of which can be corroborated and all of which contradict each other, including Gloria's. This leads to a disquieting conclusion: if paternalistic discourse is no longer possible, other discourses don't seem to be either, at least not in this story. Gloria's narrative, which ends the novella, in many ways is the least convincing of the litany of voices that make up *Sweet Diamond Dust*. Her narrative, which may or not be true, is shorter than those of all the other characters.[20] Moreover, it is contradictory, enigmatic, and, ultimately, as self-annihilating as it is destructive of the story lines set into motion by the voices of characters from more powerful subject positions in the novella.

Sweet Diamond Dust is told by different family members with conflicting points of view, as well as through the narration of a more selfconsciously "authoritative" voice: that of Don Hermenegildo Martínez, the childhood friend of the De la Valle family patriarch, Ubaldino de la Valle," and thus himself an upholder of patriarchy. The beginning of the novella—narrated, we later realize, from the biographical history Don Hermenegildo is writing about the de la Valle family—exquisitely parodies the tone of Puerto Rican nationalist discourse:

> "In the past the people of Guamaní used to be proud of their town and of their valley. From the red-ochered cliffs that pour their blood upon the valley every day at three o'clock, when the inevitable afternoon showers burst upon it, we loved to behold our town nestled on the silvery arms of Ensenada Honda bay . . .
> . . . Well-to-do families lived in elegant houses, with wood-carved lace fans filtering the afternoon rays of the sun over their doorways, balconies of marble balusters [. . .]Vulgarity and mediocrity were banished from our midst . . ."[21]

Ferré ironizes the nationalist penchant for deleting crucial historical facts (we hear about the "'well-to-do'" but not the poor) and for imposing ideology ("'Vulgarity and mediocrity were banished . . .'") here in the opening of both of Ferré's novella as well as the fictive document within the novella written by Don Hermenegildo Martínez. This fiction-within-a-fiction inscribes Don Ubaldino de la Valle as a national patriot. As Don Hermenegildo himself puts it, "'Every country that aspires to become a nation needs its heroes . . . and if it doesn't have them, it's our duty to invent them.'"[22]

Don Hermenegildo makes this cynical statement after hearing the account by "'Guamaní's last slave; Titina, the timeless one'" who has been the De la Valle's servant all her life.[23] Titina involves Don Hermenegildo in the story by telling him of a plot cooked up by Arístides, the oldest de la Valle brother, ending in the murder of the apparently rebellious Nicolás, the family's youngest son who married Gloria, the mulatta outsider. However, Don Hermenegildo quickly goes on to disclaim his cynicism by stating that there is no real need to invent Ubaldino's heroism since he himself witnessed it. We distrust him as a narrator both because of his slip and because he makes his cynical comment about inventing history in the context of the story told by Titina to whom his attitude is condescending.

Titina's motivation for telling Don Ubaldino about the goings-on at the De la Valles' is that she wants to make sure she and her husband receive the indemnity promised by the defunct patriarch. Don Hermenegildo's description of Titina as "timeless" and "everlasting," marks this former slave as both pre-temporal—prior to the De la Valle's ascendancy and thus both essential to their power if not inclusive in it—and a-temporal, because of the very lack of power that has defined her role in the De la Valle's rise according to Don Hermenegildo's narrative. Don Ubaldino's inscription of Titina follows the pattern James Clifford has highlighted among ethnographers who unconsciously allegorize when locating ethnic others in a temporally different, but identifiable, space within an assumed progression of Western history.[24] Don Hermenegildo's patronizing of Titina is characteristic of the tunnel vision of his class, preoccupied with resistance toward the colonizer but paradoxically indifferent to the poverty and suffering of their own proletarian classes.[25] I mention Don Hermenegildo's attitude toward Titina here because it will serve to contrast with Doña Laura's attitude to Gloria, which I analyze later and which also projects an allegorical figuration, of a different kind, onto her mulatta daughter-in-law.

The immediate conflict declared in chapter one, if we take it's rhetoric at face value, is between a self-sufficient paradisiacal Puerto Rican nation and a devouring, "monstrous" American colonizer wishing to appropriate the island's land and agriculture. Like some of the more significant works of the nationalist literary production, chapter one establishes an immediate dichotomy between past splendor—under the Spanish government, which many nationalist writings idealize: "'In the past the people of Guamaní used to be proud of their town and of their valley.'"—and present crisis under the "monstrous" capitalism of the Americans: "'Today all that has changed . . . Guamaní has become a hell, a monstrous whirlpool from which . . . Snow White Sugar Mills spews out sugar night and day toward the north.'"[26]

Ferré evokes and satirizes the rhetoric of the most famous nineteenth-century exponents of it—Luis Lloréns Torres and Jose Gautier Benítez, quoting from the latter's poetry as an epigraph to *Sweet Diamond Dust*. In the passage from Gautier, Puerto Rico is a "pearl the sea tears from its shell" or a "heron sleeping in the white foam/ Of the whiter waist of your shores."[27] As a pearl and living bird, the island is refined and cultivated in sharp contrast to the wildness of the (mother) ocean from which it is torn. In Gautier's Romantic vision, the amniotic immensity of mother ocean gives birth to the pearl that the ocean could very easily devour again. As Juan Gelpí points out, the ocean in the paternalist literature of Marqués and Pedreira is a much more ambivalent figure than the land:

> The ocean is . . . a menace to the equilibrium of the "gran familia," a violent space that wounds the [protagonist's] gaze and can lead to solitude, an exile figured by the high seas . . . Facing the sea Pirulo [the narrator of Rene Marqués' bildungsroman, *La víspera del hombre*, or *The Dawn of Man*] defines another aspect of his identity which is not totally divorced from patriarchal values: his nationalism. . . . On the other hand, it is near the sea where he acquires his erotic apprenticeship and has his first encounter with death.[28] (My translation)

Ferré repeats and mocks the imagery of this rhetoric, which assumes an organic, and yet distinct, relationship between the island (as "pearl," and "heron") and the nature that surrounds it, in this case the ocean. Like the Puerto Rico of the Gautier poem, the Guamaní of the opening chapter is described by the narrator as surrounded and nurtured by the ocean: "[W]e loved to behold our town nestled on the silvery arms of Ensenada Honda bay." Paternalist rhetoric establishes the ocean as a threatening limit, the domain of either Eros or death. On the other hand, Ferré's description of Guamaní as "nestling" in the "silvery arms" of the bay of Ensenada Honda's ocean is decidedly playful and this playfulness reaches its peak when at the end of the paragraph the author personifies the "gaily pealing rain" that makes the townspeople run "frantically to and fro," clearly belittling the relationship between man and nature in the paternalist literature.

The warring of the narrating voices in *Sweet Diamond Dust* insures that one doesn't know who to believe. Ultimately, what is at stake is the racial identity of Don Julio Font, Don Ubaldino De La Valle's deceased father, whom Don Hermenegildo novelizes as a blue-eyed Spaniard and whom Doña Laura, Ubaldino's dying wife, reveals was black. But there are other uncertainties. Titina and Gloria paint a picture of Gloria's romantic felicity with Nicolás, the allegedly murdered younger son who, according to Gloria, was concerned with improving the lot of the peasants working on Diamond Dust plantation. Arístides, Laura, and Don Hermenegildo construct Gloria as a type of whore who sleeps with anybody, Doña Laura even going so far as to make this whorishness of Gloria's an allegorical figuration of Puerto Rican identity:

> From the very first day of Gloria's arrival at our house. . .she soon became a sort of legendary prostitute, offering herself to all those ruined farmers who were about to emigrate to Chicago and New York, as well as to the new entrepreneurs who came from the north, and thus Nicolasito can said to be the child of all. In her body, or if you prefer in her cunt, both races, both languages, English and Spanish, grew into one soul, into one wordweed of love.[29]

At first glance Gloria, like Titina, might be identifiable with González's first storey of Puerto Rican identity. But upon reflection, and after carefully considering Doña Laura's speech one would have to separate Gloria and Titina, identifying only the latter with the more essentialized membership on the first storey. Doña Laura creates an image of Gloria that seems to correspond more accurately to González's fourth storey, the layer of Puerto Rican identity influenced by American colonization. At the fourth storey one would have to place a notion—not of an assimilated, Americanized Puerto Rican identity—but something closer to the hybrid idea Laura posits when she speaks of Gloria's cunt as bridging the gap between the north and the south. Gloria's cunt is the meeting-point "where both English and Spanish can grow into one soul, one wordweed of love," in other words, a hybrid, more potent offspring of the Anglo and Hispanic starter components.

Gloria's "world[loving]" whorishness is a projection, of course, of Laura's own frustrated sensuality and well-intentioned, if misguided, philanthropy. Gloria's love of all Others vicariously assuages Laura's guilt as the wife of a hypocritical crook. On the other hand, the kind of "partial gaze" that Bhabha describes as an effect of mimicry is evident in Laura's language, especially in her fantasies about her daughter-in-law's "cunt." This penultimate chapter narrated by Laura reveals her as far-sighted, shrewd, honest and liberal-minded. However, despite her opposition to the snobbishness of the aristocratic family she has married into, her attitude toward Gloria is symptomatic of the class divisions among Puerto Rican women. Despite Laura's apparently imaginative, even generous attitude toward Gloria's promiscuity, she shows how manipulative she is by refusing to consider Gloria as anything but a body onto which she inscribes her fantasies and idealizations. And the more em/Bodied Gloria is the more Laura reverts to a binary role as a cuntless, conniving shrew. So much is this the case that she actually hires Gloria to let the dying Ubaldino fondle her so that Laura will not have to suffer his caresses. It's not an alliance of equals Laura is after but rather the use of a younger, more sensual body. And because Laura is so identified with rationality, she allegorizes Gloria's promiscuity as an ideal state of mixing of classes and races. And if Gloria is metonymically tied to the land then Laura sells out the land as much as she does Gloria.

Nevertheless, Laura's attitude is an improvement, and a parody, of the stance displayed by Arístides, the oldest son who represents the "purist" and patriarchal point of view that sees the potential mixture (in Gloria's womb and of Puerto Rican identity) as "monstrous." Arístides can neither control nor truly know the paternity of the New Puerto Rican subject: "Once Gloria spawned her offspring one primeval night, be it reptile, fish, or fowl, she stayed home to take care of Mother."[30] In fact Arístides' attitude toward Gloria is purely the product of, on the one hand, the plantation mentality in which blacks are seen as closely allied to animals and, on the other, the nationalist, paternalist fear generated by the American takeover of the land in 1898. Arístides is a strong believer in the plantocratic "myth" of a Puerto Rican identity brought into crisis by the Americans. Because Gloria supposedly sleeps with everyone, black and white Puerto Ricans, as well as barbarous Americans, she is bestial. The bestial is the result of an inability to provide an "official" lineage and account of identity.

The way Gloria is projected upon by Arístides and Doña Laura recalls the similar kinds of projection occurring in *The Agüero Sisters* with the figure of Blanca, the murdered mother. However, unlike *The Agüero Sisters*, a story about the absent mother whose voice is more haunting because never heard, *Sweet Diamond Dust* offers us Gloria's version of events. And, unlike *The Agüero Sisters*, this is precisely the problem with *Sweet Diamond Dust*. Gloria's voice, it turns out, when we hear it, does not live up to the projections we have heard constructing her, on the one hand, as a kind of ideal and synthesized Puerto Rican (Doña Laura) and on the other as a kind of earthy, pragmatic, sensual, hardheaded Puerto Rican mulatta, the one who reveals the "identity" of Don Julio Font to Doña Laura, and who both captivates and brings the family to its crisis point through her sex appeal.

There are problems with the voice of the Gloria we hear in the final chapter. Perhaps the most disappointing thing about this closing chapter is that its tone is one of high melodrama, strangely reminiscent of the nostalgic tone in which the sisters in René Marqués' play, *Los soles truncos* evoke the past, whereas up until this point the novella has been highly satirical.[31] At the novella's end in chapter VIII, a Gloria, who seems to be headed toward madness addresses Titina as she is pouring benzene on the bagasse that surrounds the plantation house preparing for the final conflagration that will destroy not just the plantation and Don Hermenegildo, who had come to Dona Laura's deathbed, but herself and Titina as well. There is still a note of satire here. Gloria is mocking Don Hermenegildo's self-heroicizing vocation as nationalist auteur, sardonically noting that she will help him with the narrative. But the mordancy of Gloria's wit is undercut by the hysteria of her reproofs to Titina ("You should never have visited Don Hermenegildo in his office, you fool . . .") and by her very paradoxical claim that "the De la Valles and their friends are all birds of a feather."[32] This claim is contradictory because only a little later on in the chapter does Gloria declare that her love for Nicolás De la Valle was so powerful that she can only describe its intensity indirectly:

> Nicolás would have done anything for his mother, and she treated me like her own daughter. This is why Nicolás and I were married, to please her, because marriage really wasn't important to us; she knew that married or not we'd always be together, be it in the heights of heaven or the depths of hell, where Guamaní society would readily have thrown us. [33]

Nicolás's love for Gloria is revealed as indistinguishable from his love for his mother. A Girardian reading demonstrates that Nicolás loves Laura first and foremost and that it is the fact that Laura so much idealizes the mulatta that attaches Nicolás, metonymically speaking, to Gloria. That is, Nicolás loves Gloria because he imitates his mother's desire. Also, following Girard's ideas, Doña Laura's speech about Gloria's cunt shows how identified she is with the mulatta as a figuration, not just of a generalized womanhood that includes Laura, but of both the ambiguity and all-inclusiveness of Puerto Rican identity itself. In this context it is easy to see that there might be a grain of truth in Arístides' contention that Nicolás was homosexual and that the marriage with Gloria was meant to appease Doña Laura.

Of the three marginalized female voices speaking in the narrative, that of Doña Laura stands out both in terms of the accuracy of the character portrayal and the strength of her voice in the narrative. Titina is more of a plot vehicle. And though Gloria's voice ends the narrative, Gloria is given only four pages in which to speak— a good example of a subaltern whose speech is curtailed. When we do hear her, her speech, as I have already argued, is histrionic. The really subversive voice in the narra-tive is not Gloria the mulatta's, as much of the criticism on Ferré would have us believe, but the voice of Doña Laura, the daughter of a small Corsican landowner, extremely critical of the pretentious ways of the De la Valles, the old "Spanish" Puerto Rican family she has married into. It is Doña Laura's narrative, an eighteen-page chapter comprising roughly one-fourth of the novella, that reveals the truth behind the lies, mainly that Ubaldino's father, Don Julio Font, was not a blue-blooded Spanish immigrant, fresh from Extremadura, the land of the Spanish Conquistadors, but a mulatto from a nearby farm. What is revelatory and radical here, what undermines the nationalist and patriarchal presumptions of Puerto Rican literature, is the voice of this daughter of immigrant Corsican peasants.

This, however, is an idea that does not so easily construct *Sweet Diamond Dust* as subversive in the way Gelpí has argued, because for Gelpí, and other critics, and indeed for Ferré herself, Gloria's status as a mulatta is crucial. The fact that the black, female outsider burns down the plantation house is a strong symbolic act. The speeches that bolster the notion of Gloria as subversive, however, are those attributed to her by the other characters (namely Doña Laura and Arístides) not her direct discourse in the last chapter. The love she expresses for Nicolás in the last chapter conveys a strange nostalgia as well as an interesting homoeroticism revealed in her recollection of Doña Laura: "I loved her for the memories we shared and because I could conjure up Nicolás' presence more easily, when she called out to his ghost from the balconies of the house."[34] This love of ghosts evokes Rene Marqués's characters, the three sisters locked up in the Old San Juan house, recalling the good old plantation days of Papa Burckhardt before the U.S. invasion, as well as the apparitions of plantation literature in general: the madwoman in the attic who burns down Rochester's house in *Jane Eyre* and *Wide Sargasso Sea* as well as the ghost of Sutpen conjured up for Quentin by old Rosa in *Absalom, Absalom*. But the note struck seems false and it is a false note that often problematizes Ferré's work when she tries to find a bond uniting the subjectivities of women as different as Laura Latoni and Gloria Camprubí. The problem here resembles the problem in "When Women Love Men": the white woman's perspective projects a fantasy of equality that blurs the realities of subjectivies like Isabel La Negra's or Gloria's. What predominates is the feminine point of view that Ferré knows best, that of the daughter of the coffee-holding recent immigrants, Laura Latoni, or the descendant of the regal Spanish aristocracy, Isabel Luberza. The action that Gloria carries out in the final chapter of *Sweet Diamond Dust* is one of rebellion and rejection of the patriarchal ethos; her rhetoric, though, is the patriarchal rhetoric of nostalgia, of holding onto a past that was always better than the present and that contradictorily can outlive the present through the kind of rebellious act Gloria carries out.

Thus, in her "deconstruction" of the patriarchal vehicle of the house, Ferré reconfirms its solidity as a vehicle even the marginalized support just as Gloria does when "she calls out to [Nicolás'] ghost from the balconies of the house."[35] The problem with Laura's plan is exactly the fact that it emanates from Laura's subjectivity. Laura, the Corsican outsider, gets her revenge on the snooty De La Valles by forcing her adoring son Nicolás to marry Gloria, the mulatta, and then cutting all her children out of the will to leave the plantation to Gloria and the baby Nicolásito whom Laura exultantly describes as the child of "all [races and cultures]." Ferré's insight that Gloria would disagree with Doña Laura was correct but the gesture of razing the plantation is far more reactionary than Laura's liberal plan to facilitate the emergence of a New Puerto Rican race. In effect, Gloria mimetically reinscribes the class positions she supposedly rebels against. She loves Nicolás because she idealizes his mother. She burns down the plantation house, not because she rejects paternalist discourse but because she needs to identify with it by availing herself of the limited feminine agency it permits, which allows for the type of resistance voiced by Doña Laura's cantankerous and creative imaginings. By burning down the plantation house, Gloria, in fact, demonstrates an admittedly ambivalent belief in the notions of "purity" and class hierarchy that Don Ubaldino had inscribed at the beginning of the novella, and which Ferré had ironized. Gloria ends up mimicking Laura's ambivalent posturings. Burning down the plantation house then is pure mimicry: a rebellious gesture still entangled in the desires of the old order.

Perhaps Ferré sensed both that she had given the representation of Gloria's subjectivity short shrift in *Sweet Diamond Dust* and that Laura Latoni's voice was memorably eloquent for in her first real novel, *The House on the Lagoon*, which was also her first English-language book, she chose to make the dominating point of view emanate from that of a character whose subject position was similar to Laura Latoni's.

The House on the Lagoon: The Delicate Lady's Rebellion

Ferré has been soundly trounced by Puerto Rican writers and critics for writing in English. There is validity to the criticism, the gist of which is that Ferré is simply a better writer in Spanish than she is in English. Ferré herself makes no bones about it, declaring that Spanish is her first language and first love. English, which she did not learn until she was seven and then only from books, puts Ferré in a different mood entirely, slowing down the logorrhea that she says characterizes her Spanish, forcing her to write books that are more "plot driven":

> English makes me slow down. I have to think about what I'm going to say two or three times—which may be a good habit, because I can't put my foot, or rather my pen, in it so easily. I can't be trigger-happy in English, because shaping the words takes so much effort.[36]

The basic question for a Spanish-speaking Latin American and hispanophone Caribbean public is why a writer like Ferré would elect to write predominantly in a language in which she is admittedly less fluent, even though Ferré's "lesser" fluency in English is no mean gift. The desire to reach a wider audience, of course, is not so ignoble an aim. This is a subject Ferré addressed in an article she wrote for Puerto Rico's English-language newspaper, *The San Juan Star*. In reference to an audience of mainland Puerto Ricans who questioned her about her motivation, Ferré writes:

> I like to write in English, but for me there's something sacred about writing in Spanish, which is the language I dream in . . .
> . . . I wrote the novel in English and [later] Spanish because I'm ambidextrous. When I was a little girl I wrote with my left hand, but when I turned seven Mother changed me to the right. I couldn't be left-handed, she told me. Left-handed people are impaired: there were no left-handed desks at school . . . At seven I became "right-handed" *obligada*; I had to assimilate my left self into my right self. Today I write with both hands, be it with a pen or[. . .]a computer; and also in both languages.
> I think learning to speak a second language in America has a lot to do with learning how to live with *el otro*, "the other" that lurks inside us: our neighbor to the north if we come from Latin America, our neigbor to the south if we come from North America.[37]

Ferré's explanation of why she decided to write *The House on the Lagoon* in English is a kind of synthetic, dialectical, approach, not just to Puerto Rican history, but to her own literary evolution. The metaphor of being ambidextrous at first seems to be purely personal in its allusion to her education as a girl. Becoming right-handed didn't mean that the child, Rosario, need give up her select, because less usual, status as a left-handed person. Becoming right-handed implies an ascension to the public world where being left-handed is being "impaired." It also implies the acquisition of an easy access back and forth between the public world of the right-handed majority and the private world of left-handed Rosario. Bilingual fluidity provides a similar access back and forth between the more private, elemental world of Ferré's "dreaming in Spanish"[38] and the implicitly more public world of English.[39] Ferré goes on to explain that earlier, in the history of their relationship with the United States, Puerto Ricans had been suspicious of giving up Spanish to learn English ("We flaunted our singularities as weapons against assimilation by *el otro*, el americano del norte, even though we already shared a common citizenship").[40] But, she argues, this proud resistance is no longer necessary. In another article, which was lambasted more severely by critics with *independentista* leanings on the island because Ferré published it as an opinion piece *in The New York Times*, Ferré pointed out—on the occasion of the 1998 Plebiscite measuring how many Puerto Ricans favored statehood over independence—that in the past two island plebiscites she had voted for independence but in this one she would vote for statehood. Her synthetical explanation resembled the one in *The San Juan Star* article: in the past Puerto Ricans feared the other, the gringo from the mainland, but Puerto Rican identity has evolved to the point where "We no longer need fear that "el otro," the other, will swallow us up. We have become the other."[41]

Ferré's argument for writing in English is both compelling and problematic. On the one hand, it is clear that she is advocating a kind of assimilationism, if only in her use of the metaphor in which the previously dominant and marginalized left hand is "assimilated" into a subjugated position in relation to the right hand. This kind of argument bespeaks an intense power differential between the right and left hands, between Americanized Latino identity and marginalized Puerto Rican identity. In this equation, "becoming the other" is like being a mimic man, in the most denigrating, Naipaulian understanding of the term. It must be admitted, nonetheless, that what Ferré is ultimately arguing for, not just in *The Times* article, but in the evolution of her fiction, is a hybridized Puerto Rican identity, one that can perform Puerto Rican and (North and Latin) American identity. However, I feel that Ferré's first two novels in English fall short of the theory adumbrated in the *Times* and *San Juan Star* articles.

The central conceit behind Ferré's first English-language book, *The House on the Lagoon*, is that Isabel Monfort, the protagonist, starts to write a novel rendering the "herstory" of her own family as well as that of her husband, Quintín Mendizabal. When her husband finds the manuscript, he begins telling his more his/torical version of events, protesting that Isabel makes up stories because she doesn't understand or value history. Although *The House on the Lagoon* is, like *Sweet Diamond Dust*, a story of conflicting points of view, it is at the same time more ambitious in its epic sweep and more solidly constructed than the novella, if the pun may be pardoned. The solid construction, however, works to make this novel considerably less experimentally interesting since the "he says, she says" dichotomy quickly establishes Isabel as the moral center. As the story progresses the clearly archetypal features Quintín inherits as an heir to his father Buenaventura—and the latter's myth of descent from the conquistadors—become more pronounced. On the surface the novel recounts Isabel's resistance to Quintín's tyrannical and atavistic cruelty. Isabel bolsters her own tale of resistance with ancillary accounts of the rebelliousness of the women in her family.

The plantation house in *Sweet Diamond Dust* is not as important a structure as the palimpsestic house Ferré constructs in *The House on the Lagoon*, a house that is rebuilt three times to reflect structural, aesthetic, and ideological changes in the family history. As well as the house on the lagoon itself, the novel names two other houses: a country house in Guaynabo, the home of Quintín's Americanized maternal grandparents; and the house on Aurora Street, the home in Ponce of Isabel's maternal grandparents.

In *Sweet Diamond Dust* what is still figurally (or tropologically) dominant is the metaphor of the "gran familia puertorriqueña" a metaphor Ferré deconstructs metonymically. Gloria's destruction of the plantation house at the end of the novella finally and baroquely confirms a truth evident since the first of the many narrators begins telling completely unreliable stories: the *familia* doesn't exist, or rather the paternalistic notion is a myth. *The House on the Lagoon* is a dynastic story patented after the model made popular by Isabel Allende's *The House of the Spirits*, a kind of upstairs/downstairs binary tale, which reaches a dialectical synthesis through the rape of Downstairs (a black girl) by Upstairs (Isabel's husband Quintín).

Even though the social drama is mapped out in the house geography for both works, Ferré exploits and explores the house vehicle far more thoroughly than Allende. From the first, Ferré emphasizes the house on the lagoon as a symbol of the Puerto Rican family/nation by emphasizing Isabel's attraction to the cellar, which represents an "essence" that Isabel is both alienated from and attracted to:

> The cellar of the house on the lagoon mesmerized me from the beginning . . . The cellar gave the house much of its mystery, the feeling that events weren't always what they seemed but could have unexpected echoes and repercussions.[42]

Isabel, the protagonist who narrates her version of the events in her family's and husband's family's history and who incites her husband's antagonism to the feminism and social resistance evident in her own storytelling, is a character whose subjectivity is similar to that of Laura Latoni in *Sweet Diamond Dust*. Her maternal grandparents were Corsican smallholders cheated out of their farm by the trickery of her granduncle. The character's paternal grandparents belong to the aristocracy of Ponce, the town in the south of Puerto Rico that the Ferrés hail from and which is considered to be the second richest city on the island due in large part to Luis A. Ferré's investments. In particular both his creation of the Museo de Arte de Ponce as well as his continual purchases of significant works of art for the museum have established him as a Puerto Rican Macaenas and Ponce as a cultural mecca second only to San Juan, the capital. The Isabel of this narrative, however, grows up poor and afflicted for most of her life because her father is an impoverished carpenter and the family live in Trastalleres, one of San Juan's poorest barrios. Moreover, her mother, an heiress, is mentally deficient, thus negligent, and eventually goes completely mad. So, although Isabel does literally have "class," like Laura Latoni, perhaps even more so, she is completely aware of the problems with the island's political system and that is why she responds so strongly to the anatomical peculiarities of the house on the lagoon.

Knowledge of "the Puerto Rico that Jose Luis Gonzalez built" in his famous essay immediately enables us, of course, to identify the cellar as linked with black identity.[43] And, in fact, the "cellar" paragraph, which I quoted above, is taken from the chapter entitled "Petra's Kingdom," after the black servant who lives in the cellar of the house with an extended family of servants who assist her. One of the "misleading things" about the house on the lagoon is that the upstairs monarch, Buenaventura, appears to rule the roost, with his wife Rebecca. But the cellar tells Isabel another story. It tells her that Petra—whom Quintín, Isabel's husband and antagonist, refers to as "entrenched in the cellar's common room like a spider" controlling events at the house with her magic—is the locus for what Isabel constructs as a superior—spiritual—type of power.[44] This projection of Isabel's desire for power resembles Laura's projection of an idealized mulatta identity upon Gloria. The story that the cellar ultimately reveals is a more complex one, tied certainly to the master/slave dialectic in Puerto Rico, as well as to the depredations of colonialism on the land itself. In this sense the house on the lagoon's metonymic relationship with water is of supreme importance.

In *The Poetics of Space* Gaston Bachelard postulates that houses, especially the houses we inhabit as children, constitute a body of images that give human beings "proofs or illusions of stability."[45] The two most important spatial features of the house in our consciousness are, he says, its "verticality" and its "centrality."[46] The components of verticality for him are "ensured by the polarity of cellar and attic."[47] The cellar for Bachelard is the "*dark entity* of the house, the one that partakes of subterranean forces."[48] The use of Jung specifically, and psychoanalysis generally, allows Bachelard to draw the analogy between the cellar as the unconscious, and the attic as the conscious mind. Even though the cellar is the place of the unconscious mind, a cellar where there is water moves the human imagination completely "from a constructed to a dreamed world[where] reality and dream now form a whole. The house, the cellar, the deep earth, achieve totality through depth."[49]

In Ferré's novel, Buenaventura Mendizabal, a clear literary relation of Don Julio Font in *Sweet Diamond Dust*[50] founds the house on the lagoon on the grounds of a spring whose keeper is reported as murdered. Shortly before he dies, Buenaventura confesses to Petra that he committed a sin when he stole the spring, which was public property.[51] The underground spring, and the lagoon itself that surrounds the house and connects it, on the one hand with the slums where Petra's poverty-stricken family live, and on the other with the ocean, are clear indications that the "ambiguity" and "mystery" that tantalize Isabel are connected with the watery cellars Bachelard describes as linking man with "cosmic," even "anthropo-cosmic" mysteries. Petra's practice of Santería and her worship of Elegguá, the god of the crossroads, indicates that the cellar of the house on the lagoon is a cosmic place. In Afro-Caribbean religions, the deities that affect human life are identified as inhabiting the water, specifically what Haitian Voudoun describes as the "cosmic mirror"; the *loas* of Voudoun are used to crossing the cosmic mirror vertically to penetrate the world above from the world below.[52]

Petra's power, as represented by Ferré, is thus overdetermined by her heritage. As the descendant of an African Chieftain, Bernabé Aviles, described in chapter eight, whose tongue the plantation owner cut for inciting a failed slave rebellion, Petra represents the essential black identity posited by González's paradigm. However, in representing Petra as a black woman who never defies, but in fact supports and often even celebrates the white master's subject position in the house/nation, Ferré uncovers a problematic dynamic in social relations in Puerto Rico.[53] From the time that Buenaventura brought her to the house on the lagoon after she healed him from an injury in the countryside, Petra criticizes the vanities and abuses of the rich, yet ultimately supports them. For example, Petra advises another servant to overlook the fact that one of Rebecca's dresses costs five hundred dollars while the servant's monthly salary is only eight dollars. In explaining to the servant that Rebecca is the patriarch's wife and her "clothes . . . were an important symbol of her husband's position in the world," Petra clearly shows that she prefers supporting Buenaventura, and by extension the predatory system he represents, over showing solidarity with the labor concerns of her fellow servants.[54] Buenaventura's son Quintín, whom Petra herself had to raise—because his mother Rebecca rejected him, Isabel says—rapes Petra's granddaughter, Carmelina. Petra is such an upholder of the ethos of the house on the lagoon that she is prepared to drown the offspring of the union, the mulatto baby, Willie, until Isabel steps in. It is Isabel, the apparently wishy-washy wife who, after learning of the rape, threatens to leave Quintín unless he adopts Willie as his own son. This is a radical move for Isabel, who stands to gain nothing from such a socially just action. It is only after Willie grows up, and a desperate Quintín—reacting to his other, older son's decision to join a terrorist Independentista group—disowns both boys, Petra becomes enraged at Quintín's unfair actions and threatens to bring down the wrath of Elegguá on the house/nation.

Petra's threat is indeed fulfilled: *The House on the Lagoon* closes with the destruction of the house by fire, as well as the symbolic and literal death of the master, Quintín. However, it is my contention that Ferré's Petra is as unconvincing a character as Gloria was in *Sweet Diamond Dust*. Both Petra and Gloria are the result of an exaggerated political agenda in both books. Both characters represent blackness as essential Puerto Rican identity, a notion that is realized more organically in *Sweet Diamond Dust* as the contradictory voices show the impossibility of rendering the true story of the family/nation's origins. *Sweet Diamond Dust* is ultimately a more powerful literary work than *The House on the Lagoon* precisely because the political reality of Don Julio's "blackness" is never actually proven. Written in the 1980s at the height of a literary production—including works by Luis Rafael Sánchez, Ana Lydia Vega, and others—which strongly resisted a traditionalist literary patriarchalism, *Sweet Diamond Dust* showed that one of the causes of turmoil in Puerto Rican society is the whitewashing of blackness; at the same time it brilliantly unmasked history as contingent on personal desire. What happened exactly between Don Julio Font, the purported "black" father of the De la Valle line and Doña Elvira, the *criollita* of good family who married him, is ultimately unknowable if somewhat approximated by the diverging voices.

The location of Petra in the cellar of *The House on the Lagoon* informs English-speaking readers that there is indeed an important African foundational element in Puerto Rican identity. On the other hand, the problem with Ferré's design in this book is its rigidity. Puerto Rican society is far more complex and dynamic than the "upstairs/downstairs" structure of *The House on the Lagoon* can convey. Unfortunately, characters who appear marginal, such as Petra, end up actually reinforcing the stability of the structure since what Petra ultimately wants is for her great-grandson to inherit the house on the lagoon in a way that would imply his assimilation into the *blanquito* (white) Puerto Rican master narrative. The multivocality, or heteroglossia, of *Sweet Diamond Dust* best approximates a Puerto Rican society where racial mixing is dynamic, so dynamic that history has to be reconstructed to allow for mulatto plantation owners like Don Julio Font. The mistake Ferré made in *Sweet Diamond Dust* was to have Gloria react like a heroine from a previous narrative and burn down the house in order to preserve it.

If Petra, ultimately, is a disappointing character, as is her granddaughter Carmelina, whose "fire-pussy" causes the Avilés and Mendizabal bloodlines to finally mix, it is the character of Isabel Montfort who finally saves *The House on the Lagoon* from being just a picturesque rendering of the curiosities of Puerto Rican history for American readers.[55]

The burning down of the house is not carried out by Isabel but rather by Manuel, her son with Quintín, and the legitimate heir to the house on the lagoon. Manuel joins a radical independentista terrorist group, AK-47, looting then destroying the house at their instigation. Aside from the fact that AK-47 sounds dubious because radical Puerto Rican groups of this kind have traditionally carried out most of their violent activities outside of Puerto Rico, Isabel's killing of Quintín at the end of the novel, as an act of defense against his violence, is both problematic and provocative.[56] As a gesture of resistance, the killing seems extremely trite. As a mimetic gesture, it is much more interesting.

As a revelation of how Puerto Rican society oppresses black Puerto Ricans who are an essential—but denied—component of Puerto Rican identity, *The House on the Lagoon* fails in its stridency. *The House on the Lagoon* functions much more efficaciously in its representation of the ambivalence engendered in women such as Isabel as a result of their *failed* resistance to patriarchal mandates. On the one hand, the binary opposition between the husband's anger, and the wife's desire to heal the violence she blames him for, makes for an overdetermined and predictable plot (where her resistance starts in critique and ends, finally, in the repetition of his violent gestures). On the other hand, a reading of the descent to the cellar of the house as a descent into the unconscious reveals that the house is ultimately the terrain of women, even though the house in its protective role reinforces patriarchy, stabilizing the patriarch's line and keeping the family protected from the deleterious influences of the street.[57]

Bachelard affirms that the house as the first "dream-space" for the child is really a maternal space. The idea that the woman's body is the first house is an association that, as Sandra Gilbert and Susan Gubar note, creates considerable anxiety in women writers who tend to associate the symbolic confinement in houses with the way they are confined inside texts. Ultimately, Gilbert and Gubar argue, the confinement extends to the woman's body itself, since the woman's body is the first house: "To become literally a house, after all, is to be denied the hope of that spiritual transcendence of the body which, as Simone de Beauvoir has argued, is what makes humanity distinctively human."[58]

Significantly, the aesthetic beauty of the first house on the lagoon is the product of Rebecca Mendizabal's fine aesthetic taste and frustrated desire to be an artist or dancer. Buenaventura Mendizabal, Rebecca's husband, wants a disciple of

Frank Lloyd Wright, Pavel—hired by all the rich families on the island—to design a house that will add to his social prestige. Rebecca, however, colludes artistically with Pavel in designing a beautiful house that organically resonates with the natural surroundings of lagoon and ocean and that reflects Rebecca's feminine and artistic sensibility.[59] Later on, Buenaventura the Spaniard has most of this "first house on the lagoon" torn down to erect a Spanish style house with massive fort-like walls. In effect, Buenaventura turns the house on the lagoon—which was becoming too much of a woman's domain—not so much into a man's house but a house where feminine sensibility is trapped, imprisoned and constantly monitored by the panoptical windows of the Spanish fortress-like architecture. Thus trapped and monitored, feminine sensibility can express itself only subversively.

Rosario Ferré herself commented critically on the metonymic relationship between women's bodies and the houses they occupy in her perceptive study of the fantastic in the fiction of the Uruguayan writer, Felisberto Hernández. Commenting on the strange and wonderful narrative, *La Casa Inundada* ("The Flooded House"), Ferré notes:

> At the beginning of the story, the narrator compares the enormous body of the Señora Margarita with her enormous house thus establishing a correspondence between them . . . The house, according to the narrator, has a life of its own and is irrigated with water like a body nourished by blood: water flows in and out of its hallways thanks to a series of invisible valves that recall arteries and veins.[60]

Ultimately, the Señora Margarita of Hernández's story metamorphoses into her flooded house. The breaking down of the boundaries between Margarita's body and Margarita's house is a purely linguistic phenomenon that enacts Margarita's growing madness and the fragmentation of her personality, according to Ferré's study.[61]

In *The House on the Lagoon*, Isabel's psychological ensnarement, repression, and fragmentation is also an issue that gets played out in Isabel's metonymic relationship to the house on the lagoon but not in ways as linguistically provocative as in the Hernández story. Isabel, as I have noted before, is attracted to the house's cellar, partly because the cellar is the abode of Petra and Isabel regards Petra as a more authentic being, because she is black and because she wields the magic of Elegguá. Isabel's repression in the book is played out more directly in her relationship to her body.

Isabel is a privileged character in relation to Petra, Carmelina, and even Rebecca, whom Buenaventura Mendizabal literally beats into submission so that she will completely fulfill the role of mother and leave off her "artistic" ways. Isabel is also one of the characters in the book most torn by ambivalence. Isabel's alienation regarding her body is one of the best examples of her ambivalence. Isabel's alienation becomes apparent in her recounting of a story from her childhood, the narrative about the Russian ballet master who comes to Ponce to teach dancing. This is a story that deviates so sharply from the archetypal, historical, prescriptive tale Ferré set out to write in the book that, on my first and second readings, I felt perplexed by it's function in the text, since it had little to do either with the story of the family living in the house on the lagoon or even with Isabel's early history in Ponce. Unlike other stories Isabel tells, about her beloved Corsican grandmother,

Abby, for example, this is not a family story and is not obviously a tale about a strong woman's resistance to patriarchy.

Rather, the story involves a love triangle between Isabel who is the most talented dancer in the school; Kerenski, the dance master and Russian immigrant; and Isabel's best friend, Estefanía, whom Kerenski ultimately falls in love with. Significantly the reason she likes Estefanía, Isabel states, is because Estefanía, like Isabel, is also the unhappy only child of a dysfunctional, negligent couple. Isabel and Estefanía become even more attracted to each other because of their interest and skill in dance, and later by dint of their teenage crushes on Kerenski. They revere him in various ways. Like most good theorists of dance, he is able to impart a philosophy of body discipline that counters dualistic, Catholic-inflected ideas about the body. At the Kerenski school, girls from the Ponce middle class suddenly found themselves in a space in which they "could learn to interpret the soul through the outline of the body."[62]

In disciplining the girl's bodies, Kerenski displays a parental role that both girls are sadly missing in their lives. The deeper reason for loving him, however, is that Kerenski's "discipline" implies that there is a higher truth that is reachable through the physical practice of ballet: "If you let the music flood you when you dance," Andre used to say to us, "one day you'll attain enlightenment."[63] For the lonely Isabel and Estefanía, Kerenski becomes their mimetic mediator. The mimetic dynamic soon turns him into their "god" when they realize that—beyond achieving his approbation and love, they *could*, through their desire, ostensibly become just like their god.

Isabel's narrative about the Kerenski episode is the most personal story in the book, one that has nothing to do with either Puerto Rican history or the genealogy of Isabel's and Quintín's families. The episode, as Isabel recounts it, ends tragically. Kerenski plans a dramatic staging of Swan Lake for which the whole school practices assiduously. He trains Tony Torres, a boy from the slums, as the male lead because the Ponce mothers would be offended if Kerenski himself took the role and danced with the very young girls. Estefanía, who has been at the school for only six months, is chosen for the lead role much to Isabel's chagrin. During the actual performance, the dancers are masked, but Isabel realizes that Kerenski has taken over Tony Torres's role because she recognizes the "scent of crushed geraniums" of Kerenski's armpits. We realize, of course, through this bodily clue, as well as others, that Isabel is as much in love with Kerenski as Estefanía.

Kerenski and Estefanía receive all the applause: the sexual energy between them is sublimated magnificently in the artistry of the dance. After the curtain falls, Estefanía and Kerenski kiss passionately and at that moment of crisis "an invisible hand pulled a lever backstage," so that the whole town finds out about Kerenski's affair with Estefanía.[64] We are told by Isabel that several of Kerenski's students afterward accused him of molestation and he was forced to leave the island.

It seems likely that Isabel has pulled the lever but her agency in this episode is, as she describes it, "invisible." It is not until a later chapter in the novel written in third person from Quintín's point of view in which the reader's suspicion of Isabel's role is confirmed by Quintín's own bold assertions:

> "You know very well that you were the one who pulled the lever at the end of the recital at La Perla that night, Isabel! That you were the one who made the curtain rise so that

the love affair of André Kerenski and Estefanía Volmer was revealed to the world! And a few months later . . . you accused Kerenski of child molestation during a court hearing. And as a result of your testimony, Kerenski was eventually deported from the United States."[65]

The novel is heavily skewed in Isabel's favor. She observes Quintín's continual violent behavior, and also bears witness in the novel she is writing—and which Quintín is contesting—to the subjugation of women in her family and in his. At first the above passage seems like one more example of Quintín's utter self-immersion, and his insensitivity to those around him, especially women. After all, it is in this very chapter that he condescendingly points out that Isabel uses the characters in her book as "shadow players for her own personality . . . a pitfall for mediocre writers." He is completely patronizing when he tells her in one of these notes that her predilection for "rebellious" characters doesn't mean that she "should identify with them."[66]

But Quintín's annotations, however patronizing, and however revealing they are of his own patriarchal personality, do force one to rethink the Kerenski episode. Up until to the Kerenski story, readers regard Isabel as a "rebel," by association with the women characters she narrates with such gusto: her grandmother, the Corsican Abby; Quintín's mother Rebecca; Estefanía. Estefanía's hold over the more conservative Isabel is seductive. At one point both girls go out on the town wearing "Hawaiian-style see-through blouses . . . just to see people stare at us."[67] It is evident then that there is indeed a shadow play going on—between Estefanía and Isabel. Isabel constructs Estefanía as one of those "rebellious" characters Quintín criticizes: "Estefanía . . . was much more of a rebel than I."[68] Most of Estefanía's defiance tends to center around the body and sexuality: eating dessert for breakfast, not wearing underwear, going on dates without a chaperone, all these actions unheard of in the small-town atmosphere the girls grow up in. But after Isabel's description of the Kerenski episode, it becomes apparent that Isabel is attracted to rebellious women because they act out her own desires. Isabel, herself, however, seems unable to act in the same passionate and spontaneous manner she attributes to Estefanía and the other women in her stories.

Now, if Isabel has allowed herself to betray her own strong desire to rebel, it would seem that her marriage to Quintín is to blame and, indeed, Isabel does blame Quintín for many of the violent happenings that occur throughout their history together. Her final moment of blame, which is also a moment of seeming rebellion, occurs at the end of the book. Quintín disinherits the couple's younger son, Willie, who is actually Quintín's son by his rape of Carmelina and refuses to forgive their eldest son for joining the AK-47 rebels. This hardness of heart prompts Isabel to leave Quintín—taking the ailing Willie with her—an action she has contemplated for many years. But Quintín has cut her off from any funds, so Isabel arranges to have valuable paintings in the house on the lagoon stolen by a local art-dealer, so she can sell them. The night she picks for this is also the night that AK-47 attacks the house on the lagoon. In the ensuing struggle the rebels burn the house to the ground after looting it. The couple are able to escape on a motorboat after Isabel pleads with Manuel to let his father go. But on the boat, an enraged Quintín, confused by what is happening, angrily, arrogantly, and mistakenly assumes that Isabel had sided with the rebels and despite her denials begins to beat her. Isabel has an epiphany:

> I crouched at the bottom of the boat, trying to protect myself . . . Then I saw my life
> unreel before me like a film: Quintín rising from our rattan sofa at Aurora Street, taking
> off his belt and whipping the sixteen-year-old boy for singing me a love song . . .
> Margarita coming out of the operating room, pale as a statue; Carmelina and Quintín
> making love among the mangroves; Quintín unleashing his dogs so they would
> attack his own sons and making me sign a will to disinherit them[.][69]

This is one of Ferré's worst writing moments and the fact that it comes from her first
novel written in English doesn't excuse her: the clichéd metaphor of life-memories
unfurling like film is particularly regrettable. But the bad writing, when it happens
in this novel, in some sense can be attributed to Isabel, the fledgling novelist. This is
moment where Isabel, through portentous and melodramatic storytelling, distances
herself from the truth of her own participation in these violent events, just as
she distanced herself from the agency of "the invisible hand" that revealed the
Kerenski–Estefanía love affair to the world.

Quintín's whipping of the sixteen-year-old boy is the primal scene of *The House
on the Lagoon*, the event that initiates the writing of the book itself since it occurs
when Isabel and Quintín are engaged and impels their mutual avowal "to examine
carefully the origins of anger in each of our families" to avoid "the mistakes our
forbears had made."[70] Instead, however, as Isabel's filmic epiphany shows, the characters recapitulate past violence in their relationship. Isabel is just as responsible for
these repetitions of violence—from the beating of the boy, to Carmelina's rape, to the
disinheriting of the couples' sons—as her husband. For example, despite her rhetoric claiming the contrary, she rewards Quintín for beating the boy (and for the boy's
eventual suicide after this humiliation) by marrying Quintín shortly thereafter. The
beating thus takes on the nature of an erotic sacrifice. She finds out about
Carmelina's rape after the product of that rape is brought to the house. Her most
successful act of rebellion is forcing Quintín to adopt Willie as "atonement" for his
rape of Carmelina. Despite misgivings, Isabel makes no real effort to stop Quintín
from putting Isabel's cousin Margarita through the surgery that kills her, despite the
fact that the operation is cosmetic—an attempt to correct Margarita's disturbing
facial birthmark. Isabel again shows weakness in allowing Quintín to disinherit their
sons because of their political activities. Thus, Isabel's final action—the manipulation
of the motorboat in the water so that Quintín hits his head against an iron beam,
which kills him—is a rebellious act, yes, but one with a hidden agenda.

Two critical ideas, one from Judith Butler, and the other from Ferré herself, will
help clarify my idea. Butler explains the idea of agency in power relations as inher-
ently contradictory: "The paradox of subjectivation (*assujetissement*) is precisely that
the subject who would resist such norms is itself enabled, if not produced, by such
norms. Although this constitutive constraint does not foreclose the possibility of
agency, it does locate agency as a reiterative or rearticulatory practice, immanent
to power, and not a relation of external opposition to power."[71]

Following Butler's idea I read Isabel's final act of rebellion, her murder of her
husband, as enmeshed in the very chain of violence she wishes to end. It does not

indicate a subject who has finally freed herself from the confines of her subject position, but rather one who has finally learned how to use violence in the game of power, who is repeating violence with a difference, mimetically, and through mimicry, to invoke both Girard and Bhabha. But Isabel's violence as an "immanent" act if we are to understand Butler, is problematic and unsatisfying. There are other aspects of Isabel's own violence that Ferré herself throws light on.

Ferré's critical essay "How I Wrote When Women Love Men" delineates a type of irony that characterizes women's writing in general and her own writing in particular:

> As I wrote it ["When Women Love Men"] I identified myself with Isabel La Negra and with Isabel Luberza, who both talk in the first-person singular. But I was also the iron-ically detached voice which narrated the story of both women in the third-person singular. This last voice, which was also a part of me but which I could listen to more objectively as it became progressively independent, permitted me to write with a clear historical perspective about those conflicts which were to be found, not in the anec-dotes of the lives of both these women, but within my own heart. Granted, this unfold-ing of the character was, at the time, an unconscious process. In other words, I never set myself the task of writing about character doubles when I began to write "When Women Love Men." But the apprenticeship of the double-character [. . .] implied for me a search into the double nature of my own conscience (of which I had until then been unaware) . . .[72]

Ferré's insight offers us the possibility that, like Isabel La Negra and Isabel Luberza in the short story "When Women Love Men," and Laura and Gloria in *Sweet Diamond Dust*, Isabel and Quintín are doubles for each other. This also supports the doubling effect that I discussed as a feature of allegory in my introduction and in chapter two.

There are two aspects to this in my argument. The first is the notion that Girardian mimetic rivalry characterizes both the relationship between Laura and Gloria in *Sweet Diamond Dust*, with Nicolás as the object, and the relationships between Isabel and Estefanía as well as between Isabel and Quintín. The second aspect applies only to the relationship between Isabel and Quintín and is the idea that they are complements of each other, following Gilbert's and Gubar's argument about doubles in *Wuthering Heights*, which I have already described in my chapter on *The Agüero Sisters*. Gilbert and Gubar hold that Heathcliff is Catherine's "whip," recognized by Catherine herself as "an alternative self or double for her, a comple-mentary addition to her being who fleshes out all her lacks the way a bandage might staunch a wound."[73] I argue, therefore, that Isabel is not only guilty of a deeply violent passion that finally surfaces—and not a moment of "consciousness" as a superficial reading of the novel might have us think—but that, in fact, Isabel's violence has been suppressed all along because Quintín has been carrying it for her, like a strange and delicate weapon that she knew she would never be able to wield until she finally recognizes it as her own. Quintín, in effect, is Isabel's "whip," much the way Heathcliff is Cathy's. This explains Quintín's constant anger and the intense repression that allows Isabel to alienate herself from her own "invisible hand," and that exposes Kerenski 's love affair with Estefanía to the whole town of Ponce.

The novel has been built around the idea of Isabel and Quintín, writing against each other in a Puerto Rican gender war. Their rivalry deepens as the novel progresses especially, as I showed above, when Quintín starts to deconstruct Isabel's novel. Isabel's murder of Quintín, then, at the end of the novel, while clothed in the garb of an act of justice against an oppressor, is actually the most violently self-repressive moment in the book. In this way, Isabel silences the voice that has been critiquing her and pointing at this very aspect of her personality: her self-repression. Thus my contention is that the immolation of the house at the end of *The House on the Lagoon* rings so falsely and seems histrionic precisely because it is a tropological diversion by the author/narrator Isabel.

A reader who follows all the overdetermined clues of the house's structure reading the house/nation as one in which the blacks and women are oppressed by Quintín's ruses understands Quintín's demise, and the burning of the house, as the defeat of the patriarchal narrative. Nevertheless, the burning down of the house on the lagoon is even less credible and more histrionic than the burning down of the plantation house in *Sweet Diamond Dust* since at least that renunciatory gesture was rooted in other Caribbeanist narratives, irreducibly linking slaves to masters in the plantation system.[74] But the burning down of the house on the lagoon distracts us from a more important defeat, Isabel's self-defeat, her submission to participation in the patriarchalist narrative, her transformation into a violent woman in denial of her own interiority, a self-critical capacity. This interiority and critical acumen finds expression in Quintín's character, in his voice. Interestingly, in *Sweet Diamond Dust* any mimetic rivalry between Laura and Gloria finally becomes sublimated as Laura allows her love for Nicolás to translate to Gloria and Nicolasito, and as Gloria, taking up the torch of the white plantation ladies she imitates so well, burns the house down, a final act of love for Laura through the metonymic agency of her memory of Nicolás. In *The House on the Lagoon*, on the other hand, the destruction of the house amounts to an act of self-repression, since the patriarch's anger is partly the result of constant feminine evasion.

Coda: The Open Sacrifice of the Mother in *Eccentric Neighborhoods*

Eccentric Neighborhoods, a quasi-autobiographical account of Ferré's childhood, told by narrating the histories of both her mother's and famous father's families, marks a distinct departure from the anti-patriachal stance of her previous fiction and is similar in only one way. Like *Sweet Diamond Dust* and *The House on the Lagoon*, in particular, *Eccentric Neighborhoods* is a narrative that demands a sacrifice. But because the allegorical tendency linking house with nation, which characterized the two previous books, has changed to a closely autobiographical mode, the sacrifice this narrative makes is not of the the house run by the patriarch. Instead what this narrative sacrifices is the mother, as an allegorical figuration identified closely with "old Spanish" Puerto Rican identity.

Ferré's decision to write a memoir-like novel might be traced to suggestions made by critics of *The House on the Lagoon* upon its publication.[75] Although *The House on the Lagoon* received a glowing review in 1995 in *The New York Times Book Review*, the reviewer, Suzanne Ruta, also noted that the writing seemed constrained:

> A work of self-conscious brilliance, "The House on the Lagoon" has at times the feel
> of a straitjacketed tour de force. Ms. Ferré is most relaxed when writing from memory
> of the provincial life she recalls from her own childhood. Observations like this one,
> pointed and nostalgic, are at the heart of her book: "Sears wasn't a place, it was a state
> of mind; ordering from the Sears catalogue was like ordering from heaven . . . Like
> most families on the island, ours was divided politically. Carmita and Carlos were for
> statehood, whereas Abby was definitely Independentista. But we all liked to browse
> through the Sears catalogue."
> Such echoes hint that there's another manuscript hidden in this book: behind all the
> carnival masks and baroque altar screens, a gentle memoir waiting to be written.[76]

Ferré took the reviewer's advice to heart, apparently, for *Eccentric Neighborhoods* is a
quasi-autobiographical rendition of Ferré's childhood in Puerto Rico. In the book—
containing much information corresponding in interesting and provocative ways to
biographical facts recounted in the 1992 autobiography Ferré "narrated" for her
father, entitled *Memorias de Ponce: autobiografía de Luis A Ferré*—Ferré focalizes her
narration through the character of Elvira, the daughter of a well-known politician by
a woman from the island's "old Spanish" aristocracy.

Ruta ascribed the superiority of passages such as that about the Sears catalogue to
a kind of true-to-life authenticity, as opposed to the general tendency of *The House
on the Lagoon* to present a "stylized, picturesque reduction of class and racial conflicts
in two mythic families."[77] I'm not entirely sure that Ruta's correlation of literary
quality with autobiographical verisimilitude is on target. The reason the Sears catalogue passage is so powerful is because it subtly reflects the complexity of colonial life
in Puerto Rico—beyond the reductionism of political partisanship, as well as the
kind of racial and class reductionism Ruta faults. The Sears catalogue episode highlights the way images of wealth and comfort engaged the imagination of all Puerto
Ricans adapting to Americanization whether they were fanatical supporters of
Statehood or very critical of the U.S. presence. That such a perceptive image of the
complexity of colonial internalizations should be ascribed to autobiographical
elements is Ruta's misperception of good writing as a reflection of "real" life.

Eccentric Neighborhoods marks a departure for Ferré's writing in two significant ways. On the one hand it registers the abandonment of an obviously anti-
patriarchalist stance. Unlike *Sweet Diamond Dust* and all the early short fiction in
Spanish, narrated from the perspectives of all kinds of characters from different class
and racial backgrounds, as well as the dual perspectivism of *The House on the Lagoon*,
this relatively limited point of view underlines the fact that all the interesting family
stories are merely anecdotes in a narrative whose real focus is on the daughter's rivalry
with her mother, Clarissa.

Ferré has ceased to overly concern herself with the subjectivities of characters from
a different class or race. There is only one chapter devoted to Miña, the woman who
helped raise the Vernet (read, Ferré) children. Miña is an obvious but paler echo of
Petra from *The House on the Lagoon*. Miña's magic soapball, the product of years of
saving bits of soap left over from the baths of all the different family members
to produce a large iridescently colored ball containing all the family "secrets"

is a fetishistic emblem of the Vernet family.[78] The soapball recalls the magical cosmic "spiderweb" Quintín nervously accused Petra of weaving in the cellar of the house on the lagoon. An additional racial Other who receives a chapter entry is the Guatemalan maid with feet so huge that the only shoes Clarissa, Elvira's mother, can find for her, are oversized athlete's Nikes. This episode's only real thematic use is to accentuate the portrayal of the mother Clarissa as vain and superficial. She cares more about hiding the maid's oversized feet from sight than she does about the woman's complete discomfiture in the household—as an Indian from an other country with barely any knowledge of Spanish. However, the chapter is characteristic of this book's slow, anecdotal, quasi-biographical drive.

Despite the fact that the book still retains fictional features, it has a distinctly autobiographical quality that is absent in all of Ferré's earlier work, except some of her essays about writing. The first-person narrator has a different name than the author, as do all the characters that approximate the real-life figures they are derived from in the *Memorias*. For example, Abuela Adela's grotesque illness—due to a parasite that embeds itself in her leg making it swell to monstrous proportions—is clearly modeled on the *filaria* that killed Mary Aguayo, Luis Ferré's mother and Rosario Ferré's grandmother, as described in the *Memorias*.[79]

The Guatemalan maid episode is an excellent example of this anecdotal quality but even most of the stories about the Rivas de Santillana girls—Clarissa and her sisters—suffer from a tendency to focus on the picturesque facts, rather than on character development. For example, what we remember best about Tía Lakhmé— the most spontaneous of the Rivas de Santillana sisters, who always succumbs to what she calls "the positive current of the universe"—is that she is an impulsive, oversexed flibbertigibbet who married too many times and was actually once restricted to purdah by her Moroccan husband.[80] Like the superficial iridescence of Miña's soapball, it is the flashiness and color of these anecdotes that appeal to us. As a consequence, almost all the characters in the book are flat except perhaps for Clarissa.

This experiment with the hybridity of fictionalized autobiography allows the rivalrous mimetic triangle—that was submerged in *Sweet Diamond Dust* and *The House on the Lagoon*—to emerge openly in *Eccentric Neighborhoods*. The quasi-autobiographical narrator immediately posits the mother as the source of trouble, the father as the source of love. Here it is no secret that Elvira/Rosario's model, or mediator, is her father, Aurelio. Her mother is both the object Elvira wishes to win as the result of mimetic desire, as well as her rival for the love of the mediator.

:As a result of bringing the hidden mimeticism out into the open, the house as a figural vehicle is abandoned, along with a direct critique of the patriarchal narrative. Instead of women trapped and identified within houses, the book's first chapter, entitled "Fording Río Loco," draws an allegory of wild, untamable, unfathomable Puerto Rican identity through the mother:

> [W]hen the sun was nailed to the sky like a hot coal . . . [Río Loco] reared up like a muddy demon . . . enraged at everything that stood in its way . . .
>
> Río Loco always reminded me of my mother, Clarissa. We would be sitting peacefully . . . having breakfast . . . when Clarissa would suddenly rise and run to her room . . . As I left for school . . . I could hear Clarissa's sobs . . . It was as if it were raining in her mind, when all around the sun was shining.[81]

Water and hysteria are the domain of Clarissa in the child Elvira's apprehension of the relationship between father and mother. The conflict between Clarissa and Elvira's father, Aurelio—based on Luis A. Ferré—has to do with the fact that Aurelio spends much of his adulthood running for public offices. Despite his constant failures to secure the governorship of Puerto Rico, Clarissa is made insecure and jealous by Aurelio's allegiance to island politics, a direct parallel with the anxieties ascribed to Rosario Ferré's mother, Lorenzita Ramírez de Arrellano, by Luis Ferré in the *Memorias*. The binary between logos and nature that Elvira projects onto her parents in this book is very similar to the binary that Reina and Constancia, the protagonists of *The Agüero Sisters*, project onto the relationship of Blanca and Ignacio Agüero, discussed in chapter two. In this case, Aurelio is the representative of the logocentric ideals he learns from his enterprising Cuban father who closely resembles the real French Cuban Ferré scion drawn in the *Memorias*. Although Clarissa differs markedly from Blanca Agüero—she is not affiliated in any way with Afro-Caribbean religions or cultural practices and she is markedly in love with and faithful to her husband—there is the same tendency in this text, as in the García text, to both naturalize Clarissa's body and mystify her actions. She is constricted by natural boundaries like Río Loco; when she goes "crazy" her actions are unpredictable like the river's.

On the other hand it is precisely this "wildness," the excess or supplementarity in her mother's actions, that moves Elvira and that motivate this long, strange mixture of autobiography, poetic allegorizing, and history. The narrator says that she loved crossing Río Loco when it was flooded because it "broke the monotony of the trip, the silence that inevitably sat like a block of ice between Mother and me."[82] These trips to Emajaguas, the opulent home of Clarissa's family, the plantation-holding Rivas de Santillana clan, console Clarissa—who constantly feels left out of, and betrayed by, her husband's political career—by taking her back to the source of familial comfort and stability. The unusual feature of these trips is that Clarissa is always too impatient to wait long for the river's current to go down and instead usually orders the family Chauffeur to drive the Pontiac into the current, "without a quiver of fear in her voice."[83] In Elvira's eyes it is no mistake that it is precisely when Río Loco is at its peak of watery rage that the irascible Clarissa can be so calm, as if she has learnt strength from proximity with the water. It is crisis that draws strength from the unstable Clarissa.

Clarissa's identification with the "menstrual" river, and the wildness of nature contrasts with her corresponding inability to go with the flow in normal everyday situations regarding her husband and children. Clarissa is not afraid of the river's threat to her own life and her daughter's, instead she worriedly "looked at her diamond Cartier wristwatch on its black grosgrain band because she'd rather the car floated away in the river current than risk missing lunch with her mother and sisters."[84] Clarissa's loyalty to her aristocratic family can be interpreted as ambivalence toward her husband and children. Elvira's reads Clarissa as unhappy about having sacrificed her career to become a wife and mother. In this sense, Clarissa's meetings with her mother and sisters acquire importance, both because they may remind her of her premarital state of freedom and because going back home to Emajaguas and her mother is a retreat to to the support and comfort of her childhood home, an escape to the womb prefigured by Clarissa's willingness to allow the car to be submerged in the river water.

The kind of conservatism Clarissa represents Ferré previously ascribed to males like Quintín and Buenaventual Mendizabal, in *The House on the Lagoon,* who were literally descendants of the Conquistadors. Aurelio, as a Cuban immigrant, is linked to the Americans who have created a space for poor and capable men such as Aurelio's father Chaguito. In this text the Vernets—aka the Ferrés—contrast sharply with the Rivas de Santillana clan, Clarissa's family, hacienda owners who resist Yankee progressivism and uphold a more purist Spanish/Puerto Rican notion of identity. Clarissa embodies the idea of sacrifice in traditional Puerto Rican culture, the sacrifice of feminine individuality to the unity of the "gran familia." On her death bed, Clarissa adamantly advises her daughter Elvira/Rosario against divorcing the husband who beats her and who forbids her from going back to school for a graduate degree:

> "Having money, a career, is not that important. Nature, the positive current of the universe where everything is interconnected, is what really matters. Our duty is to partake of that unity . . . That's why getting a divorce . . . won't do you any good."[85]

It is clear that the price Clarissa pays for preserving the family "unity" is not just an inner fragmentation that results in periodic bouts of depression but a bodily sacrifice that leads to an early death. Aurelio, finally, after many years of running against Fernando Martín (the obvious stand-in for Luis Muñoz Marín, Puerto Rico's legendary socialist party leader turned Commonwealth promulgator), wins the elections for governor. Shortly after the elections, Clarissa's heart murmur starts to get much worse. If Clarissa, a metonymic agent for the *patria,* has been the embodied grounds for Aurelio's victory, the logic of her sacrifice implies that she should finally succumb to the final "unity". The child Elvira has always preferred her father's rational, progressive, U.S.-centered ways to her mother's reactionary Spanish conservatism. It becomes clear, however, that the father's divergence, his adaptation of some American rationalist strategies above others takes place not in a binary opposition with the mother's Spanish identity but with the mother's identity as the grounds for any divergence whatsoever. The mother is not just a body, she is the river, she is unity, she is God. She is everything and nothing at the same time.

This is Elvira's revelation in this novel/memoir. An Elvira who thought she adored her father finds herself alienated from him after the mother's death. Elvira, who has moved into her own apartment and is now studying for a graduate degree at the university (thanks to her inheritance from the late Clarissa) is given a piano by her father who then comes to her house every afternoon to play it in mourning for Clarissa's death. Realizing that the mournful piano-playing is driving away all her post-divorce suitors, an enraged Elvira finally sends the piano back to the shop, thus forcing an unwanted distance between herself and her father. The final realization is that the father's narcissism had its roots in the mother's self-annihilating devotion. The gift of the piano by the father seems like a gift celebrating Elvira's newfound independence. Instead, it is an invasive, perhaps incestuous, attempt to attach Elvira as a surrogate for Clarissa. Ultimately, the blood Elvira describes as pouring out from

Clarissa's corpse is a signifier of Elvira's sacrifice (so as not to be sacrificed by her father or by men like him) as much as Clarissa's:

> She had a death worthy of the Emajaguas philosophy of life. "If one accepts one's destiny, the pain is sublimated and there is no sacrifice," she had said to me over and over again . . .
> And then something astonishing happened. Mother was allowed one last act, perhaps even more overwhelming because it happened after her death. When the nurse turned Mother's naked body to bathe her back, *a mouthful of fresh blood spilled out and stained the white sheet a bright red.* I stared at it, horrified. The sacrifice had taken place after all. [My emphasis][86]

The mouthful of blood appears as a warning at the exact moment when a confused and angry Elvira has decided to succumb to the philosophy of unity in the "gran familia."

I want to end this chapter with this powerful image of sacrifice not just as a final example of the way Latina women characters must die in many U.S. Latino/a narratives but as an example of how these contemporary tales demonstrate their own ambivalence as English-language texts by requiring, and marking, the sacrifice of "Spanish." In this case "Spanish" identity is marked metonymically by the mother who comes from as "pure" a Spanish family as any in Puerto Rico, as well as in Ferré's decision to switch from the Latin American and Puerto Rican modalities of totalizing, multivocal texts about the familia/nation to a quasi-memoir in English, so that the stories, unmoored from the political and patriarchal obsessions of Puerto Rican identity, may attain an ambivalent freedom.

Everything that Clarissa represents, old-style "acceptance of one's destiny," a purist notion of Spanish identity and Spanish language, the idea that women must sacrifice, even efface themselves for the sake of men, runs counter to Elvira's growing sense of herself as a professor/critic/writer. The personal story of Elvira in *Eccentric Neighborhoods* is one that Ferré tells over and over about herself in her fiction, her autobiographical essays and her criticism. Like Elvira, Ferré married when she was twenty and attempted to stay with a violently abusive man in order to placate her family, eventually divorcing her husband to go back to school, at the University of Puerto Rico and the University of Maryland, to obtain a doctorate in literature and to resume writing seriously. However, all Ferré's previous work, including *The House on the Lagoon*, has tended to focus on men as the culprits in the troubles of the Puerto Rican house/nation. As I showed in my analysis of *The House on the Lagoon*, this accusatory stance wears thin in that book since it is really Isabel's own alienation from her anger that seems to create a double in Quintín. Instead of rebelling against patriarchalism by killing her husband, Isabel is fleeing even further from a confrontation with her own anger.

Eccentric Neighborhoods traces a seemingly complex family history; this time Ferré emphasizes class over race and gender: she focuses on the differences between the bourgeois Vernets—descended from a Cuban immigrant who climbs the social ladder aided by American colonialist policies—and the "aristocratic," nostalgic patriarchalism of the Rivas de Santillanas. Ferré's ambivalent quasi-memoir marks the final phase of an opus deconstructing the pretensions and myths of the purist

Hispanic upholders of the most ingrained notions of Puerto Rican identity and language. Although it would appear that the blame for the impossible sexism of Puerto Rican culture is placed on the mother in *Eccentric Neigborhoods*, the Oedipal rivalry between the mother and the daughter is sublimated by the end of the book when Elvira gains consciousness of her own contribution (by way of attachment to the father and denial of the mother) toward the maternal renunciation that has helped uphold the father's political ambitions and his stability.

Clarissa, like Blanca Agüero, represents the deeper Hispanic identity that creates self-division for both Elvira and Aurelio. It seems to be no mistake that the publication of *Eccentric Neigborhoods* in 1998 coincided with the publication of her notorious article in *The New York Times*, in which Ferré disavowed her former independentista leanings and proclaimed her support of statehood, arguing that Puerto Ricans no longer had to worry about being devoured by *el otro* because "we have become the other." Ferré's critics hold that such a statement is a refined argument for assimilation. What Ferré is talking about is not so simply a process of assimilation as one of inevitable hybridization of Puerto Ricans as a result of more than a hundred years of old colonial involvement with the United States. A hybrid identity such as the one Ferré projected onto the mulatta Gloria in *Sweet Diamond Dust* has both positive and negative valences. This can be seen in Gloria's ability to copycat the master discourse so thoroughly that in destroying it's constructions she is only repeating the discourse's nostalgic gestures. Hybrid Puerto Ricans, such as Gloria, have a remarkable ability to serve as conduits between U.S. and Latin American culture. The price Puerto Ricans have paid for this hybrid status is to be perceived as schizophrenic, monstrous, amorphous, floating, and undefined, by Latin Americans, Americans, and by ourselves. If such self-conscious assimilation kills off the Hispanic origin, it also chooses to keep on carrying and showcasing the corpse.

CHAPTER FOUR

"THAT ANIMALS MIGHT SPEAK": DOUBLES AND THE UNCANNY IN LOIDA MARITZA PÉREZ'S *GEOGRAPHIES OF HOME*

Like Cristina García in *The Agüero Sisters* and Rosario Ferré in *Eccentric Neighborhoods, The House on the Lagoon,* and *Sweet Diamond Dust,* the Dominican American writer Loida Maritza Pérez sets up an allegory in *Geographies of Home* (1999), her first novel, in which the parents substitute metaphorically for an origin that is lost or fading quickly. Three sisters, as opposed to the two in García's book, represent the possible hybridized outcomes in the New American Reality. The text begins and ends with the point of view of Iliana—the sister who has embarked upon an education at an elite private school and who feels both protective of, yet also repulsed by, her working-class family. The most memorable scene in *Geographies of Home*, however, is a flashback of a ghostly encounter in the Dominican Republic between Iliana's father, Papito, and a dying girl whose own father raped and impregnated her. As a sacrificed mother, this girl Annabelle—like García's Blanca Agüero and Ferré's Clarissa Vernet—exemplifies how past (patriarchal) violence on the island overshadows life for Latinos in the United States, even though they may not know it, just as Iliana, the assumed protagonist of *Geographies of Home*, never learns about Annabelle. However, if dead or dying women are metonyms of the dangerous, violent origin, in *Geographies of Home* we also see that female bodies aggressively engage violence as well as submit to it. In rebelling against patriarchy, Iliana and her sister Marina do not free themselves but, on the contrary, become either more repressed (Iliana) or more violent (Marina). Ultimately, rebellion against the repressive rules of Latino patriarchy carries the unfortunate consequence of a *de facto* assimilation into a U.S. culture that requires women to take on individualist, and possibly maculinist, qualities to be successful subjects.

In *Geographies of Home*, as in *The Agüero Sisters*, certain moments of magical realism, or flashbacks of uncanny events, serve as reterritorializations of life in the land of origin, in this case, the Dominican Republic, and are always associated with maternal typology or with women's ways of knowing. In *Geographies of Home*, distance from the origin and psychic repression of memories of the old country deflate the potency of the magical. While the magical is represented as a balm for the constant violence that irrupts in the character's lives, it is also mistrusted as a possible source of the violence.

Although characters who are doubles or alternate selves and who carry maternal or paternal traits are as significant in this novel as in the García or Ferré books, Pérez is breaking new ground. Far afield from the primarily middle-class characters and situations depicted by García, Ferré, and Julia Álvarez, Pérez's allegory bears more similarity to the urban stories by male authors such as Edward Rivera, Piri Thomas, and Junot Díaz.[1] Pérez, however, has taken great risks in representing the plight of an educated Latina at odds with a working-class family background so riven by violence it threatens to collapse both her mental and physical boundaries. Among U.S. Latino Caribbean writers only Rivera—whose narrator in *Family Installments* understands himself to be a "culture conscious scribe," an anomaly in the "peasant" community of his forbears in Puerto Rico—has so deeply explored the anxieties besetting working-class Latinos who try to assimilate into the system through education.[2] Like Rivera's narrator, Pérez's protagonist, Iliana, feels torn between her role as daughter of an impoverished working-class Dominican family and her newly hatched, still inchoate, identity as a privileged member of the American middle-class intelligentsia.

Iliana returns home to Brooklyn after a one-and-a-half year sojourn at an elite private institution modeled on Cornell University.[3] Despite her desire to rescue her family, it is apparent that Iliana feels estranged from them. Symptomatic of Iliana's alienation is the fact that she is tempted home by a supernatural "voice" she associates with her mother, rather than by any direct request from the family.[4] Once she is home the family responds to Iliana's presence with a surprisingly polarized mix of pride—she is their " 'jucated," "prodigal," daughter—as well as outright contempt.[5] Trying to help in the family crisis centered around the abuse of her sister Rebecca by the latter's husband, Iliana steps in with stereotypically individualist American advice, declaring that nothing can be done for Rebecca "until she's willing to help herself."[6] Iliana's mother, Aurelia, combatively responds that this advice sounds as if extracted from "a textbook" and that Iliana seems to have turned her back on her family.[7] What is apparent is that the family resents the fact that Iliana is educating herself into middle-class status. They are proud of her; but can no longer relate to her, and Iliana hides her own ambivalence (from herself, really, since the family sees through her) by wearing the mask of a rationalist authority figure.

Pérez underlines a dilemma that is very common among Latinos and other minorities of working-class origin, but which is hard to express in all its subtlety. Iliana is particularly vulnerable to psychic displacement because her working-class family is dysfunctional. On the other hand she is not able to fully avail herself of the advantages offered by the university whose "courses disclaimed life as she had known it, making her feel invisible."[8] The central metaphor of the book, described in the title, stages the notion of home as ever-changing, multiple, and unstable. But Iliana cannot help at first stubbornly identifying home with her family of origin and the house they live in. In fact, as Iliana approaches her family's house, after her relatively long absence, she senses that her absence has not made a difference. The unexpected brightness of the new coat of paint on the house highlights Iliana's feeling of being an outsider but also points to the family's self-sufficiency and renewed strength, despite Iliana's absence and the defection of another daughter, Beatriz. The small community represented by her family even regard the prodigal as a kind of enemy.

New barricades, a fence and gate, that were not there before, have been erected.[9] Eventually it becomes clear that the family depends on the mad or troubled daughters who have psychologically "stayed home" and gathers them to the hearth literally and figuratively, whereas the Americanized and apparently self-sufficient Iliana is left to her own devices. Ultimately, the family's disinterest in Iliana leaves her open to a violent attack by another family member—her mad sister and double—as if the family had agreed upon her sacrifice.

Iliana's changing but still ambiguous class status is not the only factor distancing her from her parents and siblings. She is also alienated by the rigidly patriarchal structure of her family life. Incest is the supreme signifier of patriarchal violence in the book, of its complexity and its long-lasting influence. In particular, two incidents of incest stand out: the first is the flashback I mentioned in this essay's opening in which the paterfamilias, Papito, recalls his first love in the Dominican Republic, a young girl named Anabelle, whose father raped and impregnated her, and who died. This violence is something Papito—and the text—cannot shake. The second moment of incest occurs when the mad sister Marina rapes Iliana at the end of the book. Such a violent, disturbing ending raises two questions, which I try to answer: Why is Iliana punished by the text? What is the relationship—for undoubtedly there must be one—between this final, apocalyptic, incestuous rape and the father's memory of the young Dominican girl who died as a result of being raped by her father?

The struggle between the Father's patriarchal mores and the Mother's skills and intuitions in *Geographies of Home* plays out in the conflict between Afro-Caribbean and magical beliefs and practices—handed down to Aurelia, the mother, and repressed by her when she marries Papito—and Papito's strict adherence to Adventism, which "had granted him salvation, unmediated access to the divine, and steadfast rules by which to live."[10] The idea that "within Christianity Protestantism has long been recognized as at once less authoritarian and more materially centered than Catholicism" is a commonplace among academic intellectuals, according to Elaine Scarry.[11] However anti-hierarchical Protestantism may be in theory, in *Geographies of Home,* the characters repeatedly portray Adventism as repressive, a doctrine that "condemn[s] as pagan the piercing of body parts," and encourages Aurelia's "emotional collapse and increasing deference to Papito who, in turn, placed his burden in the hand of God."[12] According to Pérez, the religion is so restrictive that when the daughters slept together in the same bed, each child had to be wrapped individually in sheets so that her skin would not rub against her sister's.[13] Adventism attracts Papito because it so clearly delineates what is right and what is wrong, very different from the animistic Afro-Caribbean religion his wife Aurelia was raised in. Papito forced Aurelia's conversion to Adventism because he felt threatened by the spirit-working of Aurelia's mother, Bienvenida: "In his mother-in-law's house invisible forces had clawed at his arm in retaliation for his attempts to exorcise the demons posing as spirits of the dead."[14] That these are "demons" is Papito's interpretation of course, not Pérez's. That Bienvenida had concourse with spirits is uncontested by Papito and by Aurelia, who both empirically encountered these spirits through the senses; Papito through the sense of touch; Aurelia, as we see in the next paragraph, through the sense of hearing.

It is clear that Pérez represents Bienvenida's spirit-working as less hierarchical and more materially focused than the repressive and authoritarian Adventism, which is revealed as joylessly denying the power of the body and the relationship between the body and ritual objects. I mean "materially focused" in the sense that Elaine Scarry argues for belief in the Judeo-Christian scriptures as "the act of turning one's own body inside-out."[15] Scarry notes:

> Belief is the act of imagining. It is what the act of imagining is called when the object created is credited with more reality (and all that is entailed in greater "realness," more power, more authority) than oneself. It is when the object created is in fact described as though it instead created you. It ceases to be the "offspring" of the human being and becomes the thing from which the human being himself sprung forth.[16]

This act of imagining, and thereby perpetuating, the belief in and concourse with spirits is exactly what Bienvenida does when she summons Aurelia to visit her because she believes she will die soon. She gives her daughter, as birthright, a series of objects that have symbolic religious power: a quilt sewn out of clothing worn by dead family members, including a patch taken from the shirt worn, when he died, by the brother who killed himself; "*a fistful of the earth to which we return to nourish those who follow*"; an earthen jug corked to contain water "*[t]o remind you that in our blood we carry the power of the sea*," and a number of other objects.[17] By discarding these objects invested with so much "power" and "authority" by Bienvenida, Aurelia recognizes, many years later in New York, that she has cut herself off from "her heritage" and also, if we apply Scarry's insights, understands she has stymied the source of her creativity, since Aurelia, like her mother, had psychic gifts.[18]

Pérez's text renders few descriptive details that would enable us to identify the cult or deities Bienvenida serves. It's hard to figure out whether the latter's religion is a Dominican variant of Voudoun or Santería—syncretic Afro-Caribbean artifacts, highly structured and hierarchized like the Yoruban, Dahomeyan, Congolese, and Catholic religions from which they take elements—or whether it is a version of Spiritism, which in fact is often practiced in Latin America alongside Catholicism. But this vagueness of representation also has to do with the fact that the religion is one abandoned by Aurelia in her youth despite her own strong psychic connection to it. She is estranged from it, as are her children: "[Papito's] God was the one spirit [Aurelia] wanted to believe in, not the spirits her mother claimed . . . It did not matter that she herself felt their presence . . . that . . . she had lain awake at night listening to their voices and hearing her mother's respond."[19] The vagueness and paucity of information about this religion in the text mimics Aurelia's repression of it.

However, the power of the origin, and of magical realism, has fragmentary potency even greater than what we saw in *The Agüero Sisters*. It is after all a benign disembodied "voice," which Iliana identifies with her mother's, that keeps Iliana "rooted" to matters pertaining to home while she is at school.[20] Interestingly, this disembodied voice disappears from the text as soon as Iliana actually arrives home. This suggests that what Iliana is in search of is a voice, an expressive vehicle as well as a form of linkage to the past. Although ironically Aurelia, the mother, projects the "voice" that lures Iliana back home, Aurelia herself has been cut off from her own voice. Early in the text, Aurelia is "conscious of something missing in the present—something her mother had possessed and passed along to her but which she had misplaced and failed to pass on to her own children."[21] This something "missing in the present and possessed in the past" is a voice connected with figures of vegetation, a voice that expresses itself in Aurelia's "perceptions" but that is "planted" in Dominican "ground," a "voice that reassured Iliana of her own existence and kept her rooted" in the stories of her family's past in the Dominican Republic when she was away at school.[22] This voice is a vestige or fragment of Aurelia's spiritually privileged past life in the Dominican Republic.

Significantly, the psychic crumbling of the daughters in Iliana's family is associated in the text with either the smell or sight of rotting vegetables. So when Marina is visited by her dream rapist—her double as I show later—she recognizes the "odor of rotting greens"; after Marina is hospitalized for a suicide attempt, Aurelia throws out all the rotting vegetables in the refrigerator.[23] A related example has to do more generally with food. When Rebecca and her children come to stay with Aurelia and Papito after Pasión's last attack, Aurelia finds rotting food all over the house because the children, used to being starved by Rebecca and Pasión, are hoarding it. The inability of the daughters to feed themselves or their children either literally or psychically is related, the text suggests, to the uprooting from the source itself. But this uprooting is one that had taken place already on Dominican soil because of the radical split between the spiritual ideologies of the father and the mother.

The text suggests that Aurelia gave up her spiritual power by denying both the material gifts her spirit-working mother gave her on her deathbed as well as the psychic gift itself, the gift of "perceptions," "la facultad" as Gloria Anzaldúa calls it in *Borderlands,* or voice. By possessing the individual, as the spirits possessed Bienvenida, a voice—such as the one that haunts Iliana at the beginning of the book—can also be owned for a sense of grounding such as Aurelia experienced on Dominican soil. In Afro-Caribbean religions when an initiate is mounted by an Orisha or Loa in a ceremony, she will start to drag a leg, a sign that her body is starting to root itself into the ground so that the spirits can climb up and manifest themselves.[24] A mounted initiate will usually speak when possessed, but her voice is the voice of the Orishas or Loas. In her celebrated text on Haitian Voudoun, Maya Deren declares that possession is the focal point of Voudoun; Migene González-Wippler has said the same of Santería. Deren notes that despite the deity's embodiment in his server, "not nearness but the distance between a man and his god" is what is highlighted.[25] The reason for possession, she states is "To be made aware, once more, that man is of divine origin . . . that at the **root** of the universe the great imperceptible principles of cosmic good endure."[26] Ultimately, in Deren's reading of Voudoun, to be rooted is to let the divine speak through one's voice. Aurelia and Iliana have experienced what it is to be rooted but in various ways lose their rootedness and their voices.

In a dialogue with René Girard, Jean Michel Oughourlian notes that there is a distinct difference between the spirit possessions that take place in tribal African religions and those that have been described in Christian narratives. The similarity between demonic or "hysterical" possession and ritual possession is that "the difference between the subject under possession and the being possessing him is never lost."[27] The difference between demonic possessions—such as those reported in Christian Europe in the sixteenth century and cited by Oughourlian—and possession by spirits in African and Afro-Caribbean ceremonies is that the latter types are "beneficent" rituals in which the individual willingly allows his/her ego to be replaced by the "mounting" deity, as the community gathers round to encourage the process (by singing and dancing and drum-playing) and to benefit from it.[28] In demonic possession, on the other hand, the subject perceives the "mimetic model" performing the possession as "an enemy and a source of pollution, as an aggressor capable of rape" as Oughourlian terms it.[29]

This distinction between Afro-Caribbean possession and demonic possession can help one understand how Papito tends to demonize the Spiritist or Voudoun cults of his island as "pagan rituals . . . [in which] bodies sway[ed] to achieve the delirium necessary for spirits to possess souls."[30] When Marina, the mad daughter, becomes possessed during a service at the family's Adventist church in Brooklyn, Papito becomes enraged at Marina for various reasons: (1) because her mental state has finally transgressed the boundary of the house and is officially beyond Papito's control; (2) because her possession occurs in the Church, which Papito so reveres; (3) because he believes that Marina is demonstrating that the "susceptibility to demons his mother-in-law had possessed had been passed on to one of his own children."[31] This tendency to demonize Afro-Caribbean religions is a symptom of double-consciousness in Papito, a character who in other ways does not seem overtly conflicted about his racial features and who in fact is hardly described in the book in racial terms. The characters who are most clearly described so we can imagine them physically are Iliana and Marina. Given the fact that we know Iliana is black and that Marina observes her own features as mulatto—"her kinky, dirt-red hair, her sprawling nose, her wide, long lips"—and that Aurelia is described as lightskinned with long wavy dark hair, it seems likely that Papito is the parent with darker skin, either mulatto or recognizably black.[32]

In another use of the metaphor of rootedness, Karin Luisa Badt states: "Given the atrocities in Afro-American history, to return to one's "roots" has the psychic resonance of returning to a subjugated position."[33] This would partially explain why Papito shies away from the African spirits worshipped by his mother-in-law. It is no mistake that Adventism, a religion brought to the Dominican Republic by American missionaries is associated with Papito and that Afro-Caribbean spirit-working is associated with the mother. In Pérez's view Papito, the father, is beknightedly cutting himself and his family off from his roots. Significantly Pérez stages Marina's rebellious bouts of madness in three settings associated with patriarchy: (1) the father's house; (2) the firm where Marina aspires toward marrying herself off to one of the lawyers; (3) the church.

If Papito seems relatively unconflicted about race, Marina, his daughter, is the character most tortured by it. She is, in fact, a classic case of double-consciousness. Because she is a lightskinned mulatta, Marina constantly denies her blackness by declaring to Iliana, "I'm Hispanic, not black."[34] Despite this declaration, however, Marina demonstrates that she has internalized the general Hispanic Caribbean tendency toward lactification, stating in the same conversation with Iliana that she really prefers whites over Hispanics: "White people have always been nicer to me than anyone else."[35] Like many Latinas, Marina fantasizes that all her problems will be solved when "a white man or at least a lightskinned Hispanic like herself would come into her life."[36] This fantasy is shattered the day Marina asserts herself when a white lawyer at the office where she works as a paralegal assistant makes an advance but then coldly spurns Marina after she tells him she wants marriage, not sex. In a rage over the lawyer's mistreatment, Marina finally crosses a certain threshold of sanity in her behavior. She is distressed, not because there was any nascent love between herself and the lawyer, but rather because he has become a mediator, in the Girardian sense, the bearer of social prestige and thus both a model and object of desire.[37] The lawyer "is also both the instigator of desire and a relentless guardian forbidding its fulfillment."[38] Significantly, the intense desire that Marina had for the lawyer transforms quickly into hatred when, on being sent to the copy room, she walks past the attorney's blonde secretary whose "green eyes and smiling lips . . . sent the bitter taste of bile rushing toward [Marina's] mouth."[39] This "pretty blonde" is a reminder for Marina that she is only a poor copy of her socially prestigious models. Ironically, Marina ends up setting fire to the *photocopy* room to which the lawyer had sent her to carry out a series of humiliating clerical duties. What sets her on the path of madness, however, is not the mistreatment by the white lawyer but her own frustrated desire.

This is not the first time that Marina has suffered from mimetic desire. As an adolescent, she was involved in a mimetic relationship with her beautiful sister Beatriz: "Everywhere Beatriz went, Marina had followed close behind. She had doted on this sister like a lover . . . eternally fascinated by her ability to attract men with cruelty and unabashed flirtation."[40] Girard provides an explanation for Marina's masochistic love for her sister:

> *Avaniteux* will desire any object so long as he is convinced that is already desired by another person whom he admires. The mediator here is a rival, brought into existence as a rival by vanity, and that same vanity demands his defeat. The rivalry between mediator and the person who desires constitutes an essential difference between this desire and that of Don Quixote . . . Amadis cannot vie with Don Quixote in the protection of orphans in distress, he cannot slaughter giants in his place.[41]

Marina's love for her sister, Beatriz, is mimetic in the sense that Marina admires Beatriz because Beatriz is admired by others (the very men Beatriz attracts "with cruelty and unabashed flirtation" also suffer from mimetic desire). Beatriz is a very different kind of model or mediator for Marina than is Amadis for Don Quixote or, referring to the anterior discussion about possession, an Orisha possessing a devotee. The distance that separates the Orisha from the devotee is lacking in the relationship between Marina and Beatriz so that the devotee, Marina, and the supposed model, Beatriz, are also rivals for the attentions of men. Marina is slavish toward Beatriz because she feels inferior to her beautiful sister. Beatriz, however, wants to defend her position of superiority from competitors and, significantly, leaves home when this position is threatened by Iliana.[42]

When they are girls, these three sisters who are closest to each other in age, form a hierarchy according to their particular identities: Beatriz is beautiful,

Iliana is a quiet nerd, Marina is ugly. In this simple hierarchy, Iliana just doesn't count. Beatriz is more powerful than Marina and in that sense there is order and distance in the hierarchy; but because Beatriz herself is a *vaniteux* (or vaniteuse) like Marina, the fact that Iliana subverts the hierarchy by going off to school deflates Beatriz's sense of self, revealing that—however beautiful Beatriz, however unattractive Marina—they are essentially the same in desire, just copies of each other. This process of breaking down the hierarchical barriers and removing the distance between mediator and imitator is what Girard calls "the exacerbation of mimesis," which ultimately "culminates in a relationship of doubles with the other. This other can take on a singular form . . . Or it can be multiple and plural, as with the cases of psychosis in our hospitals."[43]

After Iliana leaves home, Beatriz—who has already ceded her position of superiority in the family by engaging in rivalry with Marina—must also leave or concede that the new mediator is Iliana. The fact that Iliana leaves home for a year and a half lends her mystique—she is as distant from the family as a god—and privilege because her mother's projected "voice" keeps her informed of the family's activities. That is why when Iliana returns home, the half-demented Marina (who is now freer to bring her rivalrous nature out into the open) immediately confronts Iliana with envious admiration: "You look just like a model."[44] Because now, effectively, Iliana has replaced Beatriz as Marina's *model*. And: "You're in school far away from here and can do anything you want."[45] On the other hand, Marina's admiration escalates quickly into resentment: "You think you're such hot shit! . . . Reading stupid books, talking to everyone like you were better, acting like what we had wasn't good enough for you!"[46] Marina's hysterical possession in the church, and her hallucinations of the dream rapist, are complete surrenders to the reality of her doubles and the tragedy of her rivalry with the world.[47] At this point Marina has already become psychotic. As Jean Michel Oughourlian notes: "The structure of psychosis—delirium—is the mythic story constructed by one or other of the protagonists in the relationship of doubles in order to latch on to the cultural order and to try to explain himself, through without getting any closer to understanding his situation."[48] It is significant that at both these moments of supreme psychosis Iliana is present and identifies closely with Marina, particularly during the church episode during which Iliana feels alienated by the pastor's misogynist discourse decrying women who use too much makeup and wear clothes that disguise their unattractive physiques. The episode shows that both Marina and Iliana feel alienated by the patriarchal and superficial nature of the pastor's speech, condemning the "vanity of women."[49] Marina's purported possession by a God who prefers her and condemns the parishioners is a mockery of both the idea of ritual possession as well as a challenge to the pastor. Iliana's interior monologue in chapter fifteen shows she is in sympathy with her sister, and is not in awe of the Adventist God.[50] In one of the scenes in which Marina hallucinates with the dream-rapist, Iliana is ready to believe "that Marina actually saw what others couldn't" because Iliana "could not help but recall the voice she had been haunted by at school."[51] Although Iliana is disturbed by Marina's illness, she feels implicated in it. In this sense Iliana is just as afraid as Papito that Marina's madness is genetically contagious, except that, unlike Papito, Iliana doesn't know about her grandmother Bienvenida or even about her mother's, Aurelia's, "perceptions."[52]

Although there is a world of difference (the world of the educated) between Iliana and Marina, the two are both fleeing the social and economic deprivation that is their family's lot. They have similar fears but in different keys: "Marina had daydreamed of one day attracting an attorney who would support her so that she'd never again have to suffer the humiliation of being pressed against strangers and smelling their rancid breath."[53] And: "For a year and a half [Iliana] had lived in a town whose pristine appearance had deceived her into believing . . . that, having entered into the company of the elite, she would never again suffer hunger or abuse."[54] The difference is that Marina fantasizes escape as victory. Like Beatriz she simply wants to prove she is better than everybody else, which is why she constantly projects this feeling of superiority and Godlikeness onto others. Iliana, on the other hand, early on has learned to balance her fantasies with reason. This does not mean that Iliana is not as mimetic as Marina. What it may mean is that she dissimulates it better so that Marina's accusation that Iliana has airs may not be unfounded. Whether Iliana in the present suffers from the kind of envy and mimetic desires that have tortured her sisters is a moot point. That she did as a child and learned to repress these desires, however, I make apparent in the next paragraph.

Marina's rage leads to violent moments of acting out whereas Iliana's has been long-sublimated in an exertion of control over her surroundings. The particular instance the text describes as motivating this self-repression is an act of violence that Iliana carries out as a little girl against a doll, a blond-haired Hi Dottie doll. The rage, really an outburst of anger against her parents, has been long in brewing but explodes when Iliana receives a Christmas present she does not want, a moment that triggers a loss of "faith" in her parents and obviously a kind of social rage, as well, since the doll is blond-haired and blue-eyed and Iliana had asked her parents for a "gymnast," a doll with a mercurial body symbolizing the child's desire for escape.[55] Her parents gave her a doll that erased her subjectivity.[56] Unfortunately, Iliana's rebellion against the social implications symbolized by the doll have an effect opposite to the gaining of freedom. After literally tearing the doll from limb to limb, and even destroying the box (the home) it came into shreds, the eight-year-old Iliana experiences a kind of counter-epiphany that renders her so "terrified of her impulses" she decides that she must watch over herself and prevent such a thing from happening again. She tries not to reveal her emotions and allows Marina to manipulate her to the extent that she gives up her food portions to her sister. As a result, she develops "a myriad of neuroses," including sleep-walking to the refrigerator to appease her hunger.[57] Being neurotic enables Iliana to function in the poverty-stricken, difficult environment she inhabits as a child but at a certain price, that of "sleepwalking" through emotional situations. The relationship with Marina hinted at in the passage is telling: Iliana starves herself both literally and emotionally to feed Marina. In this sense their doubling is born at this moment of Iliana's self-repression. One aspect of the self (Iliana) is in control, one (Marina) will feed and manipulate until she allows her social self to whirl out of control.

In his essay on "The Uncanny" Freud throws light on the splitting that results from Iliana's attempt at self-mastery. He notes that the idea of the double was "originally an insurance against the destruction of the ego, an 'energetic denial of the power of death,'" and a product of "the primary narcissism which dominates the mind of the child and of primitive man."[58] However, Freud asserts, after the primary narcissism of the child has been surmounted, there are cases in which the critical faculty, "which we become aware of as our 'conscience' . . . becomes isolated, dissociated from the ego":

> The fact that an agency of this kind exists, which is able to treat the rest of the ego like an object—the fact, that is, that man is capable of self-observation—renders it possible to invest the old idea of a "double" with a new meaning and to ascribe a number of things to it—above all, those things which seem to self-criticism to belong to the old surmounted narcissism of earlier times.[59]

Freud would not publish his concept of the "superego" until 1923, four years after the essay on the uncanny was published.[60] However, even so, this notion of a critical agency that is so "pathological" as to split off from the rest of the self differs markedly from the idea of the superego and does seem to throw light on Iliana's "tightly lidded" personality.

A specular passage concerning a photograph of Marina, Beatriz, and Iliana and their brother Tico as children further illuminates Iliana's growing sense of disturbed identification with her sister. As she contemplates Marina's face, Iliana tries to convince herself of "their differences to persuade herself that although they had been conceived in the same womb it did not follow that she too would lose her mind."[61] Iliana sees Marina as an alternate self, fearing that her sister's madness is a mere reflection of Iliana's own latent and future condition. Because she is afraid that they are similar, Iliana entrenches herself in rigid notions of how the mentally impaired sister should be dealt with that stem from a rather Westernized and puritanical attitude toward madness: "Life was hard . . . One went on."[62] In this view Marina should be sent to a hospital, thus guarding the family from the possibility of contamination or harm. The family, on the other hand, Aurelia especially, oppose Iliana's ideas, holding that Marina should stay home and be cared for with love and a cheery repression of the disturbing nature of her behavior. The entrenchment of Iliana and her family into such diverse positions is an instantiation of how distanced they have become from each other. At the same time, it is clear that neither faction is wrong or right. If the mad sister is "taken care of," Iliana will not have to confront daily those features that remind her of herself. The family's desire to keep their obviously dangerously crazy daughter at home shows a self-defeating bravado in the face of society at large. The family claims the mad daughter as if their community mattered more than that of mainstream American society. Iliana dislikes this paternalism even though she has suffered pangs of nostalgia over it.

If, as Girard states, "being mad is a matter of letting oneself be taken over completely by the mimetic models, and so fulfilling the calling of desire . . . of abandoning oneself to a fascination with the model, to the extent that it resists and does violence to the subject," then Marina crossed this threshold after the briefly liberating episode in the law office in which the flames from the fire she lit "spoke to her . . . murmur[ing she was] free of the conventions which had kept her wobbling on a tightrope for fear of plummeting into the abyss."[63] She is fired on the spot from this job, spends her last savings on putting together a model's portfolio, but is never taken up on her attempts to acquire an object (a job as a model). In Girard's paradigm of triangulation the object is desirable to the subject because the mediator desires it. Marina desires literally to be a model, as so many young women do, because of the high prestige associated with it. But her desire reveals a deeper psychic need to become her own model, to supplant any mediator. From the individualist point of view, this desire to be different is a sign of psychic well-being. Caminero-Santangelo, for example, spends many pages in *The Madwoman Can't Speak* producing proofs of the fact that madwomen are poor focuses for discussions of feminist agency because of their failure to differentiate between self and other. But Girard's point—that the aim of mimetic desire is above all to be unique, to be supremely different, to deny sameness—highlights some of the main issues that plague Marina and, in a less dangerous way, Iliana.

After Marina fails in her attempt to become a (fashion) model she falls into psychosis because she no longer has an object (modeling, being a paralegal, going to school, etc.) This is the point where she starts to be haunted by the dream-rapist, whom she claims as real. This figure who always seems to emerge from the closet in the bedroom Iliana and Marina share in the basement of the house (the realm of the unconscious as I mentioned in the Ferré chapter) could be interpreted as the epitome of Marina's double-consciousness. The rapist in her hallucination, "a tall, lean figure absorbing the room's darkness so that he appeared only as a blacker silhouette" is dubbed "evil" by Marina.[64] This "flat-nosed, wide-lipped nigger" clearly represents Marina's own black self, which she refuses to consciously acknowledge. While penetrating her body, the man shouts at her, "Look at me!" as if her split off black self is begging for recognition.[65] This libidinal aspect of herself, from which she successfully disassociates while working at the law firm, or in conversation with Iliana, overpowers her in the darkness of the house's basement, symbolizing an aspect of both her own unconscious and that of her extended family who suffer from the same complexes but to a milder extent.

Marina's condition frightens Iliana because she is afraid of losing her hard-won self-control. But Iliana, whom Marina has taken as her mimetic model, poses an even greater threat for Marina.[66] For, as her possessions in the church and restaurant suggest, Marina has taken on the posture of a child of God to mask her failure. This religious pose necessitates constant rivals threatening her with "evil" as we saw with the dream-rapist, her double. Near the end of the book when Marina rapes Iliana, not once but twice, it would be fair to say that she projects onto Iliana the characteristics of her rapist: blackness and an aggressive masculinity, thereby conflating her imaginary double (who haunts her and threatens her with sexual and spiritual possession) with a real-life rival and double. In other words the doubles proliferate, as Girard says, the more Marina allows herself to covet the power of the Other.

These "self-seeking," "indifferent," "confident," and "volatile" qualities Marina attributes to Iliana immediately strike the reader as qualities Marina desperately envies.[67] They are qualities she projects onto all her mediators: the lawyer, the blonde secretary, Tico, Iliana. She is in rivalry with all of them. It is at this psychotic moment that Marina projects the characteristics of her dark double, the dream-rapist, onto Iliana. Because she is in rivalry with Iliana and in fear of the dream-rapist, in the scene, following the above scene at the restaurant, Marina is driven to rape her own sister, not once but twice.

Significantly, the only people the hefty Marina attacks in the book are her father, Iliana, and her "indifferent" brother, Tico, whom she accuses of attempting to rape her after she assaults him. Resentful of Papito's authority, Marina stages her possession in the church of which he is deacon; Tico, the family's youngest son, is the only brother accessible to Marina's envy and physical attacks since he occupies the basement room next to hers. Marina, then, attacks Iliana's "maleness" because it strangely resembles the maleness of father and brother, but unlike the men, Iliana is vulnerable to Marina's attack. Marina's rape of Iliana is an insane attempt to find not just Iliana's penis but Marina's penis—that is, the symbolic principle of power, the phallus, that Iliana owns and Marina desires. The rape scene, Marina's and Iliana's final encounter, echoes the scene in which Marina welcomes Iliana home by lifting her dress and "enacting a pantomime of something wriggling in her hand."[68] Later on in the text Marina barges in on Iliana in the bathroom and stares "between her legs" at the naked Iliana's genitalia. The first time she rapes Iliana, Marina yanks her hand out from between her sisters legs and yells triumphantly: "I almost had it in my hand!"[69] This creature-fetus-phallus is a principle of both creativity and power that Marina lacks and craves.

However demented Marina may be, she is not far off the mark in identifying Iliana with the phallus. In becoming an individualist like other undergraduates at her college, Iliana is free to "at moments [act] like a woman but at others like a man," a power Iliana's uneducated older sisters lack.[70] On the other hand, the text clearly punishes Iliana for her individualism. This is why she is raped twice, not once. The two rapes occur within an hour more or less of each other. The second rape happens because Iliana decides that leaving the bedroom after the first rape would be a defeat of her "willpower": "Iliana had no use for emotions now. To rail against what had been done to her would be to credit her sister's madness with having affected her."[71] And: "Besides, her sister had not meant her any harm. It was her madness that had lashed out—a destructive madness incapable of making distinctions."[72] So she denies the fact of the rape, goes back to the bedroom, is bullied, and then raped again by Marina. But she is raped again precisely because Marina can make distinctions. Marina, in her madness, is scandalized by Iliana's difference, her freedom to make choices, to dress in ways that are not provocative to men, to avoid falling into the rigid roles that have been set aside for Dominican women. It is because Iliana is too different, too much like Marina's conscious mediators (the lawyer, the secretary) and her unconscious double (the dream-rapist) that Marina attacks her. The second attack is also Marina's crazy, rivalrous attempt to prove that Iliana is not the "stronger" of the two.

The incestuous rape is also metonymically associated with the ultimate failure of the Dominican Republic as originary signifier in the book. Iliana leaves the house after she is raped in search of Ed, her gay friend, her best (and only) friend at Cornell, but returns home frustrated since Ed was not home and she was harassed by men on the street. She gets home so late that Papito, overwrought from having to deal with Marina's and Rebecca's disturbing troubles slaps her in the face and accuses her of being a slut. All these incidents—the *double* rape, Iliana's lonely wanderings afterward, Papito's beating of Iliana the same day she is raped—demonstrate the terrible bind Iliana finds herself in. Her new life, represented by Ed and Cornell University, is full of intellectual gratification, guaranteeing her a sucessful future. However, Ed is gone the moment when she really needs him and, in fact, throughout the book she has trouble getting him to listen to her when she talks about her family troubles. Her family receive her at home but they no longer understand her. In fact one of Iliana's first memories at the start of the book is of the slap she received as a child when she contradicted Papito who showed her a gift of soaps he claimed were strawberry-scented. When the child Iliana insisted the soap smelled like cinnamon, Papito hit her.[73] At the end of the book, Papito, doesn't ask his tormented, raped daughter any questions when she arrives home late. He simply beats her. In their final conversation, Iliana realizes Papito is full of fear and impotence in the face of the crises that have been tearing up the family. Iliana understands that as a child she had deified him as "Papa God" (Papá Diós), "endowing him with powers no human could possibly possess."[74] As she did with Marina after the rape, Iliana recognizes that she is stronger than her father and that it is because he never lived up to the image of "imaginary father" she'd had of him—when she was a little girl in the Dominican Republic and he was working in New York—that she is full of resentment toward him.[75] In other words, Papito always was Iliana's mimetic model and this final scene is one of confrontation and conquest of the mimetic model. If "men become gods in the eyes of each other" in mimetic desire, then when these gods fall it is only to have their place taken up by new ones.[76] In this case, Iliana acknowledges that she could fill the father's position: "She understood . . . that he was more afraid of the world than she herself had ever been."[77] That is why she needs to leave home: in search of a new mimetic model; also, she knows that her family cannot tolerate the fact that she is symbolically stronger than the father.

The father's impotence had come up before in the book in a scene in which Papito, a good Adventist who neither smoked nor drank, had just indulged his weakness for candy bars at the bodega when he ran into Pasión, the husband/abuser of his daughter Rebecca.[78] Pasión mistakes the candy bar Papito is grasping in his pocket for a gun and Papito takes advantage of this mistake by beating up the man. The candy bar is Papito's false phallus in this scene—it shows that he can pretend to have control over Pasión but ultimately neither Pasión, Rebecca, nor the rest of his family obey him. Papito does not even know at the end of the book what Marina has done to Iliana. The one who knows is Aurelia. Significantly, it is Aurelia who is able to get rid of Pasión forever through her spirit-working. Aurelia asks Papito to buy her a live chicken so that she can recreate the experience of living in the Dominican Republic where she used to kill and pluck her own chickens for meals. But what she really wants the chicken for is to perform homeopathic magic—the chicken stands in for Pasión and with each plucked handful of chicken feathers, Aurelia slowly and gradually asphyxiates the man. At that moment of magical asphyxiation, Pasión finds himself in his apartment where he had been keeping Rebecca and her children in the most miserable filth along with a small farmload of chickens. The chicken farm in the apartment is another reterritorialization of life in the Dominican Republic—we are told that Pasión bought the chickens to mimic the act of owning property in the old country, strangely and ironically embracing "a farmer's lifestyle idealized in stories told by a father who had himself abandoned it upon arriving in the United

States."[79] In effect Aurelia's magic works where Papito's phallus is shown to be fake and ineffectual. But ultimately Aurelia is as powerless to help her daughters as Papito. Although she kills Pasión with magic, she cannot keep Rebecca from desiring him even more after his death, she cannot protect Marina from madness or foresee the violence done to Iliana.

Papito's impotence is inscribed in an originary scene, one of the most powerful in a book filled with disturbing scenes, and one whose violence I argue carries over from the past in the Dominican Republic to the novel's present in Brooklyn, New York. What makes this excavated moment so interesting is that none of the other family members know anything about it except for the haunted Papito. The story: as a young man in Barahona, in the Dominican Republic, Papito is set upon marrying a young woman named Anabelle, whose striking beauty captivates him one day but whom he doesn't know at all. Upon inquiry, Papito learns that the girl's father is rumored to be very jealous and possessive of her. Papito saves up money to extend his humble little shack and builds up his willpower to ask Anabelle's hand in marriage, making sure not to "disrespect" the girl's father, in the meantime, by approaching her while she is alone.[80] Rather, he postpones getting to know Anabelle until after meeting with her father, a meeting that never happens due to tragedy. During a torrential rainstorm, flooding ruins Papito's humble home and he is driven out into the hurricane to find shelter.

As he ventures forth in the storm Pérez is careful to emphasize that Papito has an "uncanny" feeling that he has lived through this terrible storm before in a recent "recurrent nightmare . . . which, upon waking screaming, he had barely been able to recall."[81] Bereft of the protection of his shack, out in the raging storm, he comes face to face with a "mud-smeared" and barely sentient Anabelle whose ghostly demeanor and bloody, ragged dress recall Madeleine, Ligeia, Annabel Lee, and other ghostly women from Edgar Allan Poe's stories of the eroticized supernatural. In fact, in the reader's guide printed at the back of the most recent paperback edition of the novel, there is an interview with Pérez in which she describes Poe and African American novelist Zora Neale Hurston as two of her most important literary influences. In this scene, Annabelle bears the trace of Poe. The abused donkey—itself a metonym for Annabelle's victimization—recalls the mules so important in the work of Zora Neale Hurston.

Because Anabelle's garments are barely covering her body, Papito can see that she is pregnant and suddenly understands that the child has been fathered by Anabelle's own father. Then he remembers the donkey story his own father had used to tell:

> [A]n old man walked home with his donkey and his dog . . . and beat the donkey beginning to trail behind. After this had gone on from some time, the donkey squatted on its hind legs and refused to budge. When the old man raised his cane, the beast of burden opened its jaws to speak.
> "*I am tired and will lay myself down to die. Your beating me has no power to change my mind.*"
> The old man was so taken aback that he . . . ran from the donkey as fast as his legs could carry him. His faithful dog followed closed behind. When they collapsed at the edge of another field, the dog cocked its head toward its master.
> "Imagine that!" it exclaimed. "A donkey speaking!"

. . . As a child Papito had [been] filled with dread at the *possibility that animals might speak.*[82] [Italics is mine]

Besides analyzing the phenomenon of the double, in "The Uncanny," Freud examines the kind of dread evoked "when infantile complexes which have been repressed are once more revived by some impression, or when primitive beliefs which have been surmounted seem once more to be confirmed."[83] In the novel, Pérez herself underlines the "uncanny" nature of both Papito's recurring nightmare about Anabelle and his harrowing encounter with her on the road. We have already discussed how Papito demonizes the Afro-Caribbean cultural practices associated with the land of origin and how Adventism provides a structure justifying this repression. The flashback to Papito's life in the Dominican Republic and his encounter with Anabelle during the storm is one of only two scenes that dramatize the characters' lives in the home of origin. The other important scene, which also thematizes repression, is about Aurelia's last encounter with her spirit-working mother and her refusal to keep the symbolically laden items Bienvenida bequeaths her. If the rejection of Bienvenida and the repression of the Afro-Caribbean religion she practices can be termed a rejection of Dominican identity or "roots," Papito's "uncanny" encounter has the more disturbing element of an allegory of rejection by the origin itself.

Two details in particular lend the encounter with Anabelle allegorical weight: (1) the fact that in this scene, in which Papito is only nineteen years old, he is even then narrated as "Papito" suggests not just that he wishes to supplant Anabelle's father but that the structure of his desire is itself incestuous—that Anabelle is a kind of mother figure to him; in fact, not only do we not ever learn his real name throughout the course of the book, we are not even told what the family's surname is, strengthening the notion that Papito is the archetype of a father, a father always in search of inappropriate mothering from the women in his life, including his daughters. Significantly, at one point when the family is watching a video of a festivity held at their home, Papito mistakenly identifies himself as Rebecca's first husband, Samuel, who had indeed been accused of molesting his eldest daughter; (2) Anabelle is pregnant in this scene and yet "carelessly" wandering in the storm, endangering both her life and that of her unborn child. A mother rejecting or oblivious to, the child she is carrying, Anabelle is metonymically linked to mother nature, and the land itself, also shown to be in rebellious in this scene.

If, in *The Agüero Sisters,* the structure of allegory was made evident in the way the unfolding story of Ignacio's love for, and murder of, Blanca Agüero threw light on the lives of the sisters in present time, in *Geographies of Home* it is significant that so much information about past life in the Dominican Republic is repressed so that when it does surface, exactly three times—in Papito's memory of Anabelle's death, Aurelia's memory of the last time she saw Bienvenida, Rebecca's memory of sneaking out of the house to lie naked in a field and masturbate—it has the power of Othering the origin as a place of magic and sexual danger. And Pérez's representation of the origin also dismisses its potential to help heal the wounds of the present. Aurelia deliberately threw away the family mementos Bienvenida gave her; Anabelle is dead and Papito does not discuss her with his family; Rebecca's innocent sensuality has transformed into a masochistic relationship with her husband Pasión, whose name gives away his metonymic allegorical function as the embodiment of Rebecca's self-destructive desires. The more Pasión beats her, the more his wife lets him debase her and when he dies, done in by the only "trabajito" a rusty Aurelia can muster, Rebecca embraces the dead corpse in a necrophiliac frenzy.

"The ambiguity of the uncanny as both familiar and unfamiliar" characterizes the figure of Anabelle who in this scene displays both the characteristics of a ghostly being, "an apparition," as well as an all too human and suffering "body" different, in its gestational state, from the one about which Papito has fantasized in dreams, in particular the erotic dream in which Anabelle punctured the skin of a mango with her teeth and then offered it to the ecstatic Papito.[84] Although a wild-eyed, pregnant Anabelle might seem the opposite of the sensuous, inviting creature Papito had dreamed about, in this scene Anabelle's near-death status heightens her eroticism. Her "mud-smeared" torn clothing reveals her as a fallen woman (a sullied angel, in fact, "who had lost a wing") and despite his well-meaning attempts to rescue her from the storm, Papito cannot help himself from pawing at her—"He ran a palm along the base of Anabelle's spine where her dress had torn." And: "he patted Anabelle's backside to let her know they had arrived."[85] Nor can Papito help himself from continuing to associate the hurt body he has encountered with "[t]he memory of her flesh glistening in his dreams" and, metonymically, with the juicy mango— the tropical equivalent of Eve's apple—she offers him in the dream.[86] It is in fact this memory that makes him drag her eagerly to the town cathedral that is being used as a shelter from the storm.[87] On certain days Papito "knew it was he who'd killed" Anabelle but if he does kill her it is by returning her to a patriarchal setting—the cathedral—which is what she had been fleeing from in the first instance. In the cathedral the disapproval of the "old priest" and the shocked "silence that overtook the townspeople" is bound to worsen Anabelle's state of shock, not help her.[88]

Papito's encounter with Anabelle is uncanny partly because it both repeats and resolves (in death) his recurring nightmare, partly because Anabelle herself might very well be dead, and partly because it untaps memories—of the donkey story told by his dead father—and desires, for a mother figure, that Papito has repressed.

The donkey that wills itself to die rather than continue to submit to abuse clearly corresponds to the exhausted Anabelle, ridden and abused by her father. The story echoes strongly a work of African American literature, which Loida Maritza Pérez, a black Latina and former protégée of Henry Louis Gates Jr., as well as a recipient of grants for black artists,[89] is most definitely aware of—Their Eyes Were Watching God, by Zora Neale Hurston, whom she cites in the reader's guide at the end of current paperback editions of this novel. In that book the old grandmother tells Janie that "De nigger woman is de mule uh de world."[90] Nanny's point "is that if the Black man is the slave of the white man, the Black woman is the slave of a slave."[91] In the cruel and comical story Papito remembers his father telling, the donkey's status is actually lower than that of the dog who considers itself an ally of the old man and not the donkey. Papito remembers his reaction to the idea "that animals might speak" as terror in the face of a world gone awry. Papito wants to believe in is "a world where man and beast both had their specific roles and where wrongs were redressed and good deeds repaid in kind."[92] If "the impression of uncanniness" harks back "to particular phases in the evolution of the self-regarding feeling, a regression to a time when the ego had not yet marked itself off sharply from the external world and from other people," the story scares Papito not just because it hints at the monstrous collapse of boundaries in nature (speaking animals) but also because it underlines the bestial nature of human beings.[93] After all, the character with the least dignity in the story is the old man; the donkey shows patience, nobility, and intelligence and the dog, albeit clever, is a sycophant. In the story the closer the animal is to human beings, the more debased.

In his later years in the United States, however, Papito, apparently, has not absorbed either the lesson of the donkey story nor of the encounter with Anabelle—because he beats Iliana for contradicting his rules (the strawberry/cinnamon soap episode); for being too sexual (although he is wrong about this, as we have seen); and for being fearless in the face of nature (Papito spanks Iliana when, as a little girl in the Dominican Republic, she runs off to play near a river roiling with rough water). Iliana is just as fearless in the face of nature as is Anabelle who on the day of her death "made no effort to protect herself at all" in the face of the storm.[94] That Anabelle has reached a spiritual place beyond "the body she inhabited like a shell" is incomprehensible to Papito whom she inspires with both desire and fear, as a being halfway between an "apparition" and a woman.[95] Anabelle is doubly inappropriate as a love object for Papito—because she has been raped and because she is a mother, of another by another.

Freud notes "the connections which the 'double' has with reflections in mirrors, with shadows, with guardian spirits, with the belief in the soul and with the fear of death."[96] That the young Papito who thinks he is in love with Anabelle is stuck in a stage of primary narcissism is evident in the fact that, because his father has just died, he lives alone in the shack filled with old furniture including "a woman's dresser with an empty frame where a mirror should have been."[97] Papito is searching for a woman to mother, as well as mirror him. He "yearn[s] for someone . . . whose warm body beside his would remind him that he too was alive."[98] Papito himself has just emerged from a phase where he had mothered his dying father: "had bathed and clothed him . . . had held a baby's bottle to his lips and mashed his food."[99] Interestingly, Papito's yearning for mothering translates into a feminized personality. After Marina tries to commit suicide, and Aurelia and her children are trying to get her inside the car to take her to the hospital, Papito's "sobs [can be heard] from inside the house" from the bed to which he has retreated in defeat.[100]

The fact that rape and incest recur twice in the book itself can be seen as uncanny doubling. In this context, it is significant that what jogs Papito's memory of Anabelle is the uncanny event of Marina's demonic possession in the church followed by her suicide attempt. After most of the family leave for the hospital with Marina, Papito retreats further into the bedroom and in the bed "drew the blankets up under his chin" in an attempt to numb himself into a kind of intrauterine torpor. But instead "memories . . . rushed forth in waves that he was powerless to stop."[101] The "primal throb" of "his daughter's voice . . . had convinced him that she had become a medium for something else," in fact, "Satan's host."[102] Both Marina and Anabelle are associated with the sea, Marina through her name, which means "of the water," Anabelle because it is at the beach that Papito first catches a glimpse of her.[103] Both women are suicidal and both are somehow connected with the devil, Marina, directly so, through demonic possession, Anabelle metonymically through the agency of the hurricane, which is described as a "devil . . . tak[ing] possession of the world . . . sowing seeds of restlessness and instigating violence . . ." terms that recall Marina's purported rape and Anabelle's rape by her father, overdetermining the comparison between the Dominican Republic and a raped woman.[104] There is also a link here between rape and demonic possession, a suggestion that Marina's possessions by her doubles are rooted in originary patriarchal violence. Marina, the daughter of the sea, possessed by demons and doubles, is symbolically the daughter of the pregnant Anabelle, the granddaughter of Papito's mother who also "had willed herself to die" and a whole host of Latina protagonists given over to renunciation.[105] For example, in the Dominican writer's, Angela Hernández's, short story, "How to Gather the Shadows of the Flowers," the young poetess, Faride, is taken to be a madwoman by almost all the members of her family because she spends her days composing and reciting her own strange and lovely poetry. Only her mother believes she is "possessed by a woman from the past."[106] Faride, who is talented but also completely narcissistic, finally finds the "solution" to what she states are her "poetic" problems in her decision to go "to sleep definitively."[107] She sleeps soundly for six months, perhaps an allusion to Persephone's sojourn in the underworld, and then she dies.

Marina and Iliana are doubles. The name "Ana," meaning "graceful," connects both of them to Anabelle and to each other more so than to, say, their sisters Rebecca and Beatriz. Marina's "double" rape of Iliana is, as I have shown, an attempt to divest Iliana of what Marina perceives as powerful phallic qualities. However, as an episode embodying "the return of the repressed"—incest, rape, mothering—all qualities symbolized by Anabelle and, metonymically, the Dominican Republic, the rape is also an insane attempt to both find and return to the source. By reaffirming both the uncanny Otherness of the Dominican Republic as well as Iliana's equality with the Father—"[t]hose hands which had struck her with so much force were no more powerful than her own"—*Geographies of Home* seems to reconfirm American individualism as the safe harbor for Dominicanas and Latinas attempting to reconcile the desire for autonomy with the desire to nourish Latino Caribbean identity.[108]

The last lines of *Geographies of Home* transmit, in ambiguous language, Iliana's ambivalent sense of identity:

> She would leave no memories behind. All of them were herself. All of them were home.[109]

Iliana is choosing to leave the community for good, to go to college, graduate, and be in a "world" that does not seem to include her family because they have been homogenized into rootless "experience[ ]" and "feel[ings]."[110] Before the voice called her back home, Iliana's family held primacy in her life; now they are as meaningful/meaningless as anything else. "All" of her "memories" and experiences comprise "self" and "home" and are thereby equivalent and nonconflictive.[111] However, since we know Iliana has been violently raped just a few days before she comes to this conclusion, it's hard to not read the ending as a suppression of the real meaning of both Marina's action and Marina's status as Iliana's mirror or double—an ambivalent desire to throw off the shackles of patriarchy (especially Latino paternalism) while continuing to wield the symbolic power of patriarchy. Leaving "no memories behind" might mean choosing always to remember everything, all the time, but Iliana in fact seems to have already forgotten everything. The phrase takes on the meaning of erasure. Divested of the voice that haunted her at the beginning of the book, Iliana ends up more ignorant (of her family's past—still not knowing anything about Bienvenida or Anabelle) than ever, but also more powerful because, if anything, the rape and the final confrontation with Papito have taught her she has more worldly power than her proletarian blood relations; she possesses Emersonian self-reliance, American bravado. In this sense the book allegorizes assimilation through repression of Otherness but shows that such a rejection is already part of originary identity, constituting it like a kind of primal myth. Papito fears the boundary-breaking that magic and the stories of talking animals imply. Although Iliana is "fearless" and thus more of a man than her father (in the eyes of Marina and other family members), ultimately she prefers boundaries too as is shown by the final disappearance from the text of the voice that had haunted her in the book's opening pages.

In the originary scene of Anabelle's ghostly progress through the storm, Pérez is careful to show us that it is Papito's fatalistic view that represents Anabelle's ambivalence, as a mother figure determined to die before her child is even born. However, it is also significant that when Papito touches Anabelle's neck in the cathedral, his hand comes away bloodied, thereby implicating him in her death. This is a repetition of the allegorical tale of the Father killing the Mother that we saw in *The Agüero Sisters* and in Ferré's books. The bodies of the mothers in *The Agüero Sisters* and in *Eccentric Neighborhoods* also present symbolically laden wounds. Blanca is bitten on the heel—layering her association with the Afro-Caribbean deity, Oshún, with allusions to both Eve and Achilles—after which she sexually rejects her husband and goes mad. Clarissa's dead body vomits blood, marking her as a sacrificial victim of patriarchy. And, let us not forget that Iliana has been wounded too, by Marina's hand, metonymically linked to the bloodied hand Papito removes from Anabelle's neck. That Iliana has survived such hurt when all her foremothers could not, is the only hope proffered in *Geographies of Home*.

CHAPTER FIVE

LATINO RAGE: THE LIFE AND WORK OF EDWARD RIVERA

Latino rage expresses itself indirectly and goes unrecognized in U.S. culture. It is unlike African American rage, which arose from centuries of subjugation, reached an apex of fury in the Civil Rights Movement of the 1960s, and has been fully absorbed into America's cultural consciousness through art forms such as the blues, jazz, the novel, and the essay. Although Latinos, the largest minority group in the United States, suffer socioeconomic ills similar to those endured by African Americans, America does not view our struggles as equally relevant. Americans avidly consume our music, but do not yet recognize it as an American art form. Even Salsa, born in New York City—as true an American art form as any—is considered Cuban or Puerto Rican, Caribbean or Latin American; of the Americas certainly, but not of the United States. Americans do not acknowledge that our literary efforts represent American culture, while the works of James Baldwin and Toni Morrison have been taken—deservedly so—to the bosom of America and there enshrined.

It may also be that because so many lightskinned Latinos have passed for white—or tricked themselves into thinking that they had—that they believed they weren't angry. I'm not discounting the significant participation of Chicanos and Nuyoricans in the Civil Rights movement. What troubles me is the way that Latinos are so frequently ignored in discussions of the Civil Rights movement, of race, of poverty. We are often treated as if we were barely there, as if we were some kind of modifier of African American identity. We are that ghostly terrain that Americans place between black and white, between American and African American. Latino is that phantom territory.

Our ghostliness, however, has nothing to do with vision. We are not specters. Our ghostliness is aural/oral, an effect of Spanish as the linguistic double of English in the Americas. We are not properly heard, particularly not in our literature, because even when we write in English, Spanish haunts us, whether or not we use those Spanish fragments resounding in our brains.

The fact is that many U.S. Latino/a writers, of fiction as well as music lyrics, try hard to repress their Spanish.[1] In African American literature, on the other hand, black English radicalizes standard English. However distorted, extreme, or violent purists may find black English, they can understand it, because it is English. Spanish is an aural/oral ghost of U.S. history. Spanish place names came before English place names in the founding of the Americas. Latin American land—almost half of Mexico's land mass—was wrested away for the United States to incorporate itself as a nation, and U.S. interventions in Latin America determined the course of most of the Latino diasporas. And Spanish, as the great Other of English in the Americas encroaches upon American English on all sides except the north, a perceived threat to English-language dominance. Even when U.S. Latinos do not speak it properly or at all, Spanish muffles our speaking voices. We are seen, but there is a ghostliness attached to what we say, a doubling effect in language, which pure English speakers would rather not hear. When we are angry, the mainstream cannot properly hear us, because to them our rage is not loud and clear. It is not a roar, but more like a murmur, an echo, a mumbling that makes everyone uneasy, but cannot be clearly addressed because it is not a clear challenge.

It's not just the mainstream, however, that denies Latino rage. We ourselves, Latinos from all stations, middle class, working class, corporate dons, teachers, musicians, seamstresses, field laborers, don't recognize it. The direct expression of anger goes against the normative behavior passed down from our islands or countries of origin—*hospitalidad, dignidad,* courtesy, humility—codes of conduct that encourage us to hide our rage. In this way, Edward Rivera, the New York Puerto Rican writer, is exemplary in both his work and life. Ed published various stories and articles, but he is best remembered for *Family Installments,* the 1982 bildungsroman, which was marketed as an autobiography by his publisher, despite Ed's protestations that it was fiction.[2] The novel tracks the effects of suppressed rage in both its protagonist, Santos, and in his father, Gerán. A poor but hardworking *jíbaro*—a hill peasant from a Puerto Rican mountain town that Ed fictionalizes as Bautabarro—Gerán constantly fails to improve his family's situation on the island and in New York. The father's patient humility, in the face of continuing disappointments, astounds the son. As the boy matures, his incredulity turns into rage, which he can never understand or completely express. The result is a kind of self-deprecatory irony that helps the boy withstand pain and humiliation, as much as it prevents him from fully accepting himself. In his own life, Ed's self-lacerating wit similarly masked suppressed rage. Perhaps the best proof of how crippling that rage was is the simple fact that for all his talent and ambition Ed wrote only one book, a strange text exceptional among U.S. Latino novels for its figurative and linguistic doubling effects. The bilingualism throughout *Family Installments* shows how Ed attempted to heal an incommensurable rift between Spanish and English, not just as languages but as ways of being through the representation of a doubling effect in language. In addition, the madwoman at the beginning of the novel and the bisexual monster at the end of it represent partial expressions of the protagonist's and Ed's rage. As Ed's friend and colleague, as well as a critic of his work, I believe that this repressed rage haunted him and his writing and prevented him from fulfilling his brilliant promise as an author.

Egolessness

On November 26, 2001 family, colleagues, friends, and former students participated in The City College of New York Center for Worker Education's celebration of Ed's life and work. In the early fall Ed had died of a massive heart attack that doctors diagnosed to be the result of his prostate cancer. As the celebration progressed, the majority of Ed's grieving friends spun variations on a theme. Ed was humble, ironic, generous, sardonic, erudite, funny, passionate, self-effacing, a punster. One young woman, Leigh Shulman, Ed's teaching assistant in a City College creative writing class, noted with sad wonder that, contrary to most of his colleagues, "Ed had no ego." Ed's brother, Richie Rivera, about whose status as a judge in Brooklyn Ed had boasted to me, described a heroic, muscular, belligerent young Ed who protected his little brother from El Barrio's meanest hoods and raised rooftop carrier pigeons. I did not recognize that Ed. Ed—in death even more the heroic and stoical barrio tough to his brother Richie—had apparently contemplated writing a novel featuring carrier pigeons. Abraham Rodriguez struck the angriest note that evening, wondering why writers and scholars in the Latino community had forgotten Ed. In my speech I too expressed my sense that Ed's work had been ignored by his peers—U.S. Latino *and* mainstream writers and scholars—although not by his U.S. Latino readership, as the healthy shelf life of *Family Installments* has shown.[3]

Kathy Roe, a novelist-turned-psychoanalyst-in-training and arguably Ed's oldest friend, struck the most poignant note in her uncompromising sincerity about her friend of thirty years. Ed was supremely gifted, she said, but crippled by suffering and neediness. In psychic pain himself, he often could not help hurting his friends by distancing himself from them. In conversation with me, Kathy was more explicit. Ed was emotionally very demanding. If you failed to meet Ed's demands, he could turn on you. And then if you were taken aback by the surprising edges of Ed's anger, he would pull back far and deep, anticipating rejection with rejection. I asked Kathy why Ed had never married. She pointed out that she'd seen him at his happiest and healthiest when he lived with one of his girlfriends for three years. Ultimately, however, the demands of that relationship had overwhelmed him. Time and time again, he ran when confronted by another person's desire for intimacy. Kathy and I talked about Ed, discovering bits and pieces we hadn't known about his life. "He kept so many things secret," Kathy said, adding that he told friends different things, but never gave any one friend all the information, as if deliberately trying to keep everybody off track. For example, a few months before his death, he had told me that he was working on a book of autobiographical essays, but he told Kathy that his project was a novel inspired by the suicide of a childhood friend in El Barrio.

I had not dared to speak about Ed's anger, his caginess, and his suffering, surmising that these topics were too "heavy" for what, after all, was a celebration. But I briefly spoke about his frustrated writing life and the literal nightmare demons he had described to me as both stirring and tormenting his creativity and prolonging his insomnia. I mentioned Ed's need for "dreamtime," days upon days of solitude, reading and writing, or just sitting around doing apparently nothing (as a nonwriter might see it), the proper gestation period for writing articles and books. Teaching tended to rob Ed of his dreamtime—one of the explanations he'd given me for having produced only one book.

The dreamtime, however, had abysses in which Ed's demons flourished. I learned this when I was preparing a lecture on Irene Vilar's memoir *The Ladies' Gallery* (1996). The book follows Vilar's descent into madness and her relationship with her grandmother Lolita Lebrón, the Puerto Rican nationalist icon who took part in the

1954 shoot-up of the U.S. House of Representatives. One of Vilar's hallucinations during her madness involves an encounter with a grotesque, squat, familiar resembling her grandmother. This demon version of Lolita pulls the blue, elongated veins out of a wound in its wrist, thereby frightening and tormenting Vilar.

Ed said that he had been plagued by a demon like Lolita's apparition in Vilar's book. He used the term "succubus" to describe this creature, who would sometimes crouch on his back and bear down, as if trying to suffocate him. In the perfect lucidity of hindsight, I now wish I'd dared to ask Ed about the sexual implications in the term. Afterward, I also became aware of a medical condition called sleep paralysis, which often produces hallucinations and visitations of the type described by Ed.

Later, pondering my American Heritage dictionary's definition of the succubus as "a female demon supposed to descend upon and have sexual intercourse with a man while he sleeps," I wished I had asked Ed more questions about the creature that he described. *Succubare* is Latin for lying under, but Ed emphasized that his night visitor crushed him from above. However, according to the dictionary it is the incubus—the male demon deemed responsible for fathering many babies during the Middle Ages—who descends upon his victim. Yet the dictionary also allows that the incubus can be, in more general usage, "something oppressively or nightmarishly burdensome." Ed, like most writers, was precise in his use of words, so when he said the word "succubus" he must have meant a female demon. My consternation at failing to completely understand his reference would have amused Ed. I can just hear him, chuckling ruefully over my ruminations. "Ah, come on, Lyn. Don't read too much into it." This was a frequent admonition, his way of deflecting analyses that hit too close to home.

Evasive as he could be, Ed was also enormously generous, one of those rare friends who reads a book that you are reading because you need to discuss it with someone. He would do this despite the fact that his course load at City College and the Center for Worker Education had him "reading up the wazoo." He was as eager a reader of my fiction—which he loved—as he was of my academic prose, which he candidly hated ("Too much *jargon*, Lyn!"). Because he was so honest about the second judgment, I could trust him about the first. He was my first and, for a long time, my closest friend in the City College English Department, where I was his colleague in U.S. Latino and Caribbean literatures and Creative Writing. I was immediately drawn to Ed's erudition, his humor, often focused on the linguistics of Spanglish, and, of course, his passionate, omnivorous devotion to literature. We were both fascinated by the fact that he was born in Puerto Rico and had grown up in New York, while I was born in Brooklyn and had grown up in San Juan. Perhaps in each other we saw our own reflections—age and gender distorted—as if in a fun house mirror. I encountered, too, as others did, his mask of apparent humility.

He was so different in the flesh from what I had expected. I read *Family Installments* for the first time in 1996. I was a Five Colleges Fellow at Amherst College in Massachusetts, teaching a class in Puerto Rican Literature (from New York and the Island). I invited Ed to visit Amherst—his expenses would have been paid on top of a sizable honorarium. Ed never got the letter. (One of the many hazards of teaching at City College, we later joked about, was "the dead letter" situation and the many Bartleby the Scrivener types who "preferred not to" deliver messages or sort mail.) Ed didn't attend the interviews and presentation I gave at City College as part of the job application process. I assumed at the time that this Ed Rivera must have been very busy and perhaps more than a bit standoffish.

The developing personality of the young Santos in *Family Installments*—whom I identified as Ed—takes up so much psychic space in the book that I assumed Ed would have a narcissistic, solipsistic personality, like so many writers I have met, particularly male writers. How wrong I was. Ed's personality was so different from his Latino—and non-Latino—writing peers, young and old. He had a humble demeanor, as many have noted. And he seemed physically frail, in spite of his life-long training with weights, a fact I learned, after his death. It was only after his death, too, that I saw pictures of a younger Ed, brimming with vitality, sporting a mop of gloriously springy dark hair and black rimmed owlish glasses that made him look like Hector Lavoe, the famous Salsa singer, another talented and self-destructive *boricua*.

When I knew him, Ed looked pale and ashy-skinned, like the ghost of the joyous young maverick of the photos that I selected for a special section on Ed's work in the *Centro Journal* in 2002. In two of those photos, Ed looks like a self-conscious rebel, his left hip jutting out rebelliously at an angle, the corners of his mouth upturned in what might be the start of an expressive sneer, cigarette idling in the left hand, the left hand jumpy, just waiting for the photographer to finish taking the picture to scoot the cigarette back to where it belongs. So much hip, hair, and smoke: the self-confident bravado of a young writer. The Ed I knew was gentle to the point of passivity. For example, he never said anything during faculty meetings (I didn't either, though, for the most part). We both felt like outsiders, much more so than our African American cohorts, only one out of the four of whom was as silent in meetings as the two of us.

I frequently observed that Ed literally looked *down* during the meetings, sometimes because he was jotting down notes in preparation for teaching an afternoon class. But he never looked up during the meetings, a sign to me, the aspiring younger colleague, that he was obviously not looked up to. This pained me. From a certain perspective the looking down and the silence were signs of humility. But from another perspective, they seemed more like signs of weakness. I felt strongly that his weakness reflected my own, an inability to stand up to power. The mask of humility contrasted strikingly with the aggressive masks that many writers and scholars of City College's English department wore. Leigh Shulman, as a graduate student in the City College master's degree program, was well acquainted with most of the writing faculty. She told me that Ed was the only example of a type she wished she could have encountered more often in her creative-writing classes and workshops—a gentle, erudite teacher who seemed to collapse his own ego in order to nurture those of his students and advisees. But soon after I met Ed it seemed clear to me that the so-called humility was a cover for a side of him that Leigh never saw: the angry, frustrated Ed. Leigh never saw Ed as Lucifer, only the angel before the fall into paranoia and Latino rage.

The first time I encountered this quality in Ed was toward the end of 1998, when I neglected to call him back during a busy week in the school term. I was often reluctant to return Ed's calls immediately because whenever we spoke it was hard to get off the phone with him. If I tried to be polite, hinting that I had something to do,

Ed would nonetheless keep the conversation going. Our conversations were always interesting—about books we liked, writers we knew, about Puerto Rico, about Puerto Ricans in New York, about our favorite writers (his was García Márquez, "the master"). We also talked about Latin music; he loved the "old stuff," like Rafael Hernández's compositions and Los Panchos. I introduced him to slightly newer oldies like Silvio Rodríguez and Caetano Veloso.

Ed left a message on my home voicemail in the middle of the week, but I let a couple of days pass before answering it. At week's end, he left an irate message on my voicemail demanding an explanation about why I had not returned his call. I called back immediately. I tried to set the tone with him through a joke. "Ed, I didn't know you had such a bad temper." And then, somewhat reluctantly but with humor lightening his tone of voice, he told me he supposed he did have a bad temper. Later, I realized that Ed's anger was really disappointment at the level of intimacy in our relationship. We didn't speak for a very long time after that, a whole semester, and when we spoke again, it was I who called him. Thereafter, for the most part, I would have to call him. The phone chats continued, of course, to be very intense and long and, as before, it was hard for me to end the conversations.

The Saintly *Jíbaro* and the Madwoman in the Bohío

The first chapter of *Family Installments*, "Antecedentes," is in many ways one of the finest in the book, for its deft expository characterization of both sets of the protagonist's Puerto Rican grandparents, its vivid, almost naturalistic, portrayal of the Puerto Rican countryside during the 1920s and 1930s, and, most of all, its textured examination of the effects of machismo on Puerto Rican womanhood. The narrator Santos records his outright protest against the "all-fours life" that his maternal grandfather, the arch-patriarch, Papá Gigante, forced on his humble and submissive wife Socorro and planned for his daughters.[4] More interesting than the protest itself, however, is the narrator's tone through which irony tempers anger without letting go of empathy.[5] Santos deals with his own anger at Papá Gigante's abuses by identifying with "the saint" and "footstool," his grandmother Socorro.[6] As well as criticizing her for having been too humble, and for letting her husband debase her, Santos takes on the dead grandmother's point of view, as if it were a kind of mask, but judges her reality with his own eyes. This sensitive, complex approach also allowed Ed to create one of the most interesting, although short-lived, female characters in U.S. Latino a fiction. Although she takes up barely five pages of the novel's first chapter, Josefa the great-grandmother completely flouts the saintliness and *humildad* touted by her town—and her husband—as the supreme human virtues:

> His wife, Josefa, added much misery to Papá Santos' hard-luck life. She was a loca, and he had to look after her all the time. One time she tried to burn the house down. Another time she tried to kill Santos with his own machete. She put shit in the food, and sometimes, on a crazy whim, she would shit on the floor instead of using the chamber pot or making a trip to the outhouse.[7]

The novel's protagonist is named after his great-grandfather, Santos, proving just how important that character's story is to the novel, however brief it may be.

The great-grandfather adopts his grandson Gerán after the latter's father commits suicide. To be kind and humble to the point of "saintliness" is extolled by the Puerto Rican community, so much so that the characteristic is memorialized in the protagonist's name. On the other hand, the relationship between Josefa and Papá Santos demonstrates how big a strain it is to keep up the façade of *santidad* and *humildad*. In Gilbert and Gubar's classic study, *The Madwoman in the Attic* (1979), the madwoman expresses the suppressed rage of nineteenth-century British women writers who had to hide their rebelliousness if they wanted to keep their readers. The madwoman in Ed's novel performs a similar function, expressing a rage that highlights even more vividly Papá Santos's abnegation.

Papá Santos might or might not be angry at many things—at a society that watches with indifference while his family starves; at his neighbors, who won't willingly share their chickens; even at his grandsons, who can't earn men's wages but need to eat as much as wage-earning men. If he's not mad about this lousy situation, Josefa sure is. Josefa's seemingly insane actions reveal what is insufficient for the family's needs: the house (she tries to burn it down) and the food (she makes a succulent *sancocho* for the grandsons using her own piss as broth). Josefa also targets the principal cause of all her stress, the patriarchy as represented by Papá Santos (whom she tries to murder using his own machete) and his favorite grandson Gerán (whom she also tries to kill).

Josefa's craziness parodies the logic of self-abnegation in Latino communities where self-sacrifice and devotion to male children overlap. The madwoman takes the self-sacrifice of a Papá Santos to a brutal extreme. By attempting to feed her grandchildren with her own bodily emissions, Josefa shows that self-sacrifice is nothing less than the annihilation of the self for the sake of the family. At a certain point in her madness, Josefa takes to repeatedly shitting on the floor planks of the *bohío* so that the three young boys are forced to clean up after her. It is as if she is competing with the boys—losing control of her bodily functions infantilizes her and ironically forces an adult role upon them even though they are the ones who need to be cared for.

After I read Robert McCormick's dissertation on *ataques de nervios*, or the so-called Puerto Rican syndrome, Ed and I had conversations about whether or not Josefa might have been afflicted with this condition. Ed was intrigued by the idea, but had never heard of Puerto Rican syndrome, which derives its name from a coinage made by U.S. army surgeons during the Korean War. Puerto Rican soldiers exhibited strange symptoms such as partial loss of consciousness, convulsive movements, hyperventilation, moaning and groaning of varying intensity, aggressiveness to the self or to others in the form of biting, scratching, and striking, and a full range of psychotic behavior including coprophagy or shit-eating. Although the term might be a misnomer for mental illnesses ranging from schizophrenia to dissociative reactions, McCormick notes that "a certain collection of symptoms has had enough cultural specificity to lead observers to designate a unique 'Puerto Rican syndrome.'"[8]

The syndrome includes violence, which might be the result of the difficulty Puerto Ricans have in dealing with aggressive feelings—"when Puerto Ricans talk about feelings of 'nervousness' they describe situations in which they clearly feel angry."[9] Puerto Rican syndrome seems typical of stressors associated with living in the United States. Nonetheless, Ed said that his mother had told him that there were many cases like Josefa's (involving men as well as women) in their hometown of Orocovis in the 1920s, when people in the Puerto Rican countryside were literally dying of hunger, or from epidemic diseases such as tuberculosis and malaria. Although the culture change, "from a Spanish tradition where outward assertiveness and aggressiveness is discouraged, to American society where it is valued and encouraged," seems to be the principal cause of the syndrome, what Ed intuitively shows in the relationship between Josefa and Papá Santos in *Family Installments* is that the "Spanish tradition" was always already being contested by women, the poor, children, and everybody else except the Papás Gigantes of Puerto Rico.[10]

Nervioso (Nervous)

If there was a Josefa, or a succubus, pressing down on Ed's psyche, it is only because that angry part of him had to contend with the insidious sanctimony of his inner Papá Santos. The gentle, long-suffering *jíbaro* male is the model for both Gerán, the protagonist's father in the novel, and Segundo, the hero of a long short-story Ed published in *The Nation*, "The Story of Segundo and Magda." (Later, he expanded it for inclusion in the anthology *While Someone Else is Eating* (1984) as "Segundo's Benefits.") *The Nation* story was part of a series that the magazine commissioned well-known fiction writers to write about social issues. In the story a stroke incapacitates Segundo, a head shipping clerk at a dress company. Subsequently, government bureaucrats constantly deny his claims for disability benefits. In fact, this is what happened to Ed's father in real life and to Gerán in *Family Installments*. Ed frequently noted in classroom presentations, as well as in conversation, that the American public was more interested in stereotypes of Latinos (the drug dealing male, the female sex pot) than in the less picturesque reality of hard working, lower-middle- and middle-class Latinos. The story is a relentlessly bleak depiction of what it is like to meander helplessly through the civil service labyrinth of the Bronx. The irony of Segundo's situation is driven home by the story's refrain of "Segundo sympathized" whenever Segundo plays sycophant to his bosses. These men lavish Segundo with praise for being their best shipping clerk but demonstrate their appreciation through miserly five- and ten-dollar raises. In the end, Ed's meek, hardworking protagonists complement, as well as contrast with, Piri Thomas's defiant persona in *Down These Mean Streets* (1967). Double racism (in American society and in Piri's self-hating black Latino father) lends Piri's anger the resonance of African American rage. Ed's frustrated (and lightskinned) Latino anti-heroes have no such recourse. If Gerán's dogged humility infuriates the young Santos in *Family Installments*, Segundo's saintly patience ultimately irritates the reader of "Segundo's Benefits."

The last time Segundo calls to ask about the progress of his stalled case, he is told for the gazillionth time that his case is pending. "This time he almost lost his temper," the narrator tells us, "but he got hold of himself. Giving some anonymous official a piece of his mind would . . . only shoot up his blood pressure . . . So he hung up politely and distracted himself with his dominoes."[11] The anger in the narrator's tone is unmistakable, but Segundo himself remains an exasperating character, because there is no hint of fury or protest in his posture of endurance.

In "Digging In," a chapter toward the end of *Family Installments* describing Gerán's loneliness in New York before his wife and sons arrive, Santos for the first time notices Gerán's tendency to repress anger. Gerán recounts that many years ago when his family was still in Bautabarro (Ed's made-up mountain town on the island) a woman sends a telegram to him masquerading as Lilia, Gerán's wife. Upon arrival, this woman wins Gerán's sympathy with a story of hardship and lives off him for a while in order to survive. One day she disappears without a word. The young Santos is outraged when he hears this story and repeatedly asks his father why he failed to react with anger to this woman's opportunism. Gerán represses his anger because to admit to it would be to acknowledge that he has been wronged by Lilia Pompilia, whose manipulative grandiosity is implied by her grandiloquent Latinate name. Anger leads to shame, which Gerán covers with the cliché, "It happens all the time."[12] What the father hides from himself becomes a heavier burden for the son who is constantly confronting rage and shame in scene after bittersweet scene in the novel.

In chapter three, "Chuito and La Manca," Santos, barely out of long pants, is initiated sexually by his older cousin Chuito, who forces the kindergartner to have sex with a cow—La Manca. The cow responds to the boy's amorousness by shitting on him. Although little Santos is shamed to tears, Chuito laughs off the incident and Santos is relatively unscathed emotionally. If one compares this scene, however, with similar childhood initiation scenes involving bestiality (in the Cuban writer Reinaldo Arenas's *Before Night Falls* (1993), and in the Colombian American Jaime Manrique's *Latin Moon in Manhattan* (1992)) the complete absence of eroticism in the La Manca episode is striking. When Santos is older, he experiences an even greater humiliation. In chapter four, "First Communion," nervousness and anxiety make Santos pee in public as he is receiving communion. As if this is not enough humiliation, the Host breaks in half on Santos's nose.[13] This scene, hilarious and painful in equal measure, is Santos's induction, not into the mysteries of the transubstantiation of Christ, but into the rites of Latino self-repression. The brief exchange between Gerán and his.son about the incident at the end of the chapter is illuminating:

> "You was nervous, Santos," Papi said . . . "Next time," he added in Spanish, "no more accidents, okay?"
> "Okay, Papi." But didn't he know it wasn't up to me?[14]

I cannot help but repeat here the assertion in McCormick's dissertation that "When Puerto Ricans talk about feelings of 'nervousness' they describe situations in which they clearly feel angry." And, of course, if we interpret the nervousness that makes Santos piss his pants as anger it becomes clear that pissing in this scene—and shitting in the La Manca scene—are traces of the rage expressed by the constantly shitting and pissing Josefa of the novel's opening. The rage— repressed and rationalized as "nervousness"—is a response to Santos's growing realization of his lack of power, a lack expressed plaintively in the boy's lament "But didn't he know it wasn't up to me?" and in his failure to control his bodily functions.

In chapter seven, "In Black Turf," Santos is pushed around by a group of black boys whose terrain he has unwittingly invaded in Central Park. His powerlessness awakens ambivalent rage in him. The loss of control is again symbolized scatologi-cally, this time in Santos's literal immersion in a pile of shit into which he stumbles after he is pushed by one of the black boys:

> I stumbled, scraped my back on the wall and collapsed with a squeal on something soft. A swarm of flies . . . exploded around me, and in seconds I was immersed in the odor of human shit. I sat there, too overcome with disgust and rage to move . . . I began to cry . . . sucking in the thin, fibrous liquid that spilled like egg white from my nostrils. A slow accumulation of pain . . . began to tighten around my forehead.[15]

These episodes highlight helplessness, humiliation, "rage," and the "slow accumula-tion of pain." The young boy's body seems to break itself down into excreta—snot, piss, and shit—a disintegration that is the physical analogue to the more serious emotional and spiritual breakdown at the heart of *Family Installments*. Bred to be stoical and patient, Santos—Ed's stand-in—is rent deeply on the inside but does not allow himself or his father Gerán the luxury of compassion he feels for Socorro and Papá Santos. Instead he becomes alienated from both his family—his father espe-cially whose failure he fears repeating—and from the English-speaking world that he hopes to conquer through mastery of English literature.

One of the causes of Santos's feeling of alienation is racial confusion. Near the opening of chapter seven, Santos describes his fantasy of saving a "Puerto Rican dusky" or a white woman from rape by a "muscular black."[16] That the chapter ends with the black boys pushing Santos into a pile of human shit is a brilliant reversal, pointing both to Santos's masochistic identification with the white woman in his daydream and his keen, albeit unconscious, understanding of U.S. Latino/a racial identity as "dusky," that is racially situated midway—and resulting from the union— between white women and black men. Santos enters the park with a black Puerto Rican boy Panna who is his close friend. Significantly, Santos affirms that Panna is "more" Puerto Rican than Santos because he doesn't "deny his origins" by getting rid of his East Harlem accent.[17] Paulo Freire discusses the processes by which the oppressed struggle to "extroject" the slave consciousness that oppressors have caused them to "introject" in the deepest enclosures of their being.[18] Santos undergoes a similar process here regarding the blackness of his New York Puerto Rican identity. He is trying to "extroject" his negative feelings about blackness through his friend-ship with Panna (whose name, really a nickname, refers to the Puerto Rican collo-quialism for "buddy"). Santos's collapse into the pile of shit is in a sense a punishment that he feels he deserves. Barred forcibly from entry into the black section of the park by the black boys who represent both his unconscious and his punishing superego, he ends up blackened in another way by falling into the pile of shit. He feels refused by, and refuses, wholehearted identification with the blackness that he has introjected in his consciousness as "shit." However falling into the pile of shit, and the feelings of pain and humiliation that accompany this accident, usher in an unforgettable full disclosure of the blackness of New York Puerto Rican identity. The pile of shit registers both Santos's denial of the blackness of New York Puerto Rican identity, as well as a slowly emerging awareness of his "immers[ion]" in it, an illumination Santos resists and is haunted by. The moments of bodily breakdown trace this character's vertiginous interior moments of self-discovery and self-hatred.

Santos/Ed is not merely in denial, he fervently wants to understand the nature of his pain and alienation. He has a depth, an interiority, that many other U.S. Latino/a literary protagonists lack. Where better-known U.S. Latino/a coming-of-age stories—*When I Was Puerto Rican* springs to mind—are intent on tracing the journey from, say, poverty to either success in the mainstream world or heroic stature on the street, *Family Installments* confronts, and explodes, the idea of a self-possessed U.S. Latino/a hero or heroine, of New York Puerto Rican or U.S. Latino/a identities as anything but fractured, shifting, and dynamically incomplete.

The Doubling Effect in Language

The hallucinatory quality of *Family Installments*—contrasting so strikingly with the recognizable, plain frame of the U.S. Latino/a family story cum bildungsroman—is due not just to Santos's inner fragmentation as expressed by characters like Josefa or in moments like Santos's immersion in the pile of shit. It is also due to a doubling effect in language, the trace that Spanish leaves on English, as if Spanish were haunting English. Santos is acutely aware of English's ghostly presence. Because Santos fetishizes language he repeats words in both Spanish and English, holds onto them, plays with them and distorts them in ways that can frustrate readers who thought they were getting a simpler story about the vicissitudes of growing up in Spanish Harlem. This explains why both mainstream and U.S. Latino/a critics have not been much interested in the book, and it also explains why it is such an important book. *Family Installments* is an uncanny, plotless work that reveals how language forms subjectivity and how subjectivity can, in the case of both Santos and Ed Rivera, resist language. In chapter six, "Caesar and the Bruteses: A Tradegy," a half-literate Irish "Brother" attempts to teach *Julius Caesar* to Santos and his other Catholic school classmates. The students misread Shakespeare, with a little help from the echoes of Spanish and street English in their heads. Their teacher, "Bro' O'Leary," who mispronounces "tragedy" in the first place, only helps to accentuate the boys' tendency to mispronounce or hispanicize Shakespearean English. What Homhi Bhabha would call mimicry in the excerpts from Julius Ceasar, as Santos and his Puerto Rican classmate Virgilio misread them, I prefer to ascribe to the doubling effect of Spanish upon the boys:

> Caesar doth bear me hard-on . . .
> Now, good Metellus . . .
> He doth bestride the world like a *culoso* . . .
> My heart is in the coughing there with Caesar . . .
> . . .Then in my tent, Cassius, *enlarge* your griefs,[19]

Santos and his friend Virgilio sexualize and mock the archaic language of the play, as in Santos's misreading of "hard-on" and the mistranslation of coffin as "coughing." Also very much in the grain of mimicry is how the boys imitate the high-flown language even though they do not completely understand it, so that Santos, in the final instance, whimsically threatens to "enlarge [Virgilio's] griefs." He enjoys the relative authority the language gives him even though he is intimidated by it.

The boys are ambivalent about Shakespeare, as are many other eighth graders, white and black, male and female, from working-class or middle-class backgrounds. But because Santos and Virgilio also carry Spanish with them, its Latinate structure gives an added layer of complexity to the mimicry. For example, Santos's substitution of "culoso" for colossus in the phrase "He doth bestride the world like a culoso" is a usage that would strike an English-only speaker as the result of Santos's 'ignorance,' a misspelling, a mishearing, in short a deformation and phonetic rendition of the English word. But Santos's made-up word also plays cleverly with the Spanish word "culo" for ass or backside, thereby strangely and effectively allowing the boys to actually LEARN the meaning of colossus in the picture they have just painted for themselves of a big-assed, powermongering giant. Another example is the way the Roman name Metellus seems to grab Santos's attention as a homonym for the Spanish/Puerto Rican colloquialism "mételo" (as in the imperative phrasing "put it in," which can also be read sexually as "stick it in"). Of course the boys are charmed by these strange correspondences between Spanish colloquialisms and Shakespearan language but, again, in this instance and sexualizations aside, Metellus could also stand out for them as a busybody, as in associations with the phrase in Spanish, "no te metas" (roughly translated as "don't stick your nose in it").

Spanish language haunts English in a way that other minority languages cannot. In effect, there is a mimetic rivalry between the two languages that goes back to the Age of Conquest and to the creation of the Black legend, whereby the English maligned the Spanish, as one tactic among many to undermine Spanish power. This ancient rivalry between England and Spain carried over to the relationship between the Spanish- and English-speaking Americas. Then of course there is the influence of more recent history, the U.S.–Mexican War (1846–1848), and the Spanish American War (1898), as well as the interventions in Latin America and the Caribbean since then. Third, there is the similarity between the two languages, a similarity not characterisitic of other major U.S. minority languages—Chinese, for example. Spanish and English have a large number of Latinate cognates. For example, when Virgilio tells Santos not to take the Lord's name in "vainity" he is tripping up not just on English "vanity" and "in vain" but on his awareness of Spanish "en vano" (in vain) and "vanidad" (vanity).[20] Whereas W.E.B. Dubois's idea of double-consciousness emphasized that the gaze of white America split the psyche of African Americans, causing blacks to see themselves through white and black eyes, Spanish causes a hallucinatory doubling effect in language.[21] The boys are hearing Spanish, listening to it, confused and entranced by its dissimilar similarity to English.

Spanish language has a ghostly effect on English for those who can hear it. And these echoes are growing stronger and stronger as the Latino presence in the United States increases. The burgeoning of the Latino population in the United States is Latin America's revenge on the U.S. imperialist colossus (or *culoso*, as Santos would have it). Because the Latino presence is growing so quickly the ghostly effect of Spanish language is unsettling English speakers as well as many U.S. Latinos who no longer speak Spanish, having lost or repressed it for the sake of assimilation.

The overly sensitive Santos is particularly prone to hearing the strange effects of Spanish language and it is one of the reasons why, despite his effusive protestations, he is drawn to the baroque language of Shakespeare; in spite of himself so to speak.

Although Santos tells us that the boys interpret *Julius Caesar* as a play about "fags," he is not consious of the erotically charged undertone in his aggression toward his friend Virgilio, an energy that both boys project onto the play and in which they revel, as can be seen in in their very Shakespearan coinages such as "pricklickers" and "toilsuckers."[22] Santos's reinscription of himself and Virgilio as "plebeians" also underscores Santos's tacit understanding that had the boys actually lived in the time of Julius Caesar they would not have been principals in the world of the play.[23] Of course it is Santos the adult—Fanon's native looking back, remembering what he was—who whimsically describes the boys as "plebeians." The playful tone here turns gloomy and involuted when Santos reaches adulthood at book's end. As a young adult, Santos is not just self-deprecating about his class status, he seethes with an anger that shames him, and that he turns back on himself, instead of fully expressing.

Unlike Piri in *Down These Mean Streets*, however, the adult Santos is not angry about the clearly visible injustices of racism and poverty. Santos both enjoys and struggles through his college education, battling with an amorphous and tormenting situation that he himself cannot completely decipher. He comes close to identifying it toward the end of the narrative in his astonishment at how education has driven a rift between him and his familly. And by association he holds himself apart from the working-class Puerto Rican community that is indifferent to his obsession with read-ing, whether the books belong to the Western canon, the Latin American tradition, or to the island canon of Puerto Rico. He is equally dismayed that although he loves literature and has immersed himself in it, he feels somehow excluded by the high literary tradition of the Western canon. Never explcitly stated in the book, the level of anxiety that surrounds Santos's study of texts such as *Julius Caesar* and, later, *Beowulf*, reveals this fear.

Santos and the author aspire to a rich, palimpsestic representation of Santos's evolving persona, incorporating the characteristics from the island past, from the American present, from the English literature that Santos comes to venerate, and from the Spanish language too: "my shrinking Spanish, which Saint Misery's was helping me lose fast for good."[24] This disappearing Spanish leaves traces that are all the more evocative because they have to support so much more meaning. As it evanesces, Spanish paradoxically leaves a charged trace that outweighs its absence— a ghostly effect. The title of chapter eleven, "Málanguez and Son" hints at the rich-ness of the syncretic linguistic construction of *Family Installments*. The title riffs on the title of a Dickens novel, *Dombey and Son*, about a cold, cruel father's neglect of his daughter in favor of his morally fragile son. And at the end of *Family Installments*, Santos reads novel after novel by Dickens at the bedside of the ailing Gerán. The Dickens title is yet another sign of Santos's emotional withdrawl from his father. As I mentioned in my discussion of Papá Santos and Josefa, Santos's name alludeds to his great-grandfather's name, and in an ironic way to the great-grandfather's purported saintliness. There are other resonances here as well. For example, a "malanga," a tuber root native to Puerto Rico, is also used as a colloquialism for the penis. As Alfredo Villanueva-Collado notes,

> The very name of the protagonist already points to a pattern of corrosive irony, allud-
> ing to a kind of stereotypical Puertorrican phallic power (santa malanga), which the

reality of migration and the condition of exile so thoroughly described in the novel negate almost absolutely. At the same time, it points to the origins rooted in the soil; migration is, among so many other things, an up/rooting.[25]

The archetypal "phallic" father, rooted on the island and confident in his sexuality in *Family Installments* is none other than the Papá Gigante mentioned earlier; the maternal grandfather, whose very name connotes giantism of physical size as well as virility. This plenitude at the origin is not completely "negate[d]" by the new Latino reality in New York. Rather, it is rendered shadowy and ghostly by the words of Santos Malánguez's name, which some Latinos may be able to decipher and others will only wonder at, and which non-Spanish speakers by and large will find opaque. And Santos himself, as we have seen, is haunted not just by the specter of Puerto Rican masculinity but by the gendered phantoms already generated on the island by patriarchalism: in particular the mad Josefa who also haunts this most ghostly of U.S. Latino texts.

Although Santos's only chance for achieving w/holeness is the successful literary expression of all the lacks he suffers, he sets himself up for failure because deep down he accepts the notion of fixity, of an unmoveable hierarchical "disparity" between the double poles of his particular situation (as solitary reader and as working-class Latino stiff).[26] His frustration reaches a mounting point toward the end of the book. After a night of studying for final exams, Santos takes one of his "disparity" walks in his neighborhood. He is stopped by a patrol car, and frisked by a policeman who believes that the stubbed out pencil in the back pocket of Santos's pants is a potential weapon.

Santos responds in a comically ambiguous yet revealing way to the policeman's demand about what Santos is "doing with a goddamn pencil on the avenue that time of night": "'I think I put it in my pocket without thinking . . . Maybe I was going to the lavatory.' The lavatory? I must have been trying to impress the man."[27] This pencil, which doubles as a weapon (and carries phallic overtones), is Santos's instrument for gaining access to higher education, to class status, and, most urgently, to a fuller intimacy with the idealized world of literature. Although the cop mistakes it for a weapon, the pencil's "point had snapped off," and as such it is impotent.[28] Santos tries to show the policeman that his introspective midnight perambulation is an occasion for reverie, not prowling and thievery. His errant use of the word "lavatory" is a typical manuever, for Santos's obsession with language tends toward constant slippage, a real uncertainty about which word would be best in a situation, since both words and situations are so nuanced. But, like the broken pencil, which certainly cannot match the policeman's club or gun, Santos's language cannot often meet real-life situations in a direct or practical way. On the one hand Santos himself realizes that he used the word "lavatory" in order to "impress" the cops with its elevated register, to show them that he is not a street Spic but an educated, orderly Latino. On the other hand, Santos's stated intention of going to the lavatory is a lapse in logic that reveals a deeper reality. It communicates both the idea of the (broken) pencil as (defective) penis as well as the fact that Santos believes his efforts are in vain—all his studying is for naught, his literary efforts will end up in the toilet. Instead of attempting to master this legitimate fear of failure, however, Santos gives into it in a way prefigured by his use of the word "lavatory" as well as by his response to the policeman's threat to smack him in the face with the holster of his gun. To this Santos answers " 'Go ahead officer. I don't give a damn,'" acknowledging in the same paragraph that this was a "suicidal" gesture.[29] Still operating in this self-destructive mode, as soon as he gets back to the apartment overlooking an alley, which he shares with his parents, Santos throws away the poetry anthology: "That disparity between the life in the alley and the poetry in my anthology was over my head. So I simplified it by telling myself one had to take sides."[30] His renunciatory action occurs amidst the din of the alley: cats yowling, dogs barking, people cursing and shouting, the blaring of TVs and stereos. Santos sets up a fallacious binary between the aestheticized world represented by the poetry anthology and the working-class life characterized by the noise of the alley, the "screaming . . . crying and cursing" of people.[31] The sounds of animals contrasts strikingly for him with the serenity of reading poetry from the anthology. The howling of street cats allows Santos to associate the noise of "life in the alley" with the hallucinatory world of witches and the devil. The life in the alley is hellish. The poetry anthology is a palliative to this hellish existence, for it allows Santos to be quiet, to hold himself apart, to reflect and feel, to take refuge in literature. However, Santos essentializes both literature and the working class, a common reaction among U.S. Latinos. Because he believes he must be either of the working class or a scholar and writer, he is unable to embrace, or release himself from, either identity.

In Hiding

The figure that best expresses Santos's ambivalence about his relationship to English literature is the strange bisexual monster, a combinaton of Grendel from the old Anglo-Saxon narrative poem *Beowulf* and Grendel's mother, who attacks Santos at the end of the book, lying on top of him and smothering him in late night encounters that recall for me Ed's description of his own familiar, the "succubus." However, whether the phenomena of sleep paralysis, Puerto Rican syndrome, or something Other, could explain Ed's night time visitations, the Grendel monster of *Family Installments* has to be read with awareness of the toll that repression has taken on the Malánguez family in the novel up to this point. Josefa, Papá Santos's double, and the out of control shitting and pissing in the book, are foreshadowings of the Grendel/mother monster. Just as Josefa represented an anger that Papá Santos did not want to face or express, this apparition confronts Santos as a closeted aspect of himself seeking acknowledgment: "The monster, whose face I couldn't make out in the dark, would slam the door open and stand at the entrance, staring at me."[32] Santos can't "make out" the features of the creature's face, as if he cannot see himself. Although his terror paralyzes him, his "eyes move[]" as if they are the only part of him that recognizes—and answers—the creature's hypnotic and denuding gaze.[33] These visitations, which Santos also describes as attempted rapes, recall the dream in *Geographies of Home* where the mad Marina is raped by a black man who represents the blackness she denies in herself.[34] Thus, we may read the monster, on one level, like the pile of shit Santos falls into in chapter seven, as a representation of blackness.

The monster as a "dark" being points to the racial aspect of Puerto Rican identity that so many lightskinned Puerto Ricans like Santos disavow or misread.

But blackness is not the only meaning here. The "solitary" monster of the Anglo-Saxon poem also strangely reflects the outcast position that Santos both fears and desires as an intellectual and a writer. For example, Santos hurts his parents' feelings by putting a latch on his door for privacy.[35] After each Grendel nightmare, the door he locked at night is always wide open in the morning. Like Santos, *Beowulf*'s Grendel is a peripatetic and "fearful solitary" who offends the Danes by rejecting the communal order.[36] In particular, Grendel outrages the feudal society because he refuses to pay the "weregild," the monetary reparation for slaying other men. Grendel in other words is a very early precursor of a rebellious modern individualism, and this Santos unconsciously understands. So the Grendel aspect of the monster represents the side of Santos that wants to leave behind the family, and the working-class community, to indulge in the creative "privacy" promised by the indulgence in books and other solitary pleasures. The closed door that displeases Santos's family, however, also offends the aspect of the monster that is Grendel's mother.

For Santos's monster is a "mixed up" creature that is female and male, mother and son: "I merged them into one monster: Grendel with huge breasts, enormous steel claws, and stringy, hair."[37] In this context Grendel's mother is like Josefa whom Papá Santos and the patriarchy has repressed, a maternal figure, who stands in for the family that Santos has desperately been trying to lock out of his room. The monstrous maternal aspect, Grendel's mother, is also an embodiment of Santos's guilt over his desire for privacy.

Villanueva-Collado emphasizes another meaning as well: "I have always thought it entirely justifiable for Santos, a Puertorrican with severe (and probably unrevealed) identity problems, to have been attacked in his dreams by an androgynous monster fromt the beginnings of Anglo-Saxon literature. Quite a precise image for the colonial condition."[38] The figure of Grendel's mother, a layered, multivalent representation of the angry colonized motherland, Puerto Rico, as well as Mother English herself, illuminates Santos's inner turmoil. For Santos is intellectually arrogant (in this chapter he berates another student who thinks Frankenstein is a better monster than the "boring" Grendel) and insecure in equal measures.[39] About Santos's remark that the dream comes as a result of taking Literature I too seriously, Villanueva Collado notes that it is a "curiously bland" comment.[40] Although this surprisingly bland remark undermines the great degree of introspection in the narrative, it is not irrelevant to the puzzle that is *Family Installments*. In fact the disjunction between the book's tendency toward interiority and the blandness of certain conclusions Santos draws is the strongest clue leading to an explanation of the text's multiple monsters and moments of bodily disintegration. And Santos's joke that the dream results from taking Literature I too seriously reminds me of Ed's response to literary criticism, especially my own: "you're reading too much into it, Lyn." Although Santos is fascinated and repulsed by his dream visitation, he ultimately disavows it, much as Ed disavowed literary analysis. What is interesting for me here is that the young intellectual's attempt to separate from his working-class Latino community results in a strange internalization of, and identification with, that community's tendency to feel threatened by the revelations of analysis.

Again *Geographies of Home* provides a pertinent comparison. Iliana's family is proud of her achievements but they also resent them. Marina's rape of Iliana is an act of family violence that reflects the family's resentment of Iliana's new "class" status.[41] In Santos's case it is Santos himself who is divided between a hubristic desire to retreat from and best the family and a secret identification with the family's posture of humility. This provides yet another interpretation of the monster. Santos says, as if it were a joke, that "This monster didn't go in for explanations."[42] The monster is very much like Santos, then, whose bland explanation for the dream is an evasion. Despite a desire for profundity, and a sense of himself as different and better than the raucous working-class community he lives in, Santos undercuts any profound understanding of his situation. On the one hand, he is sophisticated, ambitious, and angry. On the other hand he identifies with an essentialized working-class Latino consciousness out of fear that he is not smart enough to separte completely from that background. This is an intolerable situation for his psyche, to feel at once fascinated by his origins and yet to resent the ways in which his working-class identification seems to prevent his progress; to feel gifted and special and to fear that this is only a vain illusion.

Santos's father Gerán, humble and uncomplaining, weak and abused by the world, then becomes a baffled and intolerable mirror of Santos's own condition of self-denial. Returning to Puerto Rico after a long, agonizing struggle with multiple sclerosis, Gerán finally dies. Santos, who had stayed behind in New York to finish his college education, arrives in Puerto Rico after his father has expired; he can only admit to annoyance:

> They had already sent him down to the morgue, and I began to lose my temper; he should have waited until I'd finished with my finals. I had planned on making a photocopy of my diploma and sending it to them as proof of something. Not that it would have made any difference to him . . . but it would have made a difference to me, and I was feeling selfish just then. No particular reason.[43]

The hardhearted fury in this response permits Santos to conceal his grief, even from himself. Santos focuses on Gerán all the rage he has not been able to vent on others—his cousin Chuito, the Irish nuns and brothers who educate and miseducate their Latino pupils, the black boys in the park. The father's life—and his capacity to appreciate the fact that his son has outclassed him—is summed up as ineffectual: "Not that it would have made any difference to him." The judgment against the father turns into rage against the world. But it is an impotent rage, full of denial. The son refuses to admit that he is "feeling selfish" because he is angry at his father's long-suffering posture, as well as his own inability to do anything about it. Instead of recognizing his pain and anger, he shuts down. The wounded self goes into hiding.

Santos's masochistic response to Gerán's death leads me back to Ed's so-called egolessness and his self-deprecatory irony. Ed's irony makes him pun mercilessly and, perhaps to some, opaquely at the end of the novel, referring to Thomas Browne's "Urn Burial," a Renaissance essay that is one of English literature's master narratives about death. At the end of the book, Santos, still thinking about his literature finals as he talks to a relative after Gerán's funeral, cannot recall the text's title accurately. So he riffs, producing the last lines of the novel: "Somebody's 'Brown Burial'?

'Earned Burial'? Maybe 'Bourne Aerial.' Whatever, something silly, count on it. I'd brood about it on the flight back home." Santos's lines recall Ed himself: clever, cutting, enchanted by language, but ultimately putting down his interest in all this literature—and his own sparkling Renaissance wit—as "silly."

Ed attempted to sublimate rage through this type of self-deprecatory irony. Latino rage cannot be directly expressed. Instead, it is like a language in hiding, refusing and refuting a direct and "honest" discourse of power. Apparent humility or egolessness then becomes a passive aggressive way of hiding (and yet also revealing) a degraded humanity. Pain defeats and propels Santos, as it defeated and propelled Ed, who was torn by a traumatic self-denial and a stubborn refusal. He was both passive and active, humble and proud. Hungry for intimacy, he often avoided it. His closest friends felt they did not really know him. He was driven by the tension between the thought that he wasn't "good enough," and the side that didn't want to show the world how bright and gifted he really was because people would never understand or appreciate him. So, then, fuck them.

CHAPTER SIX
MELANCHOLIC ALLEGORISTS OF THE STREET: PIRI THOMAS, JUNOT DÍAZ, AND YXTA MAYA MURRAY

The protagonists of the street allegories by Piri Thomas, Junot Díaz, and Yxta Maya Murray wear many masks. Paramount among them is the mask of the street master. In his fictionalized autobiography *Down These Mean Streets*, Piri Thomas calls his mask "cara palo," the Spanish shorthand for a face like a piece of wood, a fixed expressionless face.[1] Wearing the mask imitates, even as it undermines, a stable sense of self. Piri deceives himself into believing he knows who he is because he knows at least that he is not his masks. "I am not what I am," he might say along with Shakespeare's Iago, another great dissembler. To endure an unpleasant situation or to face an opponent, "Put cara palo on, *like it don't move you*," Piri says.[2] So important is the mask of toughness that the street macho—and the macho hopefuls, who include women—is prepared to destroy anyone who challenges the masquerade. If Edward Rivera's mask of egolessness and humility hid, but could not sublimate, his rage, the U.S. Latino/a street mask registers both pain (melancholia) at not being accepted by the social order and openly aggressive resistance to that order. In the late 1960s Piri wrote about how he grew into and out of the mask of *cara palo*. Díaz's and Murray's deployment of literary doubles thirty years later demonstrated that Latinos and Latinas in the twenty-first century are still struggling with the mask. The mask, always representing pain, aggressiveness, uprootedness, hypersexuality, racial and class marginalization for Latinas and Latinos, then is also a stereotype. Homi K. Bhabha says: "The stereotype is not a simplification because it is a false representation of a given reality. It is a simplification because it is an arrested, fixated form of representation."[3] The mask, worn by Latinos and Latinas on the street as a form of resistance weighs heavily on the Latino/a psyche in its symbolic immobility. To relieve this burden the street, perceived as a way of escaping the damaged family, becomes a palette onto which Latinos and Latinas project the psychic unrest veiled by the mask.

Fanon's Mask

Discussing masking in minority studies inevitably leads to Frantz Fanon's *Black Skin, White Masks*. Fanon emphasizes that the whitening or assimilation of the French

Antillean native is accomplished at great psychic cost. One of the most important indicators of whitening for Fanon is the mastery of the colonizer's language:

> Every colonized people—in other words, every people in whose soul an inferiority complex has been created by the death and burial of its local cultural originality—finds itself face to face with the language of the civilizing nation; that is, with the culture of the mother country. The colonized is elevated above his jungle status in proportion to his adoption of the mother country's cultural standards. He becomes whiter as he renounces his blackness, his jungle.[4]

The Martinican's education turns him into a white man with black skin, a grotesque mimicry of whiteness that Fanon expresses in his title with the powerful image of the white mask shrouding black skin. The white mask is contradictory. It marks the colonized's death in the social order even as the native subject is acknowledged as having mastered the colonizer's laguage. Fanon refers to native identity sardonically as the "jungle," implying the mythical nature of originary identity. When it dies, it is veiled by the colonized's posture of whiteness. The masked subject emerges at the expense of the unattainable origin.

This masked colonized subject, whom Fanon universalizes as male, is tormented by the incongruousness of his masks. Stereotyped by whites, blackness becomes just as much of a mask as whiteness. Bhabha finds two primal scenes in *Black Skins, White Masks*. In the first Fanon is "fixe[d} . . . in a look and word" by a white child.[5] The child exclaims:

> "Mama, see the Negro! I'm frightened!" Frightened! Frightened! Now they were beginning to be afraid of me . . . What else could it be for me but an amputation, an excision, a hemorrhage that spattered my whole body with black blood?[6]

The child's gaze turns Fanon into the stereotype of the black savage. As Bhabha notes, the stereotype allows the child to identify with her white mother by turning away from Fanon. The white child creates a fantasy of difference that is at once false and yet so powerful that Fanon feels himself to be spattered by his fictional "black blood" in the psychic dismembering of the child's gaze. And isn't it particularly devastating that it is a child's gaze that is so dismembering? The child's unmediated emotion elicits a similarly upset response from the colonized subject, producing a mirroring moment in which the colonized feels himself exposed, helpless, childlike in the white child's eyes.

As Fanon says earlier in *Black Skin, White Masks* in relation to another stereotype, the native talking "pidgin," to impose the stereotype is "to fasten [the black subject] to the effigy of him, to snare him, to imprison him, the eternal victim of an essence, of an apperance for which he is not responsible."[7] W.E.B. Dubois makes a similar point when he describes African American double-consciousness as arising from the "veil" imposed on black America by white America, rendering black Americans both invisible as well as "fastened," as Fanon would have it, to their stereotypes:

> It is a peculiar sensation, this double-consciousness, this sense of always looking at one's self through the eyes of others, of measuring one's soul by the tape of a world that looks on in amused contempt and pity.[8]

The veil or mask imposes the image of the stereotype by which black Americans are condemned to see themselves when in the company of white Americans. DuBois's idea of double-consciousness emphasizes that black Americans have their own way of seeing themselves that is not tainted by whiteness. Moreover, Dubois emphasizes that African Americans are privileged with the gift of "second sight."[9] African American double-consciousness can see white people with an accuracy not available to them, a kind of X-ray vision with a spiritual component. Like Fanon's interpretations of masking, Dubois's interpretations of double-consciousness have been very important for minority scholars in general. For example, the Latino scholar Juan Flores posits triple consciousness as a framework to discussions of Afro-Latino identity, highlighting the fact that Dubois's work emphasizes the black/white binary relationship.[10] The mask the white world imposed on black Americans tore them asunder psychically and simultaneously privileged them with the gift of "second sight." However, Piri Thomas, a black Latino, feels rejected by both white and black America. He wears the mask to create a persona that oscillates between the poles of a constructed American blackness and whiteness. As he attempts to piece together a new identity, Piri's mask of *cara palo* helps him mourn the loss of whiteness, blackness, and Puerto Ricanness.

Enter Racial Melancholia

Although Fanon uses the metaphor of the mask in his title, he rarely refers specifically to it in the essays in *Black Skin, White Masks*. Du Bois prefers the metaphor of the veil as a kind of giant curtain that falls between him and the "other world" of white America when a white classmate denies him equal subjectivity "with a glance."[11] This is another primal moment of rejection by a white child. The Latino/a street works that are the main focus of this chapter refer frequently and specifically to masks. In these works, masking is accompanied by what David Eng and Shinhee Han call "racial melancholia." Eng and Han propose that assimilation is unattainable for American minorities and that "the suspensions, conflicts and irresolutions entailed by it resemble the process of mourning."[12] Eng and Han are referring to Freud's famous distinction between mourning and melancholia. Mourning is a process of grieving that comes to an end, in which the loss of an object entails a gradual, but eventually complete, withdrawal of libido from that object. In melancholia the lost object is introjected into the psyche and mourned endlessly. According to Freud:

> An object-choice, an attachment of the libido to a particular person, had at one time existed; then, owing to a real slight or disappointment coming from this loved person, the object-relationship was shattered . . . .But the free libido was not displaced on to another object; it was withdrawn into the ego. There, however, it was not employed in any unspecified way, but served to establish an identification of the ego with the abandoned object. Thus the shadow of the object fell upon the ego, and the latter could henceforth be judged by a special agency, as though it were an object, the forsaken object. In this way an object-loss was transformed into an ego-loss and the conflict between the ego and the loved person into a cleavage between the critical activity of the ego and the ego as altered by identification.[13]

The "shadow of the object" falls upon the ego cleaving and doubling it. A part of the ego identifies with the object and a part vents critically against that object.

Freud's darkly compelling language implies a fall, a staining, and contamination. As such, it is not surprising that he would find melancholia to be a "pathological" process.[14] Freud notes that the angry feelings the melancholic could not express toward the loved/hated object then are directed toward this introjected lost object. The melancholic's self-criticism and self-impoverishment are really a raging and venting against the lost object, which is no longer an object but part of the self.

Eng and Han contend that the racialized subject cannot attain "whiteness," as Fanon and Dubois also realized. In their provocative formulation, "whiteness" is therefore introjected as a lost object that is mourned throughout the minority subject's life. For the minority the originary identity (Asianness, Blackness, Latino identity) is also introjected as a lost object, although the authors do not spell out the exact relationship between these introjected lost objects. Instead of the individual, pathological process Freud posited, Eng and Han propose that racial melancholia is social, thereby seeking to depathologize this condition as well as point to a kind of national melancholia, the result of the country's largely unconscious "loss" of the energies of its racialized subjects. In accord with Bhabha's ideas about the stereotype, Eng and Han also note that Asian Americans, in order to be acknowledged at all as American subjects, attempt to follow the model minority stereotype, "a 'positive' representation . . . [that] not only mainstream society but also Asian Americans themselves become attached to, and split by, its seemingly admirable qualities without recognizing its simultaneous liabilities."[15] But this mimicry of what is deemed to be a favorable stereotype the authors conclude only estranges Asian Americans further. One of Eng's and Han's key contributions to this discourse is to fully contradict Freud's postulation that "the shadow of the object fell upon the ego."[16] He, and Lacan after him, emphasize the importance of the ego over the object, the authors contend. Eng and Han, however, emphasize the introjected lost object (Asianness, for example) to suggest a way that marginalized others can unite in cherishing incorporated lost objects and ideals. Having forcefully argued that racial melancholia is a social condition affecting American minorities, not an individual pathology, as Freud claimed, the authors less convincingly assert that the losses and wounds of racial melancholia do not amount to "damage":

> We are dissatisfied with the assumption that minority subjectivities are permanently damaged—forever injured and incapable of ever being "whole."[17]

And:

> In most of the Freudian oeuvre, it is indubitably the ego that holds sway; his majesty the ego's narcissism reigns supreme . . . In this present formulation, however we have the loved object, not the ego, holding sway. Racial melancholia thus delineates one psychic process in which the loved object is so overwhelmingly important to and beloved by the ego that the ego is willing to preserve it even at the cost of its own self.[18]

I find these aspects of their formulation problematic; Eng's and Han's fetishism of the lost object is no more salutary than Freud's fetishism of the ego. Moreover, although the authors note that minority subjects mourn the unachievable ideal of "whiteness," which is unattainable precisely because it is a "wholeness" (a fictional identity arguably out of reach even for "white" people), they dislike the notion that racial melancholia might be viewed as "damage" because a damaged subjectivity cannot become "whole." But if whiteness and originary (Asian, Latino/a) identities are really lost objects, then "wholeness" is out of the question. The street allegorists question both notions, since street allegory, unlike the writing of a middle-class author like García or an upper-class writer like Ferré, unabashedly thematizes damage: poverty, racism, drug addiction, a life of crime, and also declares, as a new object, the street, that replaces the originary family even as it takes elements from it (paternalism, for example). Piri Thomas creatively deconstructs the fetishization of the lost object in the way he repeatedly takes new masks and identities, implicitly introjecting objects and meshing them together in his interiority.

Eng's and Han's ideas about racial melancholia help me understand the vital difference between the writers of the family allegory of divergence such as García, Ferré, Pérez, and Rivera and the writers who disavow their countries of origin, declaring that the street, which allows them to become urban Latinos, is their new home. In the previous texts the identification of the island of origin with a double character causes a sacrifice that enables a sometimes unconvincing assimilation, such as Iliana's in *Geographies of Home*, which I discuss in chapter four. Iliana, identified with her ego, purports to have done with her family, as she prepares to leave home and take on the world. If we believe the thoughts Pérez attributes to her in the third-person point of view, we must believe that she has mourned for her lost position in the family and now wishes to get on with the rest of her life. But in the school that Iliana is returning to she has already experienced racism. This leads me to believe that she follows the trajectory Eng and Han suggest, and that despite the book's openended and "positive" conclusion, she secretly turns into a racial melancholic. The writers of the street also disavow their families and the land of origin not at the end of their stories, the way Perez's Iliana does, but at the beginning of their street stories. What is different about their melancholia is that the street writers project their inner psychic landscape onto the street.

The Melancholia of the Street

Deterritorialization and reterritorialization are among the thematics of street episte-mology.[19] Having left The Dominican Republic, Mexico, and Puerto Rico for largely economic reasons, working-class Latinos and Latinas of the first generation yearn to go back.[20] The second generation, however, wants to reterritorialize, that is, to forget the old homeland and rebuild a new one. This is what Miguel Piñero's seminal "A Lower East Side Poem" declares: reterritorialization as a radical rewriting of the notion of origin. For Piñero the origin is neither Puerto Rico nor even New York, the great city on whose streets so many Latinos have suffered, struggled, and triumphed, but rather a specific and constricted space, the Lower East Side of Manhattan:

> A thief, a junkie I've been
> committed every known sin
> Jews and Gentiles . . . Bums and Men
> of style . . . run away child

police shooting wild . . .
mother's futile wails . . [ ]

So here I am, look at me
I stand proud as you can see
pleased to be from the Lower East
a street fighting man
a problem of this land . . .
this concrete tomb is my home
to belong to survive you gotta be strong . . .

I don't wanna be buried in Puerto Rico
I don't wanna rest in long island cemetery
I wanna be near the stabbing shooting
gambling fighting & unnatural dying
& new birth crying
so please when I die . . .
don't take me far away
keep me near by
take my ashes and scatter them thru out
the Lower East Side . . .[21]

Piñeiro's moving lament in "A Lower East Side Poem" quintessentially differs in conscious intention and effect from the texts outlined in the preceding chapters by García, Pérez, and Ferré. The protagonist, and/or the lyric speaker, in this literature revels in his or her *badassness* or criminality: "A thief, a junkie I've been." This is part of my identity, this speaker says. I refuse to reject my experiences; I am "proud," not ashamed, of them. The texts proclaim pride in the self's capacity to survive and triumph over the vicissitudes of street life: "this concrete tomb is my home / to belong to survive you gotta be strong." Later we will see Piri Thomas espousing this ideal of strength at any cost. The underside of this concept of strength, though, is that it usually involves taking something from somebody else. This is where the epistemology of the fictional works starts to diverge markedly from "A Lower East Side Poem." Piñero's poems do not reveal either the minutia of his interactions with other people or the temporal effects of his criminal lifestyle (the people he has hurt). In this way, there is something timeless about "A Lower East Side Poem."

Nostalgia seems to have no place in the streets Piñero describes because they are always filled with "dying & new birth crying," the whole panorama of life. Nor does he express nostalgia for or a desire to return to the island: "I don't wanna be buried in Puerto Rico." The actual island of Puerto Rico could only be the grave for this speaker, whereas "the concrete tomb" of the street, which seems so inimical to life, is the speaker's avowed proper, beloved environment. There is also an implicit critique of the desire to assimilate in the speaker's declaration: "I don't wanna rest in long island cemetery."

This is also, of course, a reference to the earlier, equally famous poem "Puerto Rican Obituary," by Pedro Pietri, in which the struggles of Juan Flores's "lowercase" Puerto Ricans who work in dehumanizing conditions are detailed beautifully and eloquently.[22] Pietri's poem is an incisive critique of the perspective of the upwardly mobile working-class Puerto Rican who works mindlessly at a job only to achieve an empty and symbolic middle-class status, marked by burial in Long Island cemetery, a status negated by death. Hence the rich irony of the poem's title, emphasizing the complicity of "Juan/Miguel/Milagros/Olga/Mañuel" in their social death.[23] Piñero's full-blown street epistemology—and the actual real-life scattering of his ashes on the Lower East Side—focuses on the street as the foundation of a sense of self that stays connected to its "real" background, however troubled, dirty, and seemingly unstable.[24]

"Dirty realism" follows from the preceding characteristics. This is a literary term that is loosely used to categorize the "grunge" fiction of white writers such as Jay McInerny and Brett Easton Ellis, as well as the contemporary urban surrealism of an accomplished novelist like Denis Johnson. The term is useful to discuss contemporary U.S. Latino/a writers. Indeed Piñero's real-life criminal persona differs from the jaded narrators of Easton Ellis and McInerny in passion as well as class status. Dirty realism for the white writers is an acknowledgment of the inability to achieve a full spiritual life. The minimalism and tonal flatness of Easton Ellis's *Less Than Zero* underscored both the aridity of the characters' lives as well as their jaded attitudes to drug addiction, sex abuse, snuff films, and so forth. For the upper-middle-class characters in *Less Than Zero,* being numb is both a response to their lives and a refusal to act. Piñero's dirty realism, on the other hand, accepts and extols the living conditions of New York for working-class Latinos, negative as they may seem from other perspectives. Piñero and Pietri, and Thomas's famous book are distinctive for the protagonists, intense feeling for the places, the streets, and urban ghettos, which have been marked by dirty realism. Piñero loves the Lower East Side and Thomas feels a passionate attachment to Spanish Harlem. The mainstream urban dirty realist Elllis has no such strong feeling for Los Angeles, and although McInerny does exalt New York in the title of *Bright Lights, Big City*, like many of the pro-tagonists of contemporary minimalist fiction, his response is weakened by self-consciousness. In that sense U.S. Latinos have concocted something unique, a rising street narrative tradition that highlights both the horrors and the beauties of street life. But, above all, the seminal works of Piñero and Thomas frequently show a tender affection for the street and its people. The old object, Puerto Rico, is relinquished and a new space, the "mean" Latino street is inaugurated.

But the poem's dark tone also ultimately undermines Piñero's celebration of new space. The speaker knows he is a New Yorker and not an islander, but he also realizes that a normative American identity is as impossible for him as a normative island Puerto Rican one would be. The old objects—Puerto Rico and Americanness—have been introjected, not mourned and then forgotten as the speaker would have us believe. However, having been removed as external objects and possibilities, they have been replaced by a new, accessible object, the street. Initially, many urban Latinos take to the streets because their actual homes are "unhomely"; I mean here to invoke Freud's idea of the uncanny, as discussed in chapter four on Pérez. The Latino home is unhomely because it is inhospitable, but also because of the suppressed past that comes back to haunt it. Although some aspects of the unhomely family may be left behind, Latinos take others into the street with them, thereby rendering the street unhomely too as tomb/home. Piñero as "a thief, a junkie" initially did not have the resources to own property. The freedom of the street helps initially to assuage the lack in property and normative identity. Nonetheless, the characters in *Locas* for example acquire property and wealth. The rage they felt at certain losses (a mother who was a prostitute and an alcoholic, for example), however, is internalized. The violent street landscape externalizes the new Latino's interior landscape, suffused with melancholia and rage.

Judith Butler notes that the process of melancholia produces psychic interiority in all subjects in the first place: "The turn from the object to the ego produces the ego, which substitutes for the object lost."[25] The melancholic ego, having absorbed the lost object, also "brings aggression against the object along with it."[26] This rage against the world, against the normative society that rejects Piñero, for example, is introjected and expressed against the self: "In melancholia, the ego contracts something of the loss or abandonment by which the object is now marked, an abandonment that is refused and, as refused, is incorporated. In this sense to refuse a loss is to become it."[27] this dynamic explains the self-destructiveness and longing for death in Piñero's poem: "this concrete tomb is my home". His love for the street is "strong"—and ambivalent. It is home inasmuch as the speaker acknowledges it as his final home, the place of both "birth" and his death.

Isn't it clear that Piñero is describing his own psyche as much as he is the street? When Piñero says "I don't wanna be buried in Puerto Rico / I don't wanna rest in long island cemetery / I wanna be near the stabbing shooting / gambling fighting & unnatural dying / & new birth crying" it becomes clear that his self-destructive choice is the exteriorization of the turmoil in the inner landscape. The objects that rejected him: a middle-class Puerto Rican subjectivity, a white middle-class American whiteness, these Piñero rejects, but also introjects, absorbing into himself the rebellion and rage against the rejecting objects. The inner landscape manifests violently everywhere as Piñero refuses to acknowledge his losses—"to refuse a loss is to become it."[28] Scattering his ashes over the Lower East Side figures his psychic explosion. He yearns for death as a moment of release from the "concrete tomb", an unbearable psychic prison.

Down These Mean Streets—The Archetypal U.S. Latino Street Story

"Every few years somebody rewrites *Down These Mean Streets*," Junot Díaz announced in the spring of 2001 to my U.S. Latino literature class of twenty-odd students. They were too awed and intimidated by the mystique surrounding this young Latino writer to ask him many questions, even after his intentionally outlandish comment. The Dominican American Díaz was referring to a recent novel, by a young Puerto Rican writer. He knew that my students had loved Piri Thomas's 1967 quasi-autobiography, just as they loved his book of short stories, *Drown* (1996). His statement was a subtle provocation, a challenge as well as a declaration of the truth as he saw it. The statement of truth: *Down These Mean Streets* is both the foundational novel of U.S. Latino/a Caribbean literature; in form, a confessional narrative written in street language with a generous sprinkling of Spanish and Spanglish; in content, the story of growing up in and out of the street. Highly influenced by African American narratives of the 1960s such as *The Autobiography of Malcolm X* and Claude Brown's *Manchild in the Promised Land*, the novel established the contours of a radical literary epistemology of the street. Often when I ride the subway in New York, I see Latinos and Latinas reading Thomas's book, but I can't say that this applies to any other U.S. Latino/a novel, at least not on the East Coast. The possible exceptions are *Drown* and *The Mambo Kings Sing Songs of Love* (1989), but I see those titles more often in the classroom than on the subway. Thomas's book still speaks to urban Latinos in a way that most of its successors do not. Díaz's provocative remark, of course, was also meant as a kind of criticism of the fictional "rewrites." Unlike many of its successors, *Down These Mean Streets* retains the ring of authenticity that derives from Thomas's status as a former "thief and junkie" in Piñero's words.

A basic characteristic of "street epistemology," exemplified in *Down These Mean Streets* is the allegorical stance itself. Piñero's poem, is not allegorical, partly because temporality holds little sway in it. It is in Latino/a fiction where we see Fanon's allegorical imperative operating (discussed in chapter one): "the native looks back and remembers what he is." In this sense the reterritorialization that we see in "A Lower East Side Poem" is complicated by the passing of time recorded in the narrative venture of *Down These Mean Streets*. Piri becomes a thief and a junkie and later critically wounds two men in two different robberies. However, both the desire to reform and the reform itself (which doesn't come until he is released from jail and then only after a frightening lapse back into the old life) also sets the stage for his decision to cut himself off from the street. Unlike Piñero in his poem and his life, after a moment of crisis Piri appears to turn his back on the street.

In her insightful reading of *Down These Mean Streets*, Lisa Sánchez González notes that in some sense Piri takes the ultimate revenge on his father by placing his faith in the Christian God. In this way "the novel forecloses the quest to constitute an omniscient, self-authorizing narrative voice in deference to the primal Word of divinity itself".[29] In this reading, *Down These Mean Streets* is a kind of to hell and back narrative of clear and final redemption. In this interpretation the street of present reality and not the remembered island constitutes the allegorized, nostalgized origin. Although this is a compelling way of reading the book, explaining its appeal as redemption narrative, I think Piri's slippery persona tends to deconstruct such a view of the novel. Piri's mask of *cara palo* enables him to weave together a variety of faces even as he mourns his originary identities.

Piri's first and pervasive dilemma in the novel is that he is torn between blackness, defined by African American identity and emphasizing race, and a Puerto Rican identity that stresses culture over skin color. Like the other Latino/a allegories I discuss in this book, the conflict here follows archetypal lines. The white Puerto Rican mother represents a "deeper" more holistic notion of Latino/a identity, partly the narrator's projection. The black Latino father represents a link to colonialist and paternalist qualities because he denies his blackness. Later in the text we encounter Brew, Piri's black American alter ego or double, who articulates the African American position on race for the text, a position about which Piri is supremely ambivalent. The main problem for Piri is not so much that Puerto Rican identity and black identity are at odds with each other, but that the black father wishes to erase his own blackness. Piri, the only child in the Thomas family who is black, is a reminder of that blackness.

The opening lines of the first chapter of *Down These Mean Streets* encapsulate the book's movement from the domestic space of a project apartment, where the father hits the son for knocking to the floor a large jar of black coffee, to the street, which mirrors the turmoil of the child's mind:

> I had been walking around since 9 p.m. My thoughts were boiling. *Poppa ain't ever gonna hit me again. I'm his kid, too, just like James, José, Paulie, and Sis. But I'm the one that always get the blame for everything . . .*
> "Caramba," I muttered aloud. "I'm getting hungry."
> The streets of Harlem make an unreal scene of frightened silence at 2 a.m.[30]

The child feels rejected because unlike his siblings he is darkskinned, but it is a feeling that he cannot articulate, that instead is objectified in the "river of black coffee" the boy spills, a correlative for the blackness that the father tries to hide from his own and his family's consciousness and which Piri, increasingly as he gets older, tries to uncover and own.[31] The inner "boiling" rage is both projected outward onto the "frightened" street as well as ultimately distracted by the drama on the street, which includes a policeman on vigil, a woman being raped, and two junkies shooting up, all of which prefigure the life on the streets for the adult Piri. But the boy turns away, eager to go back home to find out if his father has missed him. His father, typically indifferent to Piri, does not notice the son's absence until he returns. In the future narrated by the text, the adult Piri will keep his father's blackness, but give up on his father. Instead, the street becomes his "surrogate father."[32]

Father, Mother, Double

In a classic text on doubling, Otto Rank showed the correlation between the "family romance" fantasy that early psychoanalysts encountered often in small children and the duplication of parental figures in myths about such heroes as Moses, Oedipus, Gilgamesh, Tristan, Romulus, Jesus and others:

> The hero is the child of most distinguished parents, usually the son of a king . . . After he has grown up, he finds his distinguished parents, in a highly versatile fashion. He takes revenge on his father, on the one hand, and is acknowledged on the other. Finally he achieves rank and honors.[33]

In this light, Piri's desire to identify with a noble lineage is quite revealing, as is his attitude toward his father. Robert Rogers, commenting on Rank's text, notes that the "hostility of the father in the myths reflects a projection of the son's hostility toward him."[34] The hero's hostile attitude toward the father is obviously Oedipal, as is Piri's positioning. Just like the parents in *The Agüero Sisters*, the Thomas parents are locked in archetypal struggle. The mother frequently calls Piri "negrito."[35] A white Puerto Rican, the mother loves and accepts both her black husband and son. However, Piri unconsciously idealizes her white skin as much as he loves her tolerant attitude, despite his rationalizations against such an attraction. His African American friend, Brew, is literally Piri's dark double in his formulation of the race/culture debate: "[Piri's] skin is dark an', that makes him jus', anudder rock right along wif the res', of us, an', tha', goes for all the rest of them foreign-talkin', black men all ovah tha', world."[36] Despite the fact that Piri has no real memory of the island, and certainly no wish to go there, his mother represents a wholesome, white island femininity and Piri's fantastical idea of noble lineage.

Like Fanon and Dubois, Piri's black Cuban father recognizes—and is tormented by—his blackness in the eyes of white others:

> "I ain't got one colored friend," he added, "at least not one American Negro friend. Only dark ones I got are Puerto Ricans or Cubans. I'm not a stupid man. I saw the look of white people on me when I was a young man, when I walked into a place where a dark skin wasn't supposed to be."[37]

Unlike Fanon and Dubois, Piri's father constructs his identity as explicitly Latino and implicitly lightskinned. His choice of a lightskinned Puerto Rican woman as love object enables this construction. Whether father and son are estranged because the father rejects the son's blackness, which reminds him of his own, or because the son is hostile toward the father because of an Oedipal love for his mother, are actually complementary pieces of the larger puzzle. Piri's love for his mother is mimetic, in the Girardian sense; he loves her best not because she is the best parent—although he certainly presents her that way—but because the father loves her. He is first his father's rival and then his mother's lover. And the father loves the mother because she is white. The father has made a habit of pursuing white Latinas, and Piri has made a habit of trying to steal them from his father—as his theft of his father's mistress's photograph later in the novel demonstrates. Piri learns through his father both to value his mother's whiteness as goodness, and to devalue blackness. But in the process Piri also learns to hate his father, a typical move in the Latino/a street novel, as we also will see in Díaz's stories.

Rank's monograph makes another important point: in the myths of the hero, there is a tendency to duplicate the principal characters in the parents-child triangle, a tendency similar to the doubling that Fletcher observes in traditional allegories, which I pointed out in the chapter on Cristina García. Various of these duplicated characters appear in *Down These Mean Streets*: notably Brew, mentioned above as representing Piri's blackness; Trina, the idealized island girlfriend, in many ways a double for Piri's mother; two easily overlooked "motherly" characters; Lorry, who gives the young, down and out Piri financial and emotional support, and Miss Washington, the huge black woman who protects Piri from the principal of his school. She is a more fascinating double for the mother than the bland Puerto Rican beauty, Trina. In fact, at the end of chapter seven, after the formidable Miss Washington forces the principal to leave their building, Piri's mother tells him that his father will go to the school with him the next morning to resolve things. Piri privately wishes that Miss Washington would go instead of his father. Miss Washington, as a double for the maternal, reflects both parents. She has the Puerto Rican mother's tenderness without the mother's passivity and inability to speak English, and the father's strength without the father's hostility toward his son/double Piri.

Trina duplicates the mother in some of the most comforting and crucial ways for Piri. She is a beautiful white Latina, and very "island," speaking a Spanish that, like that of Piri's mother, is represented as heavily accented. That she comes to clearly represent Puerto Rico is obvious in Piri's calling her his "Marine Tiger," thereby referencing one of the first boats to transport Puerto Ricans from the island to New York. In chapter seventeen, when Piri is in the taxi that will take him and Brew to the Port Authority and from there down South to discover the roots of American blackness and racism, Brew interrogates Piri about Trina, making the point that she must be somewhat racist, since she looks so white. Piri vehemently denies this, pointing out that Trina has accepted him, that there are plenty of lightskinned Puerto Ricans who are not racist until they come to the United States and catch that "played out sickness."[38] Brew argues that racism precedes arrival in the United States. He insists that it has to do with the conflict between white and black, finally pointing out that Piri himself is "prejudiced." At this point in the text it becomes clear to the reader and somewhat to Piri that he has internalized a particularly Latino type of white/black racism and practices it.

This is especially evident in Piri's relationship with Trina; Piri never sleeps with her, choosing instead to have sex with black women like Lorry or "easy" girls like Dulcien, whom Piri easily abandons. I am proposing here that while Piri sees women in the typical Madonna/whore stereotype, for him Trina's white skin coincides with his notions of goodness, just as his father projected his mother as good and white, and as Piri himself does, haplessly, throughout the text. Trina becomes Piri's mother, an idealized, innocent white woman, angelic and basically ineffectual. Signficantly, after his return from prison, Piri goes to see her, after fantasizing about wresting her from her husband in a knife fight in which Piri is mortally wounded.[39] The fantasy, in its focus on the struggle with Trina's husband, is remarkable for its violence and complete lack of eroticism. It reveals Piri's desire for Trina as completely mimetic and self-destructive. Piri is in love with the stereotype of (a white Latina) womanhood, and the fact that the husband mortally wounds Piri in the fantasy points to the homoeroticism of Piri's desire as well as his real ambivalence about being with Trina, because their relationship would recapitulate that of his parents. When they meet again, Trina seems as blank to him in her muted emotional response as the top layer of her skin. Her elusive, human response deforms the ideal, ultimately uninhabitable mask that Piri had constructed for her.

Piri's African American friend Brew, as I have noted, is the most obvious double in the book, since his function is to clearly voice the ideas about American blackness that contradict the Latino culture over race construct. When the author removes him from the text it has the effect of leaving the race question disturbingly unresolved. Yet, in a different sense, Brew's disappearance does throw light on the race question. With the voice of his black conscience gone, Piri surrenders completely to the ambivalence of his masks. The white mother who "loves him," and the black father who is hostile to him, become figures in an extended allegory of American racial politics. In this scenario, people of color achieve social affirmation through acts of tricksterism that allow them to become harmoniously integrated into a white supremacist imaginary. Jennifer Lopez is a good example of this type of tricksterism. More than her famous butt—which after all is not very big by island or Spanish Caribbean barrio standards—it is her chameleonlike capacity to adapt that has made her a monumental success story. But JLo has the golden skin that allows her to play white, Latina, and black-inflected roles on and off screen. Piri's blackness marks him, no matter how middle class he becomes—through his last marriage to a wealthy white wife (outside the purlieus of the book) and through the success of the book itself. He is his mother's lover but ultimately his father's child.

Significantly it is in chapter eleven, subtitled "How To Be A Negro Without Really Trying," that the relationship between Piri's tricksterism and American individualism becomes apparent. At this point Piri has left his family's new home on Long Island, unbearable to him because of the racism at his school. He is contemplating bumming on the Bowery when he is taken in by a black man and his sister Lorry, a woman in her thirties with whom Piri lives for a short time. She is another obvious mother double; she gives Piri carfare and lunch money, a home, and her body. But Piri leaves Lorry for a Puerto Rican girl he describes as "a pretty bitch, with a kid and no husband."[40] His relationship with her ends when he steals ten dollars from her. A few days later, he runs into the girl:

> She made a plea for her bread back, for her kid. I said I didn't take it and brushed past her. I didn't have to look into her eyes to know the hate she bore me. But it was her or me, and as always, it had to be me.[41]

Piñero's "To belong to survive you gotta be strong" corresponds to Piri's tough mask of *cara palo*. Ultimately, however, this kind of strength often depends on victimizing an Other, as Piri does the Puerto Rican girl. Street epistemology in this context is like the survival of the fittest with the "bitch[es]" getting the lean end of the stick.[42] However, it is also clear that brutality goes hand in hand with shame, for Piri can't look his victim in the eye. This is another moment of mirroring and refraction, of loss and reformulation. The young Puerto Rican girl suddenly becomes like Piri in her "hate" and Piri takes on the colonizing role of the white principal and his father and the whole social structure. Piri's mask of *cara palo*—bolstered by the fact that he is high—allows him to acknowledge the Puerto Rican girl's pain. To the extent that he recognizes himself in her eyes he promises himself to pay her back when he's straight. But we never find out whether he does this. More importantly, his mask, and his high, give him a tremendous amount of energy and determination. "To belong to survive you gotta be strong."

Masks

Like all discourses of power, street epistemology contradicts itself from within. On the one hand, it is a "It had to be me" vision of the world, an interesting distortion of Emersonian American individualism, which highlights the individual's intuitive response to situations over group or community mandates. On the other hand, there is an ideal of community at the heart of street ethos. Having *corazón*, heart for a fight or for most anything the gang wants, is one pole of this ideal and *cara palo*, or the stick (or stone) face worn by the street tough, is another. *Cara palo* is ultimately a mask marking repression. If Piri internalizes his mother's good white Latina, and his father's bad black colonized/would be colonizer Latino as lost objects, *cara palo* is the street mask that hides these losses and the personae he purportedly disidentifies with. For a very young Piri, one of the moments that demands *cara palo* is when one of his "boys" challenges the gang to visit a group of transvestites who offer alcohol and drugs to the boys in exchange for sex. Piri is alarmed at the prospect of having sex with another man but tells himself: "Put cara palo on, *like it don't move you!*"[43] He is of course disturbed at the pleasure he feels when one of the transvestites services him. As Lisa Sánchez González suggests, the street codes that Piri subscribes to can be defined as "both homoerotic and homophobic."[44] This is a contradiction that only *cara palo* can contain as it allows Piri to ostensibly enjoy the sex while pretending not to.

Getting stoned on pot with the boys helps him keep up the "stone" face even as the high enables him to recognize, like Piñero before him, the contradictory valences of the street. On the one hand it is the place where Piri is a "king."[45] On the other, it is a violent place, mechanized "like a clip machine," with bullets, as Piri imagines while being serviced by the transvestite. The image underlines a Darwinian brutality in the way the street "takes, an, keeps on taking," preying on Piri's soul, menacing his humanity, making him want to "forget" the things that happened to him on the street, and by extension his identity.[46] The clip machine image also calls to mind the way Piri stole money from the Puerto Rican girl, suggesting that his attitude of opportunism arises from his sense of the metonymic relationship between the street and those who are of the street (Piri, the girl) who are all in sense being "taken" by its machinery, even as they in turn take others. *Cara palo* helps Piri mask both his anguish at having his humanity (his memory) taken from him as well as take pleasure in the power (the hurt) he inflicts on others.

The mask of *cara palo* is weakened by the passage of time. For once Piri returns from jail he has irremediably changed. He has created, on the surface at least, a different mask that allows him to survive an initial infraction on the outside. Arriving late to his first parole meeting, he responds to his officer's reprimands: "I made my face stay the same, relaxed and soft."[47] The new mask Piri wears when he faces the parole officer is about deference. It indicates that Piri now understands the system and is willing to work it. *Cara palo* as an indifferent mask on the verge of hostility did not brook challenges to its violent paternalist power But this new softer façade is still a version of *cara palo* in that it hides Piri's feelings of fear and resentment. However, Piri has reached a point in his development in which he feels burdened by his masks. Overjoyed at being back on the street, Piri indulges in drugs and alcohol and sex again. Then he has a moment of supreme recoil when he looks at his face in the mirror after a night of carousing:

> I pulled away from the mirror and sat on the edge of my bed. My head was still full of pot, and I felt scared. I couldn't stop trembling inside. I felt as though I had found a hole in my face and out of it were pouring all the different masks that my cara palo face had fought so hard to keep hidden. I thought, *I ain't goin, back to what I was.*[48]

In Michael Taussig's provocative revisiting of the surrealist Roger Caillois, Taussig notes that "the mimicking self, tempted by space, spaces out"—as Piri does when he is on pot and heroin or spiraling down from a high. This mimicking subject becomes, in Caillois's referenced words, "not similar to something, but just similar.

And he invents spaces of which he is the convulsive possession."[49] *Cara palo* as the mask behind which Piri's other "different masks" hide is the one that is "just similar." Up until this moment, it has been Piri's defining mask. Unlike the mask of the religious acolyte, which he assumes by novel's end, *cara palo* is not put on to imitate anything in particular, but to hold back, to repress, contain, restrain. On the one hand, it is the most spectral of Piri's masks, a stone face, a stiff face, dead. On the other hand, it is plasticity itself. When the mask of *cara palo* disintegrates, it frighteningly reveals the turmoil of Piri's inner landscape overflowing with his never mourned and introjected lost objects (mother, father, Miss Washington, Brew). He has been hiding for so long that every response feels masked to him. This moment, then, marks a crisis point for *cara palo*, whose performative space was constructed through drug and alcohol fugues. This moment of crisis forces Piri to make a choice.

Down These Mean Streets is structured as a redemption narrative, in which Piri makes the choice to leave the streets as criminal and junkie, returning in the more detached role of reformed reformer. Piri chooses the religion of his dead white Latina mother to facilitate this transition: "*If God is right, so what if He's white?*" he exclaims in the short paragraph that marks the turn to God.[50] One might interpret his choice as a further identification with his mother. Or, as Lisa Sánchez Gónzalez puts it, he "capitulates his will and word to a divine and conspicuously white father figure whose omniscience is absolute and unfathomable."[51] Sánchez Gónzalez astutely deconstructs the meaning of redemption, not as a regaining of the spiritual self, but as deference to the paternalist white power structure. However, I believe that Piri is actually playing with the format of the to hell and back redemption story. The passage in which he takes on the white God is extremely brief, facile, and unconvincing, even if we know that in real life Piri did take on religion—as many convicts do, in and out of prison.[52] I want to emphasize here that in any profound sense leaving the street is impossible. Instead, Piri accomplishes a mimetic adaptation of what he has loved and internalized—his mother and her religion, disavowing (closeting not discarding) what is shunned.

In the book's very last scene, Piri encounters one of his buddies from the old gang, a much younger man, Carlitos, who is strung out on heroin. When Carlitos offers Piri some heroin Piri, strongly tempted, refuses.[53] Piri is almost overcome by a strong desire to reenter that spaced-out performative zone that heroin promises, but whose destructiveness is revealed in Carlitos's skeletal figure and haunting eyes. In the face of Carlitos's ensuing hollow protestations of having "dignity" and "self-respect," Piri turns his back on him and the offer to fall back into the life: "I don't think my boy saw me go past him. I couldn't stand seeing my man. . ."[54] In this heartbreaking moment, Carlitos reflects the Piri of past days, pulling and pushing at him to both stay and get high and to run to a new life. The strung-out heroin addict, the mirror of one stage of Piri's life, however, is not left behind despite the signal toward exit from the mean streets at book's end, by which Piri turns his back on the specter of himself. He has acquired a new mask, a mask of obedience (to God, the church, the parole officer). Piri's ego is not a shelter for lost objects, his interiority deconstructs any kind of fetishization of the lost object.[55] The street, and its concomitant mask of *cara palo*, itself is an interior landscape that reflects the absence of other objects lost. The street in turn is rejected on the surface, only to be internalized forever in the interiority of his being. And he still lives with aspects of himself that are always hidden there, as well as the persona that he has learned to present, polished and fashioned like a play on the American obsession with the story of a re/formed street kid.

Among U.S. Latino writers, only Oscar Hijuelos, the winner of the 1990 Pulitzer Prize, has received the kind of recognition proffered to Junot Díaz, whose status as an important American writer has been ritualized by the repeated publication of his short stories in *The New Yorker*. Díaz's work merits the numerous accolades it has received as a felicitous combination of technical sophistication and the gritty subject matter found in *Down These Mean Streets*. And yet there are significant differences between Thomas's seminal narrative and Díaz's short stories. Díaz's *Drown* builds upon the framework constructed by Thomas. But as a college educated Latino who is now a professor of English, as well as a literary star, Díaz has a prestige in the mainstream that Thomas, with his police and prison record, never achieved.

If we apply the five features of street literature that I delineated at the opening of this chapter, we can see that there is a change from the values of street literature expressed by Nuyorican writers like Thomas and Piñero, whose higher education was acquired in prison and on the street and, a generation after Piñero, a more self-conscious writer like Díaz. In Díaz's work there is such a strong conflict between the macho badass and his opposite, the sensitive macho, that a doubling relationsip or a triad of characters always reflects this conflict. In Thomas all the doubles, so to speak, are discarded by the narrative, the most obvious being Brew and Carlitos. In the end, the badass macho posture wins the day even for Díaz, as we will see in one of his most impressive stories, "The Brief Wondrous Life of Oscar Wao." The younger writer does, however, carefully scrutinize the brutal self-interest that allows Piri to survive at the expense of others. In this strange Latino world of masked masculinity, racial melancholia, and ambivalence the result is that both the mother and the father are dismissed. Fathers, because they leave, are portrayed as ineffectual, and in fact are seen as ghostly figures inasmuch as they are so little known by their children. Díaz's mother characters are not just weak and passive like Thomas's women, but victims of mental breakdown ("Aguantando") and low-grade depression, much like the mother characters in the novels by García, Ferré, and Pérez, although this is not the case in "The Brief Wondrous Life of Oscar Wao." The Latina writers, however, deeply explore the psyches of their madwomen as well as those of certain male characters. Thomas produces stereotypical women characters whereas Díaz's youthful narrators leave the psyches of the older generation largely unexplored with the illuminating exception of "Negocios." What remains is the melancholic brotherhood of the street.

Yunior is the "sensitive" authorial persona who narrates five stories in *Drown*. Rafa is Yunior's macho older brother. In the story "Ysrael" we see that Rafa is exposed to the street first in the barrios of Santo Domingo, before the family arrives in the States. He mesmerizes Yunior with his stories of sexual adventure on the street. Drug dealers narrate two other stories in *Drown*: "Aurora" and the title story "Drown." The appearance of a double character in these stories reveals the ambivalence of the narrators, just as the Rafa/Yunior doubling relationship does in the dominant stories. But because of their total immersion in the darker side of street life these narrators are at greater psychic risk than Yunior whose major dilemma is whether to wear the mask of Latino masculinity that he loves in his brother Rafa but scorns in his negligent and bullying father. Despite his ultimate capitulation to the mask of machismo, Yunior, much like Díaz himself, is saved by a college education and his own distrust of the Latino father figure. For this reason, Díaz's stories, like Piñero's and Pietri's poetry and like Thomas's work, also ultimately disavow the island as a place of danger, the real origin of the psychic confusion that overcomes Díaz's characters.

All of Díaz's stories intentionally deal in the dirty realism we saw in Piñero and Thomas. Take this sentence from "Fiesta 1980": "I want to dance, she said, but now, with the sun sliding out of the sky like spit off a wall, she seemed ready just to get this over with."[56] When spit slides off a ghetto building wall, it leaves a sticky disturbing imprint. It's impossible to forget that there was spit, urine, blood, or shit on those ghetto walls, unless the stain is scrubbed off, which seldom happens. Groundskeepers, police, and the urban planners who design the projects with less interest in comfort than in packing the poor into the buildings like sardines to save the city money, are in a sense responsible for this kind of trace. Díaz's use of this simile emphasizes that the characters feel entrapped by the dreariness of their living accommodations, one factor among many that contributes to the low-grade depression periodically afflicting, in this case, Yunior's mother, and in general all the denizens of the street. But the trace of spittle is also a profane illumination, in the sense discussed by Walter Benjamin in his description of how the surrealists apprehended and represented certain everyday objects in the urban Paris of the early twentieth century: "They bring the immense forces of, atmosphere, concealed in these things to the point of explosion."[57] By metonymically echoing other stains and fragments such as skin color, language, poverty, Díaz's evocation of spit on the ghetto wall also brings the historically and socially determined energies of the ghetto world "to the point of explosion." Díaz's purported description of nature never lets us forget the ambivalent, transgressive presence of spit on the wall in the urban ghetto, which traces the movement between entrappment (drowning) and artistic production (*Drown*), between social death and subversion.

Or take another example of dirty realism, this time from the ending of Díaz's story "Aurora" about the drug dealer Lucero and his debilitating, codependent love affair with Aurora, the crack addict:

A week from then she would be asking me again, begging actually, telling me all the good things we'd do and after a while I hit her and made the blood come out of her ear like a worm but right then, in that apartment, we seemed like we were normal folks. Like maybe everything was fine.[58]

Spit in the example from "Fiesta 1980," blood in this one. The dirty realism in Díaz's work is closer to Denis Johnson's *Jesus' Son* than Piri's *Down These Mean Streets*. Piri is always conscious of the anger that drives him toward violence, toward drugs, and of the fear that finally yanks him away from the street. In "Aurora," the young narrator Lucero is always somewhat disassociated from either a direct declaration of passion for Aurora, or a clear account of why he is angry, or whether he is angry or just cynical and disaffected. This is the purpose of the simile "like a worm," for Lucero is so emotionally benumbed that the blood does not seem real to him.

Unlike Piri, Lucero, like the characters in Easton Ellis's *Less Than Zero*, is part of the T.V. generations. Whether they can talk about their anger as openly as Piri does or not, the other narrators of the stories in *Drown* are committed to an identity that is almost wholly derived from identification with life in the rundown ghettoes of urban America.

The Mask Again

In the short story "Ysrael" the narrator and his older brother have been sent from Santo Domingo, the capital of the Dominican Republic to the Dominican campo for the summer. They become obsessed with a young boy who wears a mask to cover his mutilated face. The main action of the story has to do with the boys' journey to a far-off town to see this deformed boy. Once there, they plan to tear the mask off Ysrael's face. As one reviewer noted, "Subtle parallels between the narrator and the mutilated boy (both their fathers are in America) hint that the mutilated face is a mirror image of the protagonists themselves, a grotesque emblem of their life in the Dominican Republic."[59] Although it is true that Ysrael is a mirror or double for the two boys in the story, the boys themselves are doubles.

Yunior the narrator, a persona for the author, narrates "Ysrael," as well as four other important stories in *Drown*: "Fiesta 1980," "Aguantando," "How to Date a Browngirl, Blackgirl, Whitegirl, or Halfie" and "Negocios." In all five of these stories the family dynamics are similar: the father is absent in "Ysrael" and in "Aguantando." Although he is present in "Fiesta 1980," he is a harsh character who treats his family tyrannically and is having an affair with a Puerto Rican woman. In "How to Date a Browngirl, Blackgirl, Whitegirl, or Halfie" the father is not important to the plot, even though he is still with the family. "Negocios," the novella that ends the collection, is Yunior's narration of his father's life from the moment he immigrates from the Dominican Republic to the States. It is the most technically innovative of these early stories. Although Yunior is very critical of the father, just as he was in "Fiesta 1980," the meticulous details of his father's often difficult circumstances as an immigrant shows that Yunior, as a young adult, is trying hard to understand, rather than harshly judge his father. Ultimately, the father may be condemned by Yunior less for his pernicious behavior than for his shadowy unknowability.

When we meet Rafa and Yunior in "Ysrael" the father has been in the States for six years without sending any word to his *familia*, and Rafa, the older brother, is bitter about this. At one point in the story, Yunior is fondled by a man on the bus the brothers take to Ysrael's town. On the *concho* Rafa has managed to swindle a free fare for them. Yunior bursts out crying from stress when they step down from the bus, and Rafa steps right into their father's haranguing role:

> Rafa spit. You have to get tougher. Crying all the time. Do you think our papi's crying? Do you think that's what he's been doing the last six years? He turned from me. His feet were crackling through the weeds, breaking stems.[60]

In *Drown* Rafa is the textbook melancholic who, in introjecting the boys' father as lost object, is compelled to imitate him and wear the macho mask. But he is as equally driven to rage against him, mobilizing the aggression against the father into his own ego as a lacerating self-hatred that of course the ego cannot keep in check.

Yunior's sensitivity, particularly his loving description of the mother that contrasts with his account of the father's selfishness in "Fiesta 1980," sharply throws in relief Rafa's tough mask and sexist treatment of girls, the boasting accounts of "tetas and chochas."[61] Yunior is not so hardened in his attitude toward the world. The contrast between the brothers and their relationship to each other as doubles is most acutely defined in their attitudes toward Ysrael's deformity. Rafa's drive to unveil Ysrael's face, and to violently assault the boy, is a measure of how desperate Rafa is to "uncover" and resolve the problem of his rage against the father.

Although Ysrael's pig-eaten face is an emblem of countryside poverty and devastation, Ysrael seems stronger, smarter, and definitely richer than Rafa and Yunior and the other boys. "He is faster than a mongoose, someone said, but in truth he was even faster than that," Yunior notes.[62] Ysrael himself tells how he was able to beat off, by means of physical strength and mental focus, the four boys who pinned him down and threatened to rape him.[63] And he is learning English, which he will use when he is in the States.[64] Yunior notes, moreover, that the kite Ysrael is flying is "no handmade local job," meaning it looks expensive.[65] Focusing on physical exercise helps Ysrael feel superior to the *campo* boys and fixes him as a figure to fear and envy. It also fends off his own fear of the unknown (the future in the United States) and the acquisition of a new face (a new Latino/a identity).

Ysrael reflects what all the other Dominican boys can't or don't want to see in themselves, but which fascinates them in the embodied contradiction of this boy who advertises that there is a secret side to manhood. Ysrael's mask is a physical marker of Piri's notion of *cara palo*, exaggerating the deformity of masked Latino masculinity: strong on the outside, suppressing emotion, fending off attack. No wonder Ysrael's hero is a comic book character, Kaliman, of whom he thinks "If his face were covered he'd be perfect."[66] In the end, Ysrael may stand in as a figure for Dominican masculinity and perhaps even the Dominican Republic, for he has been ravaged by the pig (poverty, imperialism), colonized by the promise of American medicine, and is haunted by nightmares of the pig's attack, like Stephen Daedalus's "nightmare of history" in *Ulysses*.[67]

The boys engage Ysrael in a conversation in which Yunior clearly identifies with the deformed boy, pleased that both their fathers have immigrated to the United States. Rafa, on the other hand, is antagonistic. When Ysrael says that "the American doctors," will operate on his face, Rafa accuses him of lying. Rafa ends Yunior's friendly conversation with Ysrael by breaking a bottle over Ysrael's head, projecting his rage against the father onto Ysrael. Yunior initially identifies Ysrael as a better model of masculinity than both Rafa and his father. However, when the boys tear off Ysrael's mask to look at his damaged face, the fearful Yunior doesn't want to look anymore. Rafa, on the other hand, is drawn to examine Ysrael's ruined face very carefully "turn[ing] Ysrael's head from side to side."[68] As if to see himself in the mirror of the Other. The story brilliantly illuminates the melancholic macho's problem: the drive to resolve the problem of his rage leads to false, as it were masked, revelations. That is, by staring into Ysrael's unmasked face he may understand, as the story's readers do, that he too is damaged, but his violent behavior only sets him up for further traumatic losses.

Yunior appears to be more self-reflective and tender in his dealings with other people than the males that surround him. In their conversation on the way home, for example, Yunior expresses the hope that Ysrael will be "fix[ed]" by the American doctors in contrast to Rafa who is bitterly certain that "They aren't going to do shit to him."[69] But Yunior as a potential "new Latino male" is ultimately crippled by the seductions and pressures of machismo. Although he turns away from examining Ysrael's exposed face (psyche), Yunior acquiesces to the whole scheme and cannot prevent the violence done to the boy. Finally, Yunior's interest and friendliness toward Ysrael is a result, an imitation, if you will, of Rafa's fascination. Ultimately, Yunior admires Rafa more than anybody else. After all, Rafa is "handsome," something that Yunior concludes for himself.[70] Ysrael, on the other hand, is deemed by the other boys, and thus the larger social structure, to be "*ugly.*"[71] And Yunior always "followed" Rafa everywhere, admiring and yearning to be like his older brother.[72] Yunior too will grow up trying to reconcile the mask of machismo with the traits that machismo is ashamed of, denigrated as the "pussy" as Rafa calls Yunior when he cries.[73] Rafa deals melancholically with the loss of his father, obsessed with the deformities that reflect his own psychic incoherence: the imagined castration that marks a weeping manchild, and Ysrael's literal facelessness.

The doubling of a macho who expresses his feelings and a macho who prefers to "drown" rather than see himself is even more complex in the collection's title story "Drown" because of its homoerotic thematics. In this story the young narrator, a nameless drug-dealer, recounts episodes from his past friendship with Beto, who is now in college. The narrator ended the friendship because Beto is a "pato," gay.[74] We never see the narrator intimately involved with a woman in the course of the story, suggesting to the reader that the narrator may be gay and has difficulties face/ing it. His inability to acknowledge his sexuality parallels his inability to get on with his life.

Further, Díaz shows how the narrator's unacknowledged attraction to men and his love for Beto is a consequence of his enduring attachment to his mother; the narrator is a *mamao*. Past high school, he still lives with his mother, supporting them both by dealing drugs. The father, like the fathers in most of the stories in "Drown," absent or unfaithful scoundrels who mistreat their children, lives with another woman in Miami and occasionally calls the mother. Whenever the narrator catches the mother talking to the father he hangs up the phone, because, he says, the father's words "wreck [the mother's] sleep."[75] The mother is a creepy, silent figure who never protests the narrator's machista attitude. But if the mother is "wrecked" and zombie-like as a result of the father's abandonment, so is the son who reacts to the loss of the father by introjecting the lost object. But although this character may be filled with rage, like Rafa in "Ysrael," unlike Rafa his reaction is to stifle his rage to the point of paralysis. And, like Piri, he assumes the father's psychic role as his mother's lover. He and the mother watch T.V. together rather than talk, the son thus submerging himself in silence and repressed hostility:

She has prepared dinner—rice and beans, fried cheese, tostones. Look what I bought, she says, showing me two blue t-shirts. They were two for one so I bought you one. Try it on.

It fits tight but I don't mind. She cranks up the television. A movie dubbed into Spanish, a classic one that everyone knows. The actors throw themselves around, passionate, but their words are plain and deliberate . . .

We watch the movie and the two hours together makes us friendly. She puts her hand on mine . . . You can't be anywhere forever, was what Beto used to say, what he said to me the day I went to see him off. He handed me a gift, a book and after he was gone I threw it away . . .

I let her sleep until the end of the movie and when I wake her she shakes her head, grimacing. You better check those windows, she says. I promise her I will.[76]

By story's end the narrator has clearly chosen to be not Beto's but his mother's lover, which holding hands with her emphasizes. To be Beto's lover would entail both sexual self-awareness, and participation in the world that Beto has entered; college, the world of the "book" that the narrator throws away, a universe of mobility, learning, change, growth. The narrator rejects Beto's warning that "You can't be anywhere for ever" for the womb-like comfort of the apartment whose windows he will symbolically shutter by story's end, just as he has closed himself down.[77]

Spanish, too, becomes a symbol of stasis. At the beginning of the story the narrator recalls how Beto's "voice" had the power of "rousing my mother from the Spanish of her room and drawing me up from the basement."[78] Spanish, the mother's language and the language of a history the narrator does not or prefers not to remember, is identified with stasis and sleep, with drowning. Ultimately the narrator, choosing submersion in his mother's static world, becomes like her, just as he wears a shirt just like hers, constricting and tight, at story's end. Struggling against the feminized identity of *pato*, he has become both lover to and clone of his mother.

Beto's voice "that crackled and made you think of uncles or grandfathers" echoes the paternal origin.[79] Its booming manly sound simultaneously draws the narrator "up from the basement" and the mother from her bedroom, showing that both mother and son have projected the lost father figure(s)—not just the father but all the absent and shadowy "uncles" and "grandfathers"—onto Beto, in whom the narrator and his mother see the stereotype, the mask, of Latino masculinity. In this sense, Beto's function in the story combines aspects of those of Ysrael and Yunior in "Ysrael." Beto will not "drown" in the ghetto like the narrator but, like Yunior, he inevitably succumbs to the macho mask. Like Ysrael he becomes an ambiguous symbol of masculinity reflecting not so much the projection of the desires of others but the refractions of the narrator's ambivalent desire.

Beto's training in masked masculinity begins, predictably enough, with his own father. Throughout his youth Beto and his father had watched pornographic movies together in a silent camaraderie that recalls how the narrator and his mother watch television together: "neither of them would say a word, except to laugh when somebody caught it in the eye, or the face."[80] Pornography is a form of sex devoid of feeling that makes a fetish of the object of desire. It is not surprising that the macho would prefer fetishistic sex, because he is concerned above all with his mask. And, inasmuch as the macho mask is a stereotype of masculinity it is also a kind of fetish. The following quote from Bhabha allows me to compare the macho's preference for fetishistic sex with his fetishization of his own identity:

> The fetish or stereotype gives access to an "identity" which is predicated as much on mastery and pleasure as it is on anxiety or defence, for it is a form of multiple and contradictory belief in its recogniton of difference and disavowal of it.[81]

Fetishistic sex does not require that the macho drop his mask or "defence" to expose his anxiety. He need not feel or express emotion, including love, in the sexual relationship with the fetishized object of desire. Beto's father had modeled "mastery and pleasure" in showing Beto how to enjoy sex without emotion as they watched pornographic movies together while Beto's mother pretended not to notice by devoting herself to the kitchen. Just as the men repressed emotion, she repressed her rage. In Beto's family emotion is submerged in a parallel to the narrator's "drowning." Inasmuch, as every family member bolsters Beto's father's fetishistic behavior, they all wear masks—the hypersexual machos, the submissive housewifely Latina "taking hours to cook a pot of rice and gandules."[82] In the latter example it is particularly clear that, despite her emotional turmoil, the wearer feels locked into the masked response.

Beto's first seduction of the narrator is fetishistic in the same way and occurs while the two of them are watching a porn movie. It is an experience characterized by both fear (the narrator is "scared") and pleasure (the narrator "came right away").[83] The next time Beto performs fellatio on the narrator the experience is much less fetishistic. Beto asks if he should stop. The narrator—like the silent, passive–aggressive mothers in the story—"didn't respond."[84] Beto lays his head on the narrator's lap, the most tender gesture of affection in the story. The powerful effect of this experience also makes more complex the meaning of drowning, since the narrator describes his state after this sexual experience with Beto as "caught somewhere in between [sleeping and waking], rocked slowly back and forth the way surf hold junk against the shore, rolling it over and over."[85] Instead of drowning in the soporific Spanish television whisper laden silence of his mother's bedroom, the narrator could allow himself to fully enter the erotic/oneiric landscape Beto has opened up for him. But instead he ends up choosing his mother.

This is a choice that demonstrates the narrator's dilemma, his desire to assume the emotional emptiness of the macho mask worn by his and Beto's fathers, and his powerful impulse to refuse it. In the end the narrator gives up Beto because he is afraid of growth and knowledge, sexual and otherwise, afraid of leaving his mother. The narrator, however, is just as mistrustful of machismo, which is why he ends up identifying with his mother more than with his father. In defending the mother value, the narrator gives up the male that he desires. He does not have a lover, and he is not looking for one. Rather, he is as asexual as he is nameless by story's end, having ultimately sacrificed himself to preserve himself from the way of all (macho) flesh. What is left is a particularly frightening mask, more restrictive than Piri's *cara palo*, which at least admits of a fetishistic sexuality. By story's end the narrator turns into a nonentity.

Saints and Machos

The struggle of Latino men to reconcile with macho values is nowhere portrayed with more complexity, humor, and understanding than in Díaz's story,

"The Brief Wondrous Life of Oscar Wao," as an enticing preamble to the author's much awaited first novel.[86] This story is narrated by Yunior, the most important voice in *Drown*. Now he is an adult, telling a story about Oscar de León, his college roommate at Rutgers and clearly his double—which Yunior emphasizes by protesting their differences too much:

> You never met more opposite niggers in your life. He [Oscar] was a dork, totally into Dungeons and Dragons and comic books . . . I was into girls, weight lifting and Danocrine . . .[87]

They are different, but complementary. Yunior feels sufficiently involved in Oscar's fate to tell Oscar's story just as Nick Caraway told Jay Gatsby's. And, actually, there is a striking similarity between "The Brief Wondrous Life of Oscar Wao" and *The Great Gatsby*. Oscar and Gatsby are total idealists who die in the name of love for women who are beneath them, Yvón literally a prostitute and Daisy a lovely, wealthy girl with no spiritual and moral depth. Although Oscar is not glamorous for Yunior, as Gatsby is for Nick, Yunior ultimately admires the dead, heroic Oscar like Nick admired Gatsby. The momentum in the story comes from Oscar's relentless search for love and a girlfriend. Yunior is touched first by Oscar's romantic quest for a woman and then by Oscar's heroic behavior when he dies for love.

Oscar is to this story what Yunior was to "Ysrael," a sensitive person drawn to machista values but effectively, in Rafa's words, a "pussy." However, ultimately they choose different destinies. Yunior cannot resist the mask of machismo ("Fiesta, 1980") and is repeatedly unfaithful to his long-time girlfriend Lola, Oscar's sister. Oscar has, perhaps, less choice, influenced if not determined by his unattractive appearance, outward lack of confidence, and introversion. Oscar keeps himself sexually and spiritually "pure," remaining a virgin and never relinquishing his belief in love. When Oscar finds his long sought for love, he deems it worthy of the ultimate sacrifice—his life.

That Díaz sacrifices Oscar demonstrates that in his work thus far the macho always wins. Oscar is chivalrous, tender, and tenacious in the face of his family's opposition to his pursuit of Yvón. In the end Oscar's behavior looks like foolish idealism. The woman for whom he sacrifices himself s unworthy. She continues to work at the brothel/nightclub that she'd been working at before, despite having been the object of Oscar's potentially redeeming love.

One detail among many that make this story important is the attempted reversal of judgment and value at the story's end in Oscars words: "The beauty! The beauty!"[88] This recalls Kurtz's final words in *Heart of Darkness*: "The horror! The horror!" Kurtz's realizes the "darkness" in the hearts and psyches of Europeans and other whites who colonized Africa and other parts of the world. Kurtz projected his own darkness onto the Africans whom he mastered and brutalized. Finally naming what he did as "horror," Kurtz proves capable of a moment of self-understanding, a true epiphany.

How is Oscar de León like Kurtz? He returns to the Dominican Republic as the home of origin. It is not the white colonizer's usurpation of a land inhabited by people of another race and culture. Nonetheless, Oscar is returning to the "Native Land" as an Americanized Dominican.[89] As an American Oscar has a status on the island that he does not have in the United States, despite Yunior's hilarious assertion that Oscar "couldn't dance, he didn't have loot, he didn't dress, he wasn't confident, he wasn't handsome, he wasn't from Europe, he wasn't fucking no Island girl."[90] But Oscar is an "American citizen" as he tells the Capitán in their first time meeting, an identity that carries both positive and negative weight on the island. Yvón perceives Oscar to be an outsider. She calls him an "idiot Americano" when she is in a bad mood.[91]

An outsider in the Dominican Republic, Oscar is even more an outsider in the United States among U.S. Latinos. Yunior develops this aspect of Oscar's persona, showing how he fails with one U.S. Latina love object after another: his Dominican American childhood sweethearts; Ana Acuña, his Dominican American high school love interest; and the hilariously presented Catalyn Sangre de Toro Luperón, the vampirish Puerto Rican Goth, for whom Oscar falls in college. This last love interest is particularly illuminating, it is what makes Yunior start to respect Oscar. Yunior is also attracted to Catalyn. She rejects him outright, while she tolerates Oscar as a friend and confidant. Díaz makes clear that Oscar is the mirror image of Yunior as he once was, the "nerd" trying desperately to be a macho in "Fiesta 1980."

Both characters are sensitive, bookish. This is evident in Yunior's allusions to Fanon and postmodernism as well as the science fiction and comics Oscar and Yunior (by implication) love. They are both also boyish and immature, but Yunior has been successful at donning the mask with the help of weight training and acceptance by his "boys." Oscar simply can't figure out how to be street and hip. His sincerity enables him to forego the masks. This throws in relief how complex the figure of the New Latino Male is. Yunior, college-educated and drawn to girls like Oscar's sister, the enlightened Lola, still behaves like a macho, sleeping with woman after woman until Lola dumps him. Oscar, on the other hand, who criticizes Yunior's behavior— "You should never have had carnal relations with that Paraguayan girl" he tells Yunior at another one of the story's endlessly comical (and yet tender) moments—ends up dead when he tries to be sincere and transparent.[92]

Díaz's criticizes the origin, the Dominican Republic, as a place of danger, of "mind-boggling poverty" where Haitians are treated with an antediluvian racism and where the corrupt police harass people, and often murder them, as they did under Trujillo's reign of terror.[93] Yunior's observation that Oscar's murderer, the Capitán, is "one of those very bad men who not even postmodernism can explain away" is an interesting joke for the Capitan's evil nature is simple on the surface of it.[94] It is not that he so loves Yvón; it is that he simply doesn't want Oscar, his rival, to have her. The corrupt Dominican political system allows men like the Capitan to commit murder and evade justice. A postmodern critic might have trouble understanding the positioning of these two doubles—heroic Oscar and macho Yunior—in relation to the dangerous origin that kills Oscar, but does not harm Yunior. Yunior—college education notwithstanding—is the male in the story who behaves more like the island machos in his incapacity to be loyal to a woman, the way the Capitán will fuck but not marry Yvón. By dint of survival, Yunior, not the enlightened Oscar, represents the New Latino male. Oscar, in his homeliness, simplicity, and total naivete about macho values, can, yes, ultimately fuck an island girl (courtesy of his American status) but he cannot survive the island because he's not macho enough to beat down the Capitán. And he can't survive in New York Latino culture because those conservative island values (can't dance, has no loot) have been reinscribed in the United States. Ultimately, although this story questions machista values in the figure of Oscar, it shows that Oscar's route, respect for women, is viable only for saints, not "real" Latino males. The New Latino Male, Yunior, obsessed with the mask/façade of his Danocrine inflated body, seems to be headed for an identity crisis.

The intertextual relationship between "The Brief Wondrous Life of Oscar Wao" and Conrad's *Heart of Darkness* represents Ocar's problematic voyage back to the origin, but also suggests how *Heart of Darkness* reveals a White masculinist impulse to return to an originary mother in Africa, the space of a devouring maternality that cannot be grasped or comprehended because it does not really exist. The violence in "Oscar Wao" has a ritualistic feeling to it, as if the police are resorting to it in order to stay in control, artificially, of an origin (the public secret that is not a secret and does not actually exist) that must be mythified and controlled by violence for "order" to be maintained. This "order," though is really chaos, manipulated by the Capitán, and others like him, to stand in for order.

The prostitute Yvón represents for Oscar and the Capitán a fetish mother, a substitute for the origin, whose meaning must be circumscribed and contained. Of course, the story shows that the origin, as Antonio Benítez Rojo has observed about Caribbean identity, extends beyond the island's geographical borders and changes, despite the Capitán's attempts to ossify it into an anxiety-ridden possession.[95] That is why the violence is necessary, precisely because Latino machismo has the impossible project of trying to contain and retrieve something forever lost by attempting to close and suture the ruptured connection to the m/other. Moreover the origin kills Oscar (in a way that Africa may or may not kill Kurtz), but there is, I think, in both these stories a yearning to die, to be killed by the origin, to be swallowed up by the m/other, thereby allowing this fragmented, migrant Latino self to be made whole again.

Why does Oscar fall in love with a prostitute? Isn't the prostitute the ultimate wielder of the m/other mask? Do Oscar (and Kurtz) die because they make the wrong ontological decisions of trying to create a unity where there is none (with a prostitute on the one hand, and in mastery over an enslaved and brutalized people on the other)? Instead of letting themselves develop their freakish disjointedness, they force on themselves a mask of unity, ultimately a mask of death. They die not because they are outsiders, but because they are outsiders forcibly trying to recover an origin that they assume others have. Ahab does this as well in *Moby Dick*. Toni Morrison's Sula in *Sula*—of whom Morrison says that she is an artist without an art—is also a good example of this tendency. An alternative position for Oscar then is to be an author, an artist. He has been writing a gargantuan science fiction novel, which is left unfinished at his death. This is also a parable of what happens to those (e)strange(d) people who try to force themselves into society instead of expressing themselves through artistic forms. Ramón Yunior, Oscar's double, chooses writing over death.

Gender and The Street

Piri's fictionalized autobiography and Díaz's stories have in common the character of the emotionally unavailable Latino father who is frequently absent from home and, in the case of Yunior's father, is an inveterate womanizer. Because our literature is so allegorical, these two characters have many of the features of the stereotyped macho Latino male. However, Thomas and Díaz have not simply created stereotypes. Both these father figures become vivid and complex through exposing their interiority. Piri's father's complexity surfaces in the passage already discussed in which he confesses to Piri that he was ashamed of being black. Ramón de las Casa's interiority emerges in Díaz's novella "Negocios," the last piece in *Drown*. Yunior narrates this long story from his father's perspective, a technically sophisticated approach, which allows the reader access to the father's viewpoint but includes the son's effort to understand the father. Ramón Yunior stops trying to understand his father suddenly at the end of "Negocios" when he meets with the woman with whom Ramón Sr. had lived in the States. The absent father at this point has started a third family. This perspective partly vindicates the hated father figure. We witness Ramón's struggles firsthand through his point of view, as well as Yunior's, who also tells us what other characters say about his father. It allows Yunior to wear his father's mask, to enter his father's perspective, as he tells his father's story. Nonetheless, the Americanized protagonist reestablishes his own resentful perspective at the story's end, thereby silencing—and taking revenge against—the absent father.

Women characters do not generally fare well in street allegories written by men. We have seen how the women characters in *Down These Mean Streets* are doubles of the mother. Piri glorifies the mother figure as good and reclaims her as lover, as do most of the male protagonists of *Drown*, in which the only other female character of note is Aurora, the sexualized junkie who serves as a scapegoat for the drug-dealing narrator of that story. Although the mother characters in *Drown* do resemble the stereotyped passive, submissive Latina, they are a little different from the sweet-tempered mother of *Down These Mean Streets*. Their silence stems from depression and repressed rage. In this sense Díaz's silent mothers are potentially interesting, especially Yunior's, of whom we learn in "Aguantando" that she has suffered a nervous breakdown, after her husband abandons her and she retreats to a sanatorium. However, the persona of Yunior is incapable of doing for his mother in "Aguantando" what he does for his father in "Negocios": that is, take on the third-person point of view to sound the depths of the elusive character's interiority.

Among the male writers who have written street allegories, Abraham Rodriguez is the only one to show an interest in strong women characters who are also hip to the ways of the street.[96] To my mind, his most successful portrayal occurs in "No More War Games," in his book of short stories *The Boy Without a Flag*. The story is told in the third person through the perspective of the prepubescent Nilsa, who loves "warring" with rocks and glass bottles against some of the boys in her neighborhood in the empty lots and buildings of the South Bronx. But as puberty approaches, her best friend and sidekick in the war games opts for makeup and dating. The story is a rare and wonderful exploration of a young girl's conflicted feelings as she realizes she is going to have to abandon the street games she loves to capitulate to her own and other people's notions of femininity. This is a successful depiction of the interaction between street identity and gender concerns among urban Latinas.

Abraham Rodriguez takes greater risks, for questionable payoff, in his novel *The Buddha Book*. The story begins with the accidental murder of a teenage Puerto Rican girl who is the wife of a gang leader. She has abandoned a young neighborhood boy for the wealth and prestige of being a posse leader's girl. Lucy is a Latina "material girl" who constantly flaunts the diamond studded "tag" or bracelet that the gang leader gives her to mark her as his own. The male protagonist José kills her accidentally, buttressing my contention that Latina characters are often sacrificed in our fiction as a scapegoat for Latino culture's materialism and violence.

Another female character shows Rodriguez's enduring interest in gender and the street. Anita is a strip dancer and serial killer. Her fascination with Angel the gang leader suggests that she is an angry double for the murdered Lucy and is perhaps avenging the sacrifice of the dead girl. However, where "No More War Games" successfully probes the depths of its character's psyche, *The Buddha Book* does not offer a convincing portrait of Anita. We never understand this character's allegedly traumatized psyche and are left somewhat baffled by her desire to be the "first" Puerto Rican female serial killer. Anita says: "So everybody on the streets thought I was small, this victim. But it wasn't no mistake he drew the bullet . . . Was an execution . . . I have power. I make my own life."[97] While Rodriguez is trying to make a point about a woman's capacity to resist violence and victimization, Anita's words and actions do not add up to a serious portrayal of a psychically wounded woman. They create only the flat, vivid texture of comic book stories (with which the book's characters are obsessed). As well, Anita's idea that "power" derives from killing men for the sexual thrill and being celebrated as a serial killer is merely a disturbing imitation of phallocentric (and criminally warped) notions of power and agency.

The only novel thus far that offers a serious portrayal of Latinas on the street is Yxta Maya Murray's account of the rise of a *chola* gang leader in the East L.A. of the 1980s in *Locas* (1997).[98] Although this study focuses mainly on U.S. Latino/a Caribbean literature, *Locas*, written from a Chicana perspective, deploys in an exemplary way the traits of U.S. Latino/a allegory that I describe in chapter one.

Doubles are an important aspect of the literary methodology of *Locas*, as crucial to the workings of this book as they are to *Down These Mean Streets* and *Drown*. In *Locas* the doubling manifests in the split between the calculating, driven Lucía and her *chola* counterpart Cecilia, who is maternal and tender. Lucía, like Lady Macbeth, "unsexes" herself to become hard like the men in the gang she aspires to lead, to "work it hard for la number one," as she perceives they do.[99] At the book's climax, Lucía finally demonstrates her mettle when she orders that a rival ganglord's wounded baby brother be finished off by her *locos*. Both these female narrators are very close to Manny, the leader of the Lobos gang. Cecilia, Manny's little sister, has loved him fiercely since childhood, and Lucía starts off as Manny's girlfriend. Cecilia is Lucía's opposite: darkskinned, "Indian," short, self-hating, and candid in her narrative about her quest for love and affection. The *locos* consider Lucía to be beautiful because of her light skin and tall stature, but she makes power, not love, her external goal. Cecilia's fate is closely linked to Lucía's, underlined by the fact that the women have uncanny knowledge about each other. Lucía knows about Cecilia's relationship with Chucha when nobody else knows or cares; Cecilia brings Lucía the news of her mother's death, when nobody else knows or cares. Both women love Manny in different ways, and later both women are sexually involved with Beto who replaces Manny as jefe. Lucía goes as far as a woman can in the gangland world by being the gangleader's woman, controlling Manny's—and later Beto's—gang in a subversive way, and by having her own *clika*. Cecilia, who had also been drawn to the glamor of gangbanging, renounces the gangland because she understands that ultimately it is a destructive world.

For Thomas and Díaz the street allegory is the story of how a young male rejects his father's ways and usurps the father's place as the mother's protector, while simultaneously taking the street as substitute father. Murray's Lucía rejects the submissiveness and passivity of the "sheep"—the women whose function it is to "sex" the gang boys and make babies for them—in favor of macho behavior. Thus, Lucía is in the same category as Rodriguez's phallocentric serial killer character Anita, for both characters mimic male aggression and violent behavior. Lucía has convinced herself that it is her will to power over the gang that drives her: "I'm the only winner around here . . . See that street. That street's mine."[100] But over and over again, the melancholia that overcomes her, the "black water [that] closes up over me," as she puts it, reveals the price Lucía pays for maintaining a violent control over her own "Fire Girls" and Manny's gang.[101]

Like Piri, and Díaz's male characters, Lucía is driven to wear masks to get ahead and to hide her feelings. At first Lucía cleverly wears the mask of the good girl: "Said baby and smiled so my teeth showed."[102] Sex interests Lucia as the guise under which she can be secure as Manny's woman. In *Locas* the women telling the story don't like sex for its own sake. Rather, in *Locas* sexuality is always marked by the "dirty realism" I discuss earlier in the chapter. Lucía; her mother, who remains nameless; and Lucia's double, Cecilia all have sex with men to either survive on the street or because it is the very narrow gender role available to them as "sheep." Lucia's declaration that "sex is in a Mexican woman's blood" describes her subjectivity as a young "jalapeña," as she puts it, discovering the world through her first sexual relationship.[103] Once Lucía figures out that power over a group is what really rules her world, she resorts to sex rationally to acquire power. Similarly, Cecilia regards sex as a means to a quite different end, a child who will perhaps respond to her the way Manny never has.

Just as Piri and the nameless narrator of "Drown" seek to become their mothers's lovers, Cecilia is in love with her brother Manny. She fawns over him protectively, as if she wanted to be his mother, but the leader of the Lobos gang barely notices his plain, stolid little sister. After miscarrying her first child due to a beating by her lover, Cecilia never realizes her desired goal of motherhood. It is Lucía who, as *jefa*, wears the mother mask, "my mama smile," to rally both the gang girls and boys over whom she wields control.[104]

The mother figure, introjected as lost object, is at the basis of Lucía's ambivalence. Lucía, who sees "a little Manny in [herself]," a talent for wearing the gang leader mask, imitates her model faithfully, seeking to drastically sever herself from her mother, a prostitute and an unkempt drunk.[105] The only time Lucía visits her after moving in with Manny, she is humiliated and infuriated by her mother's drunken half-conscious state and dirty living conditions. Her reaction points to the multivalent meaning of the word "loca" in the text. On the one hand the term refers to the "vida loca" of gang life. As an adjective, it accentuates the bravado of the street thug.[106] The term most importantly refers to the rage, bordering on insanity, that

Lucía feels when she contemplates her mother's abjection:

> I'm getting this good *mad* feeling burning up low in my chest, a wildfire spreading that makes me wanna hit something, and that makes me strong. She's as good as dead and might as well be. (My italics)[107]

Murray's switch from the Spanish "loca" to the English "mad" when Lucía contemplates her mother's debased state points to the ways in which U.S. Latino/a street identity is a reform(ul)ation of psychic damage as to be a *loca* is to be "crazy," out of control, but to be "mad" as Lucía means it in the passage is to be both angry and "strong." Ultimately, we understand that the identity of "*loco*" is one way of resisting the madness of failed assimilation by channeling rage. Lucía rejects the deviant mother by both pronouncing her dead psychically and by refusing to be like her (a mother, a passive woman). If her mother was a *loca* in the sense of dysfunctionality and deviancy, Lucia takes on the guise of street *loca* to compensate for that lost identity.

Even though Lucía and the other *locos* and *locas* read Lucía's angry aggressiveness as strength, it is clear that her rejection of the mother figure devastates her. She is the character in the book most affected by and obsessed with parental absence. All the Americanized protagonists, Lucía, Manny, and Cecilia distance themselves from their parents—physically in the case of Lucía and emotionally in the case of Manny—because their parents are too old world and too powerless. Cecilia does seek out her mother's approval only to receive ambivalent treatment. The allegorical split is actually much sharper, clearer, and definitive in this text than in either Díaz or Thomas, both of whose protagonists revere their mothers and obsess over their emotionally inaccessible fathers. In *Locas*, all the fathers are long gone, barely remembered by the children, and mothers are barely tolerated. Manny offers his mother money from his arms sales, but when she realizes that it's tainted and remonstrates with him, he threatens to hit her. Cecilia, who knows Manny better than their mother, reads her brother as "sick of listening to what women were going to tell him . . . No patrón lets his mama tell him what to do."[108] What Cecilia does not say is that somewhere on the street, in the process of gangbanging, Manny has also lost any reverence, traditional or otherwise, for the mother. He has cut himself off from the past, a melancholic whose inner drama the text does not examine, who has introjected the father he never knew and the mother he despises.

Murray represents Lucía's melancholia as particularly hard to overcome because, unlike Manny and Cecilia, she had previously identified strongly with her mother. This is apparent in one of two defining moments for Lucía:

> Way back when I was a little niña and she ran me over the border she held onto me tight, so tight its hard to breathe . . . and when I looked up at her face in that dark night, she looked like the pretty moon, smiling down at me.[109]

The urgency of this moment, which contains elements of birth and death, is emphasized by the sudden switch from past to present tense. Lucía's feeling of suffocation at this moment of crossing subtly evokes how a child perceives the mother as capable of both sustenance and destruction, of omnipotence. But when the baby actually looks at her, her mother's smile is unequivocal. The moment replicates itself in Lucía's adult life through metonymic associations between its elements (the moon, the night time) and the jumping in rituals with her gang, as well as similar metonymic displacement of the mother's best physical and psychological traits onto certain gang girls, doubles for Lucía's mother, to whom she will feel lasting attachment since, like Stargirl, they remind her "of somebody," or like Turtle, of "something."[110] In particular, Stargirl's resemblance to the mother, as remembered in the moment of border crossing at night, is highlighted by her "linda face that sometimes . . . looks like the full moon."[111]

Later as an adult, Lucía experiences a similar moment of renewal when she "jumps in," or initiates, the girls in her *clika* or gang:

> "There, you mine now," I told them, and smiled wide . . . We sat there on that grass, all bloody and bruised and loving each other, my chest sore with that feeling. The sky was black and big above our heads, little pin-point stars thrown up there, . . . it was just us three feeling brand new.[112]

When Lucía feels at one with the world she reaches out (and as it were away from both the constrictions of the domestic space, and the violence of the street) to nature, the "stars" in this case, as she did in the originary passage about her mother, whom she identified with the moon. Here she makes clear that the curtailed violence of the jumping in, or initiation, ritual is for the dual purpose of bonding the girls into a gang and creating a family in which she can feel both free and beloved. Coming together as a group, the girls feel creative, as if they are remaking the world, making something "new."

There is also a passionate, homoerotic charge to the relationships with her favorite girls that stresses Lucía's yearning to recuperate the tender and open maternality for which her most significant double, Cecilia, actively yearns. "You mine, now" Lucía tells her girls after the jumping in, but her attempt at ownership, at controlling her Fire Girls in a way she could never control her mother, is doomed. If the gang is a way for these marginalized *cholas* to find the family that their dysfunctional backgrounds never gave them, then Lucía's gang is a failure. The violence of the gangland world destroys most possibilities for fulfilling relationships, as Stargirl's fate—paralyzed for life as the result of a gunshot wound—demonstrates. Because Lucía needs to control her gang by impressing them as all powerful, and because she wishes to avenge Stargirl whose feistiness and edgy streetwise beauty reminds Lucía of her mother as a young woman, she avenges the shooting that cripples Stargirl by finishing off the killing of a child who belongs to the gang that did the shooting. Lucía tells the crippled girl that she has avenged her mightily, but Stargirl points out that no revenge or violent act can give her back her healthy body and her life. Or her man, who has been murdered by the rival gang. Stargirl's lingering attachment to her dead man is an example of how impossible Lucía's goal is to transcend the heterosexist boundaries of the gangland world and make the girls "mine," as she dubs them by virtue of the jumping in.

When Stargirl rejects the *clika* despite Lucía's sacrificial action, Lucía's grieving response is telling: "I ain't gonna loca out for anybody no more. I killed that Llorona and buried her deep in the ground."[109] Lucía, experiences the loss of Stargirl as a second loss of the mother, always associating "loca[ing] out" with rage, love and an object (a woman) whose love she cannot control. Lucía tries to forget and psychically "bur[y]" the lost mother, and the second lost object that she associates with her mother, Stargirl, equating both lost figures with the Mexican "Llorona," the archetypal Mexican devouring mother, whom she then tries to repress.[114]

One of the Chicano variants of the *La Llorona* folk legend overlaps with the U.S. Latino literary tendency to allegorize the story of family origins as embedded in the history of conquest, rape, and betrayal. *La Llorona* was an Indian or Mestiza woman who refused all suitors until an arrogant ranchero of noble blood arrived in her town. She seduced him by pretending indifference until she won him over, but, eventually, the ranchero, an archetypal macho, lost interest in her and pursued other women, including women of his class. One day riding in a carriage with one of his new women, he saw his estranged wife walking with his children by the river. He spoke to the children affectionately, but ignored his wife who became so angry she hurled their children into the river. As the children were drowning, however, she repented and tried to save them, but failed. She then threw herself into the river. Later, the townspeople could hear *La Llorona* (the crying woman) wailing for her children by the river.

In her unique dialectical opus, *Borderlands/La Frontera* Gloria Anzaldúa suggests that the mother archetype has three aspects in Chicano/a culture: Guadalupe the virgin mother who has not abandoned her children; *La Chingada*, Doña Marina or Malintzin, better known as La Malinche, the seduced Indian mother and Cortés's translator reviled by Mexicans and Mexican Americans for having handed Mexico over to the Spanish conquerors; and *La Llorona*, "the mother who seeks her lost children," in many ways a combination of the other two maternal figures.[115] She adds that in seeking her children *La Llorona* is symbolically searching for the lost parts of herself.[116] This throws light on Lucía's situation in *Locas*. The Indian or mixed blood *La Llorona* responded to the (Spanish) landowner's betrayal by in turn betraying their children. This story refers to the national Mexican allegory embodied in the everyday curse "La Chingada" (literally "The Fucked One" or La Malinche) that refers the ills of Mexico to La Malinche's decision to let Cortés fuck her, and through her, Mexico and its history. The *La Llorona* character avenges the white man's betrayal by killing her children, a disturbing allegory of the way conquest and betrayal is internalized and passed on through generations. *La Llorona* killed a part of herself to both express and avenge the pain of abandonment, but her revenge destroyed the family. Then she returned to mourn her losses as a ghost. Like the character in the *La Llorona* story, Lucía needs to love and be loved, to own and feel owned, to feel whole and unified. Lucía seeks love from others, wearing the mama mask for the *locos* and *locas*; in other words, nurturing them.

The *La Llorona* figure that haunts Lucía results from the introjection of the mother as part of her split ego and her raging against it, "That old monster," the devouring mother.[117] Lucía is riven by contradictory impulses: the desire to assume the role of "a mama to all these locos;" in the gangland; and the denial of physical childbearing that underlines her rejection of her alcoholic mother's existence and that accompanies her donning of a street boy's clothes and her aggressive "manly" posture as a *loca*.[118] Hence "loca[ing] out," going crazy on the outside to combat the craziness within that Lucía calls her *La Llorona*.

This figure, this introjected mother, of course, is not precisely Lucía's mother. It is the part of Lucía's ego that attached to and rages against the mother as lost object, that later adds and rages agains Stargirl as lost object. The buried mother evokes for Lucía "hearing rancheras in my head and talking crazy in the mirror."[119] This image like so many others in *Locas*—the sexy "jalapeña," the drunken, abusive parents, the Mexican maid—both invokes stereotypes and reveals the power they exert in U.S. Latino/a culture. The ghostly *rancheras* evoke Lucía's Mexican parents who listened to wailing music as they fought, beat each other, and drank (to death in the case of Lucía's mother); whose rage was out of control. Lucía evinces a confusion that results from, as it were, becoming a bigger monster than the monster that haunts her. Talking crazy in the mirror is meant somehow to shake the fixity of that stereo-typed—but also very real—ghostly figure: "That old monster I usually stare down wicked and break to my own use comes back dark and windy, and the black water closes up over me."[120] She has reached a moment comparable to Piri's point of disso-lution wherein the *cara palo* mask breaks apart to unveil other masks and a fluidity of identity, the fragility of the fixed thug mask Piri thought could shield him, above all from himself. Although we know that Lucía utilized her masks more fluidly when she first became Manny's girl, as an adult she remains caught in the nightmarish situ-ation of letting herself be taken over by the "wicked" mask of the devouring mother, which ironically she assumes to fend off the monstrous *La Llorona* figure that haunts her, and that she disavows after the Stargirl debacle. To no avail, because it is the fate of this archetypal killing mother to keep returning until it is acknowledged. Lucía's mistake is one that Anzaldúa defines as the driving force behind the construction of negative Latina archetypes, from the Aztec deity Coatlicue to *La Llorona*. As arche-typal figures they project aspects of a composite fluid feminine identity. But they are stereotypes, fossilized negative feminine images. Although her mother was loving at a crucial phase in Lucía's life, Lucia ossifies her as a *La Llorona* figure. Even more grievously, Lucía has become largely overwhelmed by this introjected negative image of the maternal. Lucía recognizes only the petrified mask of the devouring mother, the bereft figure that she turns into by the end of *Locas*, too fearful in the face of her losses to recognize her own yearning behind the rigidity of this particular mask.

The fictions by Thomas, Díaz, and Murray show that U.S. Latino/a masking reflects racial and gender melancholia, aggressively (re)forming cultural archetypes and mainstream stereotypes to present a hardened façade (*cara palo*) that masters the street, hides pain, and finds double characters on which to project rage and other emotions. Representations of minorities on the street usually focus on the conflict between the criminals and the police, but these three writers shift their focus from that external drama to the internal dilemmas that give rise to it and that make working-class U.S. Latino/a subjectivities so richly complex. Almost forty years after Thomas published his fictionalized autobiography, Latinos and Latinas continue to explore the relationship between the street, as a reflection of the conflicted U.S. Latino/a psyche, and the mask as an ossification of the psyche's defensive posture. These allegorists of the street reveal how the pieces, objects, and persons introjected into the U.S. Latino/a street psyche appear, merge, fade, and reappear as the figures and faces of marginalized identities. Although the street mask may recede in favor of a mask that mimics assimilation, just as Piri's *cara palo* breaks apart so he can re/form. But Piñero, Piri, Lucía, and Díaz's narrators can never fully transcend their pain to be made "whole." These artists and philosophers of the street offer a valuable critique of theories that fetishize objects and selves as pieces that fit harmoniously into mythically "whole" identities. Their focus on the formation of urban, working-class, marginalized subjects highlights the injuries sustained by the street's denizens. But their work transforms the street into more than just a backdrop for the story of damaged minority identities. Rather, these writers reveal the Latino/a street as an American terrain of myriad creative possibilities—an allegorical territory like the American West and the Italian American gangland, its stories driven by the productive energies and intensities of ambivalence.

NOTES

Chapter One   Introduction: Toward a Typology of U.S. Latino/a Literature

1. The term, "U.S. Latino Caribbean literature," was coined by William Luis in his 1997 book, *Dance Between Two Cultures: Latino Caribbean Literature Written in the United States* to designate Cuban, Dominican, and Puerto Rican writing as a U.S. form of expression. This is the first work of literary criticism to attempt a comprehensive appraisal of this category of literature beyond the particular group—U.S. Cuban American, Dominican American, etc.—boundaries.

2. The typology applies, for example, to the murdered Guatemalan woman in the Guatemalan American writer Francisco Goldman's excellent novel *The Long Night of White Chickens*, as well as to *Locas* by the Chicana writer Yxta Maya Murray, which I address in chapter six: "The Allegorists of the Street," since it is the only street allegory written by a woman about women.

3. See Angus Fletcher, *Allegory: The Theory of a Symbolic Mode* (Ithaca and London: Cornell University Press, 1964) 195; and Robert Rogers, *A Psychoanalytic Study of the Double in Literature* (Detroit: Wayne State University Press, 1970) 16.

4. See Lisa Sánchez González's discussion of *Cantando bajito*, *The Line of the Sun*, and *When I Was Puerto Rican* in which she calls them "failed allegories." Lisa Sánchez González, "I Like to Be in America" [sic] in *Boricua Literature: A Literary History of the Puerto Rican Diaspora* (New York and London: New York University Press, 2001) 134–160.

5. See Marta Caminero-Santangelo, *The Madwoman Can't Speak: Or Why Insanity is not Subversive* (Ithaca and London: Cornell University Press, 1998).

6. In chapter five of her book, "Murdering Mothers in Morrison, García and Viramontes," Caminero-Santangelo uses texts written by women of color to further develop her argument. The "madwoman figure of the murdering mother," she says, "preempts not just individual subjectivity but the building of collective resistance as well." Caminero-Santangelo, *The Madwoman*, 179.

7. Asunción Horno-Delgado, Eliana Ortega, Nina M. Scott, Nancy Saporta Sternbach, eds., *Breaking Boundaries: Latina Writing and Critical Readings* (Amherst: The University of Massachusetts Press, 1989) 3.

8. Gayatry Chakravorty Spivak, *A Critique of Postcolonial Reason* (Cambridge, Ma. and London: Harvard University Press, 1999) 118. In her revisiting of the Caribbean/Latin American Caliban/Ariel disjunction, Spivak points out the danger run by intellectuals or educated "natives" who presumptuously take on the Caliban mask: "If, however, we are driven by a nostalgia for lost origins, we too run the risk of effacing the "native" and stepping forth as 'the real Caliban.' . . . The stagings of Caliban work alongside the narrativization of history: claiming to be Caliban legitimizes the very individualism that we must persistently attempt to undermine from within."

9. For most of the time I was writing this book, I focused on writers with "origins" in the Spanish Caribbean. However, once I started to write about "street allegory" in the work of

Junot Díaz and Piri Thomas, I had to also take into account the Chicana Yxta Maya Murray's *Locas* since it is the only street novel written by a woman. I included Murray in this project, ultimately, to drive home the point that the temporal, allegorical divide (manifested in the literary works) has turned U.S. Latinos into (ambivalent) Americans. And the inclusion of Murray need not detract from the emphasis here on the Spanish Caribbean as origin. For discussions of divergence from the origin, also see Juan Flores, *From Bomba to Hip Hop* (New York: Columbia University Press, 2000) and Lisa Sánchez González, *Boricua Literature* (New York: New York University Press, 2001). In informal conversation with me about U.S. Latino/a literature, Silvio Torres-Saillant (*Caribbean Poetics* [Oxford University Press, 1997]) has observed that most U.S. Latino/a writers come from an English language formation.

10. Ana Lydia Vega, "Pollito Chicken" from *Vírgenes y mártires*, a collection of stories by Vega and Carmen Lugo Filippi (Río Piedras: Editorial Antillana, 1988). Nicholasa Mohr, "Puerto Rican Writers in the U.S., Puerto Rican Writers in Puerto Rico: A Separation beyond Language (*testimonio*)" in *asunción* et al., *Breaking Boundaries* (1989).

11. The Nuyorican Tato Laviera's memorable reinscription of "En Mi Viejo San Juan" (considered a classic Latin American song text) in the poem "Migración," for example, is one of the best examples of the flexibility and imaginative potential of Spanglish or bilingual poetry. See "Migración" in *Mainstream Ethics/Ética Corriente* (Arte Público Press, 1988).

12. The Guatemalan American writer Francisco Goldman is also another notable artist who works at artfully reproducing the rhythms of Spanish in English in novels such as *The Long Night of White Chickens* and *The Ordinary Seaman*.

13. Edward Rivera, *Family Installments* (London, New York: Penguin, 1983) 17.

14. Díaz paid homage to Rivera and Thomas during a public lecture at The City College of New York in 1999, and in a visit to my U.S. Latino/a Literature class at The Center for Worker Education in 2001. During the latter visit, Edward Rivera was present—unbeknownst at first to Díaz—and the two met for the first time, much to their mutual delight.

15. From the entry for "Allegory" in Alex Preminger and T.V.F. Brogan, eds., *The New Princeton Encyclopedia of Poetry and Poetics* (Princeton: Princeton University Press, 1993) 31.

16. The Romantic poets preferred the symbol to allegory. "This appeal to the infinity of a totality constitutes the main attraction of the symbol as opposed to allegory, a sign that refers to one specific meaning and thus exhausts its suggestive potentialities once it has been deciphered. Paul de Man, "The Rhetoric of Temporality," *Blindness and Insight: Essays in the Rhetoric of Contemporary Criticism* (Minneapolis: University of Minnesota Press, 1983) 188.

17. In "Pascal's Allegory of Persuasion" de Man explains allegory's "lopsided, referentially indirect mode" as the result of the unknowability of the target toward which signs direct themselves. "Pascal's Allegory of Persuasion," in Stephen Greenblatt, ed., *Allegory and Representation* (Baltimore and London: The Johns Hopkins University Press, 1981) 1. de Man values allegory over the symbol. Unlike the symbol, allegory "prevents the self from an illusory identification with the nonself, which is now fully, though painfully, recognized as a non-self." "The Rhetoric of Temporality," 207.

18. Fanon goes on to describe allegory as an inferior kind of literary production, which marks the native writer's ruptured relationship with his people: "But since the native is not a part of his people, since he only has exterior relations with his people, he is content to recall their life only." Frantz Fanon, *The Wretched of the Earth* (New York: Grove Press, 1968) 220–223.

19. Homi K. Bhabha, *The Location of Culture* (London: Routledge, 1994) 86. Before Bhabha, the most famous proponent of mimicry was the Trinidadian writer V.S. Naipaul who, in two novels in particular, *A House for Mr. Biswas* (1961) and *The Mimic Men* (1967), used

the term to refer to the marginality and relative inferiority of Third World artistic production in relation to metropolitan production. This is one of the reasons that Naipaul is
such a controversial writer and why Bhabha's reevaluation of mimicry has gained such
currency.

20. de Man, "The Rhetoric of Temporality," 207.
21. Walter Benjamin, *The Origin of German Tragic Drama* (London, N.Y.: Verso, 1998) 176.
22. Ibid., 183–184.
23. Jenny Sharpe, *Allegories of Empire: The Figure of Woman in the Colonial Text* (Minneapolis,
London: University of Minnesota Press, 1993) 14.
24. *Benjamin, German Tragic Drama,* 12.
25. See Ahmad, Aijaz. "Jameson's Rhetoric of Otherness and the 'National Allegory.'" *Social
Text* 17 (1987): 3–25.
26. Frederic Jameson, "Third-World Literature in the Era of Multinational Capital," *Social
Text #15* (Fall 1986) 69.
27. Ibid.
28. Patrick McGee, "Texts Between Worlds: African Fiction as Political Allegory," in Karen
Lawrence, ed., *Decolonizing Tradition: New Views of Twentieth-Century "British" Literary
Canons* (Urbana and Chicago: University of Illinois Press, 1992) 241.
29. Carpentier, *The Kingdom,* 86.
30. Jose David Saldívar reinscribed Carpentier's argument in *The Dialectics of Our America*
(Duke 1991) stretching the idea to cover U.S. minority writing. Stating that Latin
American magical realism's expression of the extreme disjunction between worldviews has
strongly influenced the younger field of U.S. minority literature, Saldívar makes the long-
awaited argument that there are several points of linkage among the literatures of the
disenfranchised of the Americas.
31. Carpentier, *The Kingdom,* 88.
32. Carpentier's mother, however, was a European—a Russian—immigrant to Cuba just like
his father. The identification, as Benítez Rojo argues, took place along the lines of a binary
where the law of the Father/realm of the Mother were identified with Reason and Music
respectively. Antonio Benítez Rojo, "Alejo Carpentier: Between Here and Over There,"
Caribbean Studies, Vol. 27, 3–4 (1994): 183–195.
33. Carpentier, *The Kingdom,* 83.
34. Ibid., 87.
35. Richard Slotkin, *Regeneration Through Violence: The Mythology of the American Frontier,
1600–1860* (New York: HarperPerennial, 1996) 16. Slotkin makes the following observation, and then quotes from Bernal Díaz del Castillo's *Conquest of New Spain,* p. 413:
"The accounts of the conquest of Mexico written by Cortés, Gómara, and Díaz del
Castillo . . . reflect the strong influence of secular chivalric romances." Díaz's Indians, view-
ing the ruins of Mexico City, speak 'in much the same way we would say: '*Here stood Troy.*'"
36. Among others: Fletcher, 222; and Abdul R. JanMohamed, "The Economy of Manichean
Allegory: The Function of Racial Difference in Colonialist Literature" in Henry Louis
Gates, Jr., ed., *Race, Writing and Difference* (Chicago: University of Chicago Press, 1985)
78–106.
37. Fletcher, *Allegory,* 182, 185, 187.
38. Fletcher contends that "the criterion of realism is wasted on the theory of allegory"
because allegories are replete with naturalistic, realistic detail, but such detail tends to be
"cosmic, universalizing, not accidental." Fletcher, *Allegory,* 198–199.
39. In a highly instructive essay on ghosts in Latin American and U.S. texts, Lois Parkinson
Zamora distinguishes the major characteristic of both Latin American magical realism
and what she calls American romance as a universalist, transcendent (archetypalizing)
impulse. Although Parkinson Zamora admits that "archetypes often encode dominant
cultural stereotypes, rather than contest them," (504) she stresses that this kind of
universalizing makes these texts political, counterhegemonic, resistant to "the abuses of

individualism" (504). (Parkinson Zamora also notes that Borges's creation of universalizing tales in the 1920s, 1930s, 1940s, was a political act because it meant opposing the
then-dominant Argentine mode of literary realism, *costumbrismo*, or the naturalist depiction of everday customs.) I cite Parkinson Zamora to underline my point that both Latin
American magical realism and the realism of U.S. Latino/a texts have their roots in allegory. Lois Parkinson Zamora, "Magical Romance/Magical Realism: Ghosts in U.S. and
Latin American Fiction," in Lois Parkinson Zamora and Wendy B. Faris, eds., *Magical
Realism: Theory, History and Community* (Durham and London: Duke University Press,
1995) 504.
40. Junot Díaz, *Drown* (New York: Riverhead Books, 1996) 28.
41. Miguel Piñero, *La Bodega Sold Dreams* (Houston, Texas: Artc Publico Press, 1985) 8.

Chapter Two: When Papi Killed Mami: Allegory's Magical Fragments in Cristina García's *The Agüero Sisters*

1. From a phone conversation with Cristina García at her California residence (May 1999).
   Walter Benjamin, *The Origin of German Tragic Drama*, trans. John Osborne (London:
   New Left Books, 1977) 181.
2. Cristina García, *Dreaming in Cuban* (New York: Ballantine Books, 1992) 235–236.
3. Sandra Gilbert and Susan Gubar, *The Madwoman in the Attic: The Woman Writer and
   the Nineteenth Century Literary Imagination* (New Haven: Yale University Press,
   1979) 444.
4. This does not represent the critical response to the book when it was first published.
   See Ilan Stavans, "Swooning in Cuban," *The Nation* Vol. 264, 19 (1997). Stavan feels *The
   Agüero Sisters* fails because it is a melodramatic reprise of *Dreaming in Cuban*.
5. Joel Fineman, "The Structure of Allegorical Desire," in Stephen Greenblatt, ed., *Allegory
   and Representation* 32.
6. Constancia's obsession with the quest that leads to the manuscript fits a category that
   Fletcher describes as "daemonic agency," which "implies a *manie de perfection*, an impossible desire to become one with an image of unchanging purity." Fletcher, *Allegory*, 65.
   Both Constancia in her present-day investigation of the past, and her generally suspicious
   "research" of events (such as, for example, following her husband Heberto because she
   suspects him of clandestine acts). Fletcher says is typical of allegorical protagonists. In this
   sense, Ignacio Agüero is also a typical allegorical hero because he is obsessed, to the death
   so to speak, with his wife.
7. Cristina García, *The Agüero Sisters* (New York: Alfred A. Knopf, 1997) 105. All the ensuing Cristina García citations refer to *The Agüero Sisters*.
8. Fletcher speaks of the "principal of magical contagion" as controlling the way allegorical
   characters act, "infecting each other with various virtues or vices." *Allegory: The Theory of
   a Symbolic Mode* (Ithaca and London: Cornell University Press, 1964) 207.
9. In reference to Spenser's *The Faerie Queene*, Fletcher comments: "From being a person
   with a vague mixture of good and bad in his character, Sir Guyon is divided into partials
   of himself, and against each evil he has to fight the identical war. Spenser's favorite
   way of getting the doubling effect, however, is to play on man's illusion that he has a
   well-defined, unified ego." Fletcher, *Allegory*, 207.
10. Fletcher, *Allegory*, 207.
11. García, *Sisters*, 44.
12. Ibid.
13. Ibid., 126–127.
14. Ibid., 125.
15. To be specific, Blanca's mother was a mulatta. From Ignacio Agüero's buried manuscript:
    "*Later, I learned from Damaso Mestre, the youngest of [Blanca's] brothers, that their mother*

was a mulatta descended, in part, from French colonists who'd fled Haiti after the slave revolt of 1791." (187). García has chosen to italicize Ignacio's narration in order to differentiate it from the focalized narratives in present tense in the rest of the text.

16. Fletcher, *Allegory*, 195.
17. Actually, Blanca is technically a quadroon because her mother is a mulatta.
18. Constancia who was rejected by her mother at birth always hated her mother as a child and loved her father obsessively. Reina, a tall, sensual Amazonic beauty who favors the unknown mulatto who steals Blanca away from Ignacio, is sensual in a way that the text seems to identify, rather archetypally, with the Mother's qualities.
19. Fineman, "Allegorical Desire," 33. Fineman's reference to allegory as the "courtly figure" comes from George Puttenham's *The Arte of English Poesie* (1589), facsimile reproduction (Kent, Ohio: Kent State University Press, 1970) 196. Quoted in Fineman.
20. Fineman, "Allegorical Desire," 196.
21. García, *Sisters*, 4.
22. "This dual theory of the sign," says Foucault, "is in unequivocal opposition to the more complex organization of the Renaissance; at that time, the theory of the sign implied three quite distinct elements: that which was marked, that which did the marking, and that which made it possible to see in the first the mark of the second . . . It is this unitary and triple system that disappears . . . and is replaced by a strictly binary organization." Michel Foucault, *The Order of Things: An Archaeology of the Human Sciences* (New York: Vintage Books, 1994) 64.
23. The beginning of Ignacio Agüero's manuscript cites the fact that he was born the same day that Cuba's first president of the Republic, Estrada Palma, visited his province, Pinar del Río. However, he asserts that the Platt Amendment "which permitted Americans to interfere in the country from the day it was born" was still in effect that year, 1904. So Ignacio is born into a contradictory situation, a "free" Cuba with the United States keeping quasi-colonial rule. García, *Sisters*, 28.
24. Ibid., 114.
25. Ibid., 119–120.
26. Fené, *SDD*, 24.
27. Ibid., 116.
28. Ibid.
29. Tim Cahill describes this process at length in his insightful, disturbing study of the serial killer, John Wayne Gacy, who could not remember most of the thirty-odd murders he had committed. Tim Cahill and Russ Ewing, *Buried Dreams* (New York: Bantam Doubleday Dell, 1986).
30. García, *Sisters*, 134.
31. Ibid., 99.
32. Ibid., 183.
33. I am following Gilbert's and Gubar's reading of *Wuthering Heights*' Catherine and Heathcliff as male/female doubles in *The Madwoman in the Attic*, 275, 293.
34. In the same phone conversation cited at the beginning of these endnotes the author stated that she tried to make Santería work on "another level" in *The Agüero Sisters*. García said she did not grow up within the religion and knew much less about it when she wrote *Dreaming in Cuban* than she did when she worked on the second book.
35. García, *Sisters*, 110.
36. Giral depicts a Maria Antonia who sins against Santería and who is rejected by its patriarch, *the babalawo*, when her *madrina* tries to have her taken back after numerous transgressions. Because she is interpellated so harshly by the *babalawo*, Maria Antonia responds with even more outlandish behavior such as resorting to spells of witchcraft in order to prevent her lover from leaving her and, eventually, murdering her lover.
37. This I've gleaned from attending Santería ceremonies in Villa Palmeras, Puerto Rico, as well as from conversations with Santero Remedios Herrerra and Afro-Cuban Religions Scholar Ivor Miller.

38. However, she did precisely this in *Dreaming in Cuban* in which her descriptions of Santería ceremonies are replete with folklorically accurate details.
39. García, *Sisters*, 111.
40. *The Origin of German Tragic Drama*, 175.
41. Patrick McGee, "Texts Between Worlds," in Karen Lawrence, ed., *Decolonizing Tradition* (Urbana and Chicago: University of Illinois Press, 1992) 239–260.
42. Jenny Sharpe, *Allegories of Empire: The Figure of Woman in the Colonial Text* (Minneapolis, London: University of Minnesota Press, 1993) 13.
43. García, *Sisters*, 223.
44. The legends of Santería.
45. From Genesis 3:14: "And I will put enmity between thee and the woman, and between thy seed and her seed; it shall bruise they head, and thou shalt bruise his heel." Let us say there's a metonymic relationship between Eve's heel and the heels of her daughters.
46. García, *Sisters*, 227.
47. Ibid., 265.
48. Ibid., 261.
49. Ibid., 262.
50. Ibid.
51. Ibid.
52. My own experience in observing Santería initiation ceremonies or *tambores*.
53. Saldívar quotes from Immanuel Wallerstein's book, *The Modern World System*, II, 1980. José David Saldívar, *The Dialectics of Our America: Genealogy, Cultural Critique, and Literary History* (Durham and London: Duke University Press, 1991) xi.
54. Although this is Saldívar's contention, he only reads one work of U.S. minority writing as magical realist: African American writer Ntozake Shange's *Sassafras, Cypress and Indigo*. Saldívar 87–104.
55. Saldívar, *Dialectics*, 89.
56. Ibid., 90–96.
57. Alejo Carpentier, "On the Marvellous Real in America," in Lois Parkinson Zamora and Wendy B. Faris, eds., *Magical Realism: Theory, History, Community* (Durham and London: Duke University Press, 1995) 75–88.
58. Carpentier, "Marvellous Real," 86.
59. García, *Sisters*, 104–105.
60. Ibid., 25.
61. Carpentier, "Marvellous Real," 75–88.

Chapter Three: Killing "Spanish": Rosario Ferré's Evolution
from *autora puertorriqueña* to U.S. Latina Writer

1. Some notable commentators are: Juan Gelpí, Frances Aparicio (both cited here), and Jean Franco, Lorraine Elena Roses, Debra Castillo, and Sandra Cypess.
2. If length is one of the features of the novel, *The House on the Lagoon* is not just Ferré's first novel in English but her first novel in either English or Spanish. *The House on the Lagoon* is 407 pages long, whereas *Sweet Diamond Dust*, at 79 pages, seems to hover in the gray genre boundary between novel and novella. Ferré's most novel-like book in Spanish is *La batalla de las vírgenes* at 121 pages.
3. For a magisterial discussion of the link between a nationalist agenda and paternalist rhetoric in Puerto Rican literature see Juan G. Gelpí's *Literatura y paternalismo en Puerto Rico*, Editorial de la Universidad de Puerto Rico, 1993.
4. A book on Julio Cortazar's short stories, one on the lesser-known Uruguayan writer Felisberto Hernandez's fiction and *Sitio a eros* (1980), on writers as diverse as the famous Puerto Rican poetess Julia de Burgos and the American Lillian Hellman, as well as the

British patroness of feminism and modernism, Virginia Woolf. Ferré pointed out in her preface to *Sitio a eros* that she had written an easily accessible book of criticism "without one footnote" that was written not for academics but for her then seventeen-year-old daughter, and young women like her daughter. Despite her father's political notoriety, in her early career as a writer, Ferré openly advocated independence for the island.

5. In "The Blessing of Being Ambidextrous," an article Ferré wrote for *The San Juan Star* (January 12, 1997), the author emphasizes the importance of writing over translation in her approach to turning *The House on the Lagoon* over to a Spanish readership: ". . . I wrote the novel in Spanish a few months later [so that it] . . . would soon be published in Spain and later the United States."

6. Her role as one of the principal editors of the radical Puerto Rican literary journal, *Zona de carga y descarga*, from 1972 to 1975, is also significant in this context. See Gelpí, *Literatura*, 171.

7. For one of the most virulent critical attacks on Ferré's oeuvre in English see Juan López Bauzá, "Rosario Ferré: el debate del idioma, los escritores de ayer y hoy" (*Palique*, February 19, 1999). López Bauzá is an emerging fiction writer in Puerto Rico.

8. Gelpí, *Literatura*, 121.

9. Rene Marqués is a famous Puerto Rican playwright, novelist, and critic, a patriarch of Puerto Rican letters. His two most important works are *Los soles truncos*, a play about the three daughters of a ruined plantation owner, the ruin having set in with the American invasion of Puerto Rico; *La carreta*, a play about a poor family that emigrates from the starving countryside to the city and later to New York. His work tends to nostalgize the plantation past and identify the fate of Puerto Ricans who left the island for New York as filled with poverty, humiliation, and loss of identity.

10. Frances Aparicio, *Listening to Salsa: Gender, Latin Popular Music, and Puerto Rican Cultures* (Hanover and London: Wesleyan University Press [University Press of New England, 1998] 50.

11. Ibid., 56. Aparicio cites Rafael Falcón noting that "the struggle" of black Puerto Ricans has not yet been adequately represented in Puerto Rican literature in Spanish. See Aparicio's footnote regarding Falcón: ibid., 257. And see Rafael Falcón, "El tema del negro en el cuento puertorriqueño," *Cuadernos hispanoamericanos: Revista mensual de cultura hispánica* 451–452 (January–February 1988): 97–109.

12. Double mediation intensifies the mimetic triangle; it is the result of the contagion of desire and the breakdown of hierarchy. René Girard, *Deceit, Desire and the Novel* (Baltimore and London: The Johns Hopkins University Press, 1965) 101.

13. González's *Puerto Rico: el país de cuatro pisos* was not published in English until 1993.

14. "It is also well known, because it has been documented, that the composition of the Spanish group was exceptionally unstable throughout the first two centuries of colonial life. For example, it is worth remembering that in 1534 the governor of the colony gave an account of his efforts to stop the Spanish population's mass exodus to the mainland in search of riches. The island, he wrote, was "so 'depopulated that one sees hardly any people of Spanish descent, but only Negroes.'" From José Luis González *Puerto Rico: The Four-Storeyed Country and Other Essays*, trans. Gerald Guinness (Princeton and New York: Markus Wiener Publishing, 1993) 10.

15. The only "original" Caribbean Indian population intact are the Caribs who inhabit the center of the island of Dominica, in the eastern Caribbean. González also makes the argument that the few surviving Taíno Indians tended to mix with Africans, so that black culture on the island subsumed the remnants left of Indian culture. Ibid., 9.

16. Ibid., 12.

17. Ibid.

18. The irony of claims to aristocracy on the island escapes neither Ferré nor González, whose insightful argument rests on a description of the alienation felt by the black, white, and mulatto a description of peasantry when confronted with the behavior of the mid-nineteenth-century European immigrants.

19. Gelpí claims that the voices that critique patriarchy reach a climax of multivocality in *Maldito amor* (*Sweet Diamond Dust*): "That narrative practice, initiated in *Papeles de Pandora*, continues in her later work. In *Maldito amor*, Ferré takes heteroglossia to its extreme: the enunciation of the different voices that complement and contradict each other undermines any possibility of a totalizing impulse at the level of the narrative voice. Therefore, the paternalist logos is abandoned. The crisis of the canonical metaphor is inscribed in *Maldito amor*, just as it was in the stories in *Papeles de Pandora*; the text concludes with the burning of the house by a marginal character, the mulatto nurse Gloria Camprubí. Her voice closes the text and unmasks the patriarchal discourse of the other narrative voices." (My translation); Gelpí, *Literatura*, 170–171.

20. Except Titina, the "timeless" old black servant whose voice is heard for only two pages as compared to the four allowed Gloria's account.

21. Rosario Ferré, *Sweet Diamond Dust* (New York: Plume, 1996) 3–4. Published in Spanish as *Maldito amor* by Editorial Joaquin Mortiz, S.A. de C.V., Mexico, 1986. Hereafter given as *SDD*.

22. Ferré, *SDD*, 24.

23. Ferré, *SDD*, 24.

24. James Clifford quotes Johannes Fabian to articulate this idea. See "On Ethnographic Allegory." James Clifford and George Marcus, eds., *Writing Culture: The Poetics and Politics of Ethnography* (University of California Press, 1986).

26. Ferré, *SDD*, vi:

Pearl the sea tears from its shell
as its pleasing waves hasten home
heron sleeping in the white foam
of the whiter waist of your shores. (My translation of the original as quoted in the novel)

27. Gelpí, *Literatura*, 89.

28. Ferré, *SDD*, 76.

29. Ibid., 49.

30. I say "strangely" because Ferré's short works in Spanish, especially *Maldito amor* (*SDD*), have always been read as subverting the patriarchal totalizing of writers such as Pedreira and Marqués. Yet Gloria's tone is also strangely reminiscent of the nostalgic, histrionic tones of Emilia in *Los soles truncos*.

31. Ferré, *SDD*, 81–82.

32. Ibid., 84.

33. Ibid., 86.

34. Ibid., 84.

35. Rosario Ferré, "Writing in Between," *Hopscotch: A Cultural Review*, Preview issue (Duke University Press, 1998) 49.

36. Rosario Ferré, "The Blessings of Being Ambidextrous," *The San Juan Star* (1998) 9.

37. Note the identical terminology used in both Ferré's article and in the passage from Cristina García's first novel, which I briefly examine in chapter one, wherein Pilar starts "dreaming in Spanish" upon the return to Cuba at the end of *Dreaming in Cuban*.

38. For a similarly controversial designation of English as a "public" language and Spanish as pertaining to the domestic sphere, see Richard Rodriguez's *Hunger of Memory: The Educationa of Richard Rodriguez*.

39. "The Blessings of Bein Ambidextrous," 9.

40. *The New York Times*, March 19, 1998.

41. Rosario Ferré, *The House on the Lagoon* (New York: Plume, 1996) 235.

42. This is also the title of an essay deconstructing González's argument published by the New York Puerto Rican critic and scholar Juan Flores in *Divided Borders*.

43. Ferré, *The House on the Lagoon*, 249.
44. Gaston Bachelard, *The Poetics of Space*, trans. Maria Jolas (Boston: Beacon Press, 1964) 17.
45. "A house is imagined as a vertical being. It rises upward. It differentiates itself in terms of its verticality. It is one of the appeals to our consciousness of verticality. A house is imagined as a concentrated being. It appeals to our consciousness of centrality." Bachelard, *Poetics of Space*, 17.
46. Ibid.
47. Ibid., 18.
48. Ibid., 23.
49. That is, the Don Julio Font that Don Hermenegildo constructs as the white, Spanish husband of Doña Elvira. However, in *SDD* we come to understand that Don Julio was a mulatto. Buenaventura and Don Julio Font both have striking blue eyes and black hair.
50. Ferré, *The House on the Lagoon*, 258.
51. Maya Deren, *Divine Horsemen* (New York: McPherson and Company, 1953, 1970) 34–37. The Voudoun deity, Legba, is the same as the Santería orisha Eleguá or Elegguá.
52. The narrative telling how Petra arrives from the countryside at the house on the lagoon supports this. Petra heals the original Spanish patriarch, Buenaventura's, swollen ankle. He brings her to the house because he believes she has unusual powers of healing. The obvious sexual link between white masters and black female slaves is absent in Buenaventura's attachment to Petra, which Ferré seems to want to construct as a relationship of equals (Petra's otherworldly power is equal to Buenaventura's capacity to accumulate worldly riches, and in fact even helps it along). But this sexual link will surface later, almost like an atavism, in Quintín's (Buenaventura's son's) rape of Carmelina, Petra's great-granddaughter. This rape definitively unites Petra's and Buenaventura's bloodlines.
53. Ferré, *The House on the Lagoon*, 236.
54. Carmelina, Petra's daughter, and the namesake for the granddaughter who gets raped by Quintín to produce Willie, the very light-skinned mulatto child Isabel raises as her son, is as stereotypical a black character as Petra. This is Petra explaining the cause of Carmelina's death: "Next to our house in Guayama there was a royal palm tree, and right after Carmelina was born a bolt of lightning struck it. The fire ran down the tree trunk and jumped into our house through the window; it missed Carmelina's crib by inches. But the spirit of the god of fire entered her body, anyway. Except, instead of in her heart, it lodged in the wrong place: her pussy. When she grew up, every time Carmelina crossed her legs, men were struck by lightning and fell in love with her. Many of them had been friends before they met her, but once they saw her they burned with desire and jealousy, and finally one of them killed her to eliminate the problem." *The House on the Lagoon*, 243.
55. The Macheteros and the FALN—in the news often in 1999 because of President Clinton's offer of clemency—are the possible models for AK-47. But these terrorist groups conducted their activities mostly in the United States and not on the island itself (outside of the heyday of the nationalist uprisings led by Pedro Albizu Campos in the 1930s).
56. Gelpí notes that this is the quintessential function of the trope of the house in the classic works of Puerto Rican literature by Antonio Pedreira and Rene Marqués.
57. Sandra M. Gilbert and Susan Gubar, *The Madwoman in the Attic: The Woman Writer and the Nineteenth-Century Literary Imagination* (New Haven and London: Yale University Press, 1979, 1984) 88.
58. Pavel—based on a historical figure who was indeed a disciple of Frank Lloyd Wright, and created "versions" of Wright mansions in Puerto Rico—is a mimic man who finally creates something original, Isabel holds, because of his sublimated love for Rebecca. Therefore, the house on the lagoon is not a mimic mansion but one designed, mindful of Rebecca's highly original specifications, to meld with the natural surroundings of lagoon

and ocean. Pavel, we are told, "created the house on the lagoon as one would create a poem or a statue, breathing life into its every stone." *The House on the Lagoon*, 47–49.

59. Rosario Ferré, *El acomodador: una lectura fantástica de Felisberto Hernández*, (Editorial Tierra Firm, Fondo de Cultura Económica, S.A. de C.V.) 60; my translation.

60. Ibid.

61. The House on the Lagoon, 159–160.

62. Ibid., 166.

63. Ibid., 177.

64. Ibid., 193.

65. Ibid., 189.

66. Ibid., 165.

67. Ibid., 164.

68. Ibid., 407.

69. Ibid., 5–6.

70. Geographics, 277.

71. Judith Butler, *Bodies that Matter: On the Discursive Limits of Sex* (New York: Routledge, 1993) 15.

72. Rosario Ferré, "How I Wrote When Women Love Men," in *The Youngest Doll* (Lincoln and London: University of Nebraska Press, 1991) 147–148.

73. Gilbert and Gubar, *Madwoman in the Attic*, 265.

74. The house on the lagoon certainly alludes to the old plantation houses of Caribbean slavery times; but part of the reason its extremely vertical hierarchy seems so artificial is because it is located in the heart of the city, San Juan.

75. Ferré quotes an interesting passage from *Coto vedado*, by Juan Goytisolo, to introduce Part II of *Eccentric Neighborhoods, The Swans of Emajaguas*: "Writing a memoir is the same as making an appointment with the dead. A meeting of ghosts takes place, a series of familiar décors passes by, where those absent repeat the same gestures over and over, as they patiently await their turn to be explained" (*Eccentric Neighborhoods*, 40). Of all the dead whose gestures Ferré/Elvira repeats in order to understand, the most important is her mother whose final gesture upon her death—the vomiting of blood—obsesses this narrative.

76. Suzanne Ruta, "Blood of the Conquistadors: A Novel about the Rise and Fall of a Puerto Rican Dynasty," *New York Times*, September 17, 1995.

77. Ibid.

78. Ferré, *Eccentric Neighborhoods* (New York: Farrar Straus & Giroux, 1998) 99.

79. Ibid., 57. This disease also inspired Ferré's first, and possibly most sensationalist, short story, "The Youngest Doll," in which the infection in the old aunt's leg—caused by a river prawn—spreads to the doll she gives her youngest niece and symbolizes the repressed rage both the aunt and niece feel over the way the men in their lives have used them.

80. Ibid., 77.

81. Ibid., 4–5.

82. Ibid., 5.

83. Ibid.

84. Ibid., 6.

85. Ibid., 334.

86. Ibid., 338.

Chapter Four   "That Animals Might Speak": Doubles and the
Uncanny in Loida Maritza Pérez's *Geographies of Home*

1. Julia Álvarez is often criticized for both an elitist focus on an upper-middle-class feminine subjectivity as well as for a kind of picturesque, opportunistic translation of U.S. Latino/a life. Roberto González Echevarría, for example, criticizes Álvarez's novel *In the Time of the*

Butterflies on the grounds that it privileges Álvarez's American self, engendering an exploitative narrative where "her American self learn[s] what it was really like in her native land, the Dominican Republic." See Roberto González Echevarría, "Sisters in Death," Review of *In the Time of the Butterflies*, by Julia Álvarez, *New York Times Book Review*, December 18, 1994, 28.

2. The narrator of *Family Installments* notes, "The people of Bautabarro were peasants, not history-minded, culture-conscious scribes." Edward Rivera, *Family Installments* (New York: Penguin, 1983) 14.

3. Pérez herself is a Cornell graduate. The description of the College, as an elite private institution, located on " a hilltop location" in upstate New York gives away the identity of the school, even though Pérez never states outright that it is Cornell.

4. "The voice was her mother's—authoritative but hinting mischief as when she had taught her to dance merengue on a Sabbath morning while the rest of the family attended church." Loida Maritza Pérez, *Geographies of Home* (New York: Penguin, 1999) 2.

5. Loida Maritza Pérez, Geographies of Home (New York, London: Penguin, 1999) 49, 311.

6. Ibid., 64.

7. Ibid., 65.

8. Ibid., 4.

9. Ibid., 27.

10. Ibid., 149.

11. Elaine Scarry, *The Body in Pain: The Making and Unmaking of the World* (New York: Oxford University Press, 1985) 242. Scarry points out, as well, that the Christian scripture "is at once less authoritarian and more overtly material than the Hebrew." And she adds "that Luther's rebellion against and revision of the older version of Christianity was anti-hierarchical in its essential impulse is as widely accepted as is the identification of modern Western materialism with what has come to be called 'the Protestant work-ethic'. [Here she footnotes, Max Weber's *The Protestant Ethic & The Spirit of Captialism*.] In turn, within Protestantism various denominations can be differentiated from one another by the same counterparts: Quakerism, for example, has been elaborately and persuasively shown by sociologist Digby Baltzell to have been at once more egalitarian and more materially centered than Puritanism, and to have been the religious ideology that eventually came to hold sway in the obsessively democratic, obsessively materialistic, United States. Thus certain characteristics of the revision of Judaism by Christianity may themselves have been repeated and extended in the revision of Catholicism by Protestantism, and in turn by the successive revisions within Protestantism that occurred through the emergence of various sects."

12. Pérez, *Geographies*, 324.

13. Ibid., 282.

14. Ibid., 147.

15. Scarry, *Body in Pain*, 190.

16. Ibid., 205.

17. Pérez, *Geographies*, 134.

18. Ibid., 135.

19. Ibid., 133.

20. Ibid., 2.

21. Ibid., 23.

22. Ibid., 1, 4, 23.

23. Ibid., 16.

24. Maya Deren, *Divine Horsemen: The Living Gods of Haiti* (New York: McPherson and Company, 1953) 248.

25. Ibid.

26. Ibid.

27. René Girard, *Things Hidden Since the Foundation of the World* (Stanford University Press, 1987) 319; henceforth referred to as *THFW*.

28. Jean Michel Oughourlian, *The Puppet of Desire: The Psychology of Possession, Hysteria and Hypnosis* (Stanford University Press, 1991).
29. Girard, *THFW*, 319.
30. Pérez, *Geographies*, 148.
31. Ibid., 148.
32. Ibid., 18.
33. Karin Luisa Badt, "The Roots of the Body in Toni Morrison: A Matter of 'Ancient Properties,'" *African American Review* 29 (Winter 1995) 583.
34. Pérez, *Geographies*, 38.
35. Ibid., 39.
36. Ibid., 17.
37. The lawyer plays a similar role as Proust's mother in the first volume of *Remembrance of Things Past* as analyzed by Girard in his description of mimetic desire. René Girard, *Deceit, Desire and the Novel: Self and Other in Literary Structure* (The Johns Hopkins University Press, 1965) 35; henceforth referred to as *DDN*.
38. Ibid., 35.
39. Pérez, *Geographies*, 98.
40. Ibid., 42.
41. Girard, *DDN*, 7.
42. Pérez, *Geographies*, 42.
43. Girard, *THFW*, 315.
44. Pérez, *Geographies*, 36.
45. Ibid., 39.
46. Ibid., 39.
47. In response to René Girard's request that he define hysteria, Oughourlian notes, in their dialogue, that the term has been overused almost to the point of meaninglessness but that the term helps distinguish pathological possession from beneficent ritual possession: "I think we are dealing with hysterical phenomena in cases of 'pathological' possession, which our culture associates with 'devils'—if we take 'hysteria' to mean something midway between psychosis and ritual possession . . . It shares with ritual possession the fact that the difference between the subject under possession and the being possessing him is never lost . . . But hysteria has in common with psychosis the fact that the mimetic model is perceived as an antagonist . . . I believe that this shows why any exaggeration of aggressive and antagonistic tendencies can turn into psychosis." Girard, *THFW*, 318–319.
48. Girard, *THFW*, 315.
49. Pérez, *Geographies*, 106.
50. Ibid., 105–106.
51. Ibid., 45, 46.
52. Ibid., 298.
53. Ibid., 97.
54. Ibid., 71.
55. Ibid., 188.
56. Iliana's reaction is healthy compared—to use a celebrated example—with the desire of Toni Morrison's Pecola in *The Bluest Eye* for blue eyes, which, in addition to the fact of her father's rape, drives her to madness.
57. Pérez, *Geographies*, 188–189.
58. Sigmund Freud, "The 'Uncanny'," in *Writings on Art and Literature* (Stanford University Press, 1997) 210, 211. Freud is quoting from Otto Rank's comprehensive research on doubling in *The Myth of the Birth of the Hero* and in "The Doppelgänger," an essay originally published in German in the magazine *Imago*.
59. Ibid.
60. However, Freud's 1914 essay "On Narcissism" anticipates the concept of the superego with the idea of the ego-ideal. See "On Narcissism" in Peter Gay, ed., *The Freud Reader* (New York and London: W.W. Norton and Company, Inc., 1989, 1995) 558.

61. Pérez, *Geographies*, 41.
62. Ibid.
63. Girard, *THFW*, 311; Pérez, *Geographies*, 98.
64. Ibid., 16, 17.
65. Ibid., 16.
66. Girard makes a fascinating comparison between the mimeticism that is characteristic of manic-depressives and that which "in a slightly milder form characterizes 'the ordeal . . . of most intellectuals,'" 308. He says: "The manic-depressive has a particularly acute awareness of the state of radical dependence that people occupy vis-à-vis one another, and the lack of certainty that results. As he sees that everything around him consists of images, imitation, and admiration (image and imitate derive from the same Latin root), he passionately desires the admiration of others. He wishes for all mimetic desires to be polarized around himself, and he lives through the inevitable lack of certainty—the mimetic character of what develops—with a tragic intensity. The smallest sign of acceptance or rejection, of esteem, or disdain, plunges him into dark despair or superhuman ecstasy. Sometimes he sees himself perched on the top of the pyramid of being—sometimes, by contrast the pyramid is inverted and, as he is still situated at the point, he is in the most humiliating position of all, blotted out by the entire universe. *Things Hidden Since the Foundation of the World*, 307–308.
67. Pérez, *Geographies*, 277.
68. Ibid., 31.
69. Ibid., 284.
70. Ibid., 285, 287.
71. Ibid., 287.
72. Ibid., 7–8.
73. Ibid., 319.
74. Ibid., 320.
75. Girard, *DDN*, 53.
76. Ibid., 320.
77. Ibid., 239.
78. Ibid., 53.
79. Ibid., 154.
80. Ibid., 155.
81. For the full scene, see ibid., 156–162.
82. Freud, "The 'Uncanny,'" 226.
83. Robin Lydenberg, "Freud's Uncanny Narratives," *PMLA* 112.5 (October 1997) 1073. Also, see Pérez, *Geographies*, 153.
84. Ibid., 159–160.
85. Ibid., 153, 160.
86. Ibid., 160.
87. Ibid., 156–162.
88. Ibid. In the acknowledgments page at the end of *Geographies of Home* , Pérez thanks the U.S. Africa Writer's Project and Henry Louis Gates Jr. (among other organizations and individuals) for their support.
89. Zora Neale Hurston, *Their Eyes Were Watching God*, 29.
90. Carla Cappetti, "The Beast in the Garden: History and Nature in *Their Eyes Were Watching God*," 8. The quote is from a forthcoming article by Cappetti, the author of *Writing Chicago* (Columbia University Press, 1993). This article points out, that contrary to current critical consensus which holds that Janie has become an autonomous self by the end of the novel, Janie is still caught between the "alienated objectivity of bourgeois society and the irrational subjectivity attributed to nature and the proletariat (23). Cappetti demonstrates this through an ingenious focus on animal imagery in the book that shows how proletarian subjectivity is Othered as bestial. Janie's subjectivity is not so dissimilar from Iliana's. Rather than a Teacake associated with a rabid dog at the end of

Their Eyes, Iliana's Other is her double, Marina, who is proletarian but desperately wants to climb up.

91. Pérez, *Geographies*, 159.
92. Freud, "The Uncanny," 212.
93. Ibid., 156.
94. Ibid.
95. Freud notes that Rank notes this.
96. Pérez, *Geographies*, 151.
97. Ibid., 151.
98. Ibid., 150.
99. Ibid., 125.
100. Ibid., 149.
101. Ibid., 148.
102. Ibid., 151.
103. Ibid., 155.
104. Ibid., 150.
105. Angela Hernández, "How to Gather the Shadows of the Flowers," in Margarite Fernández Olmos and Lizabeth Paravisini-Gebert, eds., *Pleasure in the Word: Erotic Writing by Latin American Women* (Fredonia, NewYork: White Pine Press, 1993) 265.
106. Ibid.
107. Pérez, *Geographies*, 320.
108. Ibid., 321.
109. Ibid.
110. Ibid.

Chapter Five: Latino Rage: The Life and Work of Edward Rivera

1. See Raquel Rivera, *New York Ricans from the Hip Hop Zone* (New York: Palgrave Macmillan, 2003) 154–157 for a discussion on New York Rican rap artists' fear of the "overuse" of Spanish or Spanglish in their lyrics. The norm for the rappers is the urbanized hip-hop inflected language of African American rap music. Just as Latino/a rappers fear deviating from the perceived authentic language of rap, many Latino/a writers repress Spanish from the dominant English-language discourse of their novels.
2. See Lyn Di Iorio Sandín, "Edward Rivera, the Culture-Conscious Scribe"; Edward Rivera, "Stable Manners; or How the Publication of Family Installments was Stalled for Three Years and $3,000.00"; Gary D. Keller, "The Pioneering Bilingual Persona of Eduardo/Edward Rivera"; all in *Centro Journal*. XIV, no. 1 (Spring 2002) 102–109,119–123, 127–139.
3. As this book was going to press, I learned with dismay that *Family Installments*, in print since 1982, may be going out of print.
4. Edward Rivera, *Family Installments: Memories of Growing up Hispanic* (New York, London: Penguin, 1982) 23.
5. Rosario Ferré uses a similar tone in much of her writing, a technique she calls "the art of dissembling anger through irony," which she points out is also typical of the work of nineteenth-century British women writers such as Ann Radcliffe, Mary Shelley, and the Brontë sisters, who "personified in their Gothic monsters and deranged heroines the frustrations they themselves experienced as women." Rosario Ferré, "How I Wrote 'When Women Love Men,'" in *The Youngest Doll*, trans. Diana Vélez (Lincoln and London: University of Nebraska Press, 1991) 147.
6. Rivera, *Family Installments*, 23.
7. Ibid., 16–17.

8. Robert McCormick, *Personality Concomitants of the Puerto Rican Syndrome as Reflected in the Minnesota Multiphasic Personality Inventory* (A doctoral thesis submitted in 1986 to the Psychology department at Rutgers University) 22.

9. Ibid., 26.

10. Ibid., 26—27.

11. Edward Rivera, "Segundo's Benefits," in Earl Shorris, ed., *While Someone Else is Eating: Poets and Novelists on Reaganism* (New York: Doubleday & Co., 1984) 47.

12. Rivera, *Family Installments*, 186.

13. Ibid., 103.

14. Ibid., 106.

15. Ibid., 158.

16. Ibid., 148.

17. Ibid.

18. The quoted terms are Freire's; the characterization is Denis Goulet's in his introduction to Paulo Freire, *Education for Critical Consciousness* (New York, London: Continuum, 1998, 1973) viii. See also Paulo Freire, *Pedagogy of the Oppressed* (New York, London: Continuum, 2003, 1970).

19. Ibid., 124–125.

20. Ibid.

21. See W.E.B. Dubois, *The Souls of Black Folk*, Henry Louis Gates Jr. and Terri Hume Oliver, eds. (New York, London: W.W. Norton & Company, 1999, 1903). Also, see chapter six.

22. Ibid.

23. Ibid.

24. Rivera, *Family Installments,* 30.

25. Alfredo Villanueva-Collado, "Edward Rivera's *Family Installments*: An Agonistic Reading," *Centro Journal* XIV, no. 1 (Spring 2002) 161.

26. Rivera, *Family Installments*, 238.

27. Ibid., 237.

28. Ibid.

29. Ibid., 238.

30. Ibid., 238–239.

31. Ibid., 238.

32. Ibid., 264.

33. Ibid.

34. See chapter four of this book.

35. Rivera, *Family Installments,* 264–265.

36. Ibid., 264.

37. Ibid., 264–265.

38. Villanueva-Collado, "Agonistic Reading," 165.

39. Rivera, *Family Installments*, 264.

40. Ibid., 264–265 and Villanueva-Collado, "Agonistic Reading," 165.

41. See chapter four of this book.

42. Rivera, *Family Installments*, 264–265.

43. Ibid., 286.

Chapter Six: Melancholic Allegorists of the Street: Piri Thomas, Junot Díaz, and Yxta Maya Murray

1. The exact Spanish colloquialism for "wooden face" is "cara de palo."

2. Piri Thomas, *Down These Mean Streets* (New York: Vintage Books, 1991; Knopf, 1967) 55.

3. Homi K. Bhabha. "The Other Question: Stereotype, Discrimination and the Discourse of Colonialism," in *The Location of Culture* (London and New York: Routledge, 1994) 75.

4. Frantz Fanon, *Black Skin, White Masks* (New York: Grove Press, 1967) 18.

5. Bhabha, "Other Question," 76. The other primal scene occurs when the Antillean child encounters racial and cultural stereotypes in children's fictions and identifies with the white hero, turning away from his own blackness.

6. Fanon, *Black Skin*, 112.

7. Ibid., Fanon, 35.

8. W.E.B. Dubois, *The Souls of Black Folk*, Henry Louis Gates Jr. and Terri Hume Oliver, eds. (New York and London: W.W. Norton & Company, 1999, 1903) 11.

9. Ibid., 10.

10. Juan Flores's "Triple-Consciousness? Afro-Latinos on the Color Line" was a talk presented at the Opening Roundtable of "100 Years of W.E.B. Dubois' The Souls of Black Folk" held at Michigan State University, April 2, 2003. He notes that "the centrally important instance of the Afro-Latino indicates that the proverbial 'double counsciousness,' pronounced by DuBois 100 years ago, can take the form of what we might call a, 'triple consciousness,' for, to paraphrase, in studying the historical and contemporary experience of the US Afro-Latino, 'one ever feels his three-ness—a Latino, a Negro, an American; three souls, three thoughts, three unreconciled strivings; three warring ideals in one dark body, whose dogged strength alone keeps it from being torn asunder.' I have no intention of trumping or one upping the African American particularity and struggle, but only to point to increased complexities in light of the thorough-going transnationalization of social experience, and of the endemic, 'problem,' in the 21st century. Maybe we would do well to scrutinize the term, 'consciousness' itself, and explore its compatability with notions like historical perspective, or identificatory fields, or social positionality."

11. Dubois, *Souls*, 10.

12. David Eng and Shinhee Han, "A Dialogue on Racial Melancholia," in *Loss*, David Eng and David Kazanjian, eds. (Berkeley, Los Angeles, London: University of California Press, 2003) 345. See also Anne Anlin Cheng, *The Melancholy of Race: Psychoanalysis, Assimilation and Hidden Grief* (New York and London: Oxford University Press, 2000).

13. Freud, "Mourning and Melancholia," in *The Freud Reader*, Gay, Peter, ed. (New York and London: W.W. Norton and Company, Inc., 1989, 1995) 586.

14. Ibid., 587.

15. Eng and Han, "Dialogue," 351.

16. Freud, "Mourning and Melancholia," 249; cited by Eng and Han, "Dialogue," 364.

17. Ibid., 363.

18. Ibid., 364.

19. For a discussion of deterritorialization see Gilles Deleuze and Félix Guattari, *Kafka: Toward a Minor Literature,* trans. Dana Polan (Minneapolis: University of Minnesota Press, 1986).

20. I'm thinking particularly of Puerto Ricans and Dominicans, but first-generation Cubans expelled from Cuba by Castro fit this equation too, despite the fact that so many of them were not working class.

21. Miguel Piñero, "A Lower East Side Poem," in *La Bodega Sold Dreams* (Houston, Texas: Arle Público Press, 1985) 7–8.

22. Juan. Flores, *From Bomba to Hip-Hop: Puerto Rican Culture and Latino Identity* (New York: Columbia University Press, 2000) 180.

23. From the version of "Puerto Rican Obituary" found in Augenbraum, Harold and Fernández Olmos, *The Latino Reader: an American Literary Tradition from 1542 to the present* (Boston, N.Y.: Houghton Mifflin Company, 1997) 36.

24. For an informative and moving account of Piñero's funeral cortege, see Miguel Algarín's introduction to Algarín, Miguel and Holman, Bob. *Aloud: Voices from the Nuyorican Poet's Café* (New York: Henry Holt & Co., 1994).

25. Judith Butler, *The Psychic Life of Power: Theories in Subjection* (Stanford: Stanford University Press, 1997) 168.

26. Butler, *Theories in Subjection*, 186.

27. Ibid., 187.

28. Ibid.

29. Lisa Sánchez González, *Boricua Literature: A Literary History of the Puerto Rican Diaspora* (New York and London: New York University Press, 2001) 118.

30. Piri Thomas, *Down These Mean Streets* (New York: Vintage Books [Random House], 1997, 1967) 3.

31. Thomas, *Mean Street*, 4. One of the ways in which Thomas fictionalizes his life story is by rendering the mother and his brothers "white" in contrast to Piri's and the father's blackness. However, *Every Child Is Born a Poet*, the 2003 documentary film by Jonathon Robinson based on *Down These Mean Streets* and on Thomas's performance poetry, shows photographs of Piri's family that reveal the whole family as lightskinned mulattoes with the exception of Piri who is much darker than the others.

32. Sánchez González, *Boricua Literature*, 110.

33. Otto Rank, *The Myth of the Birth of the Hero* (New York: Vintage, 1932) 65.

34. Robert Rogers, *A Psychoanalytic Study of the Double in Literature* (Detroit: Wayne State University Press, 1970) 12.

35. As the last two lines of Pedro Pietri's "Puerto Rican Obituary" tenderly assert "negrito" is often an affectionate epithet in the Spanish Caribbean: "Aqui to be called negrito/means to be called LOVE." Pietri, in Augenbram and Fernández Olmos, *Latino Reader*, 337.

36. Thomas, *Mean Streets*, 159.

37. Ibid., 153.

38. Ibid., 167.

39. Ibid., 324–325.

40. Ibid., 97.

41. Ibid., 98.

42. Ibid., 97.

43. Ibid., 55.

44. Sánchez González, *Boricua Literature,* 113.

45. Thomas, *Mean Streets*, 58

46. Ibid.

47. Thomas, *Mean Streets*, 320.

48. Ibid., 321.

49. Michael Taussig, *Mimesis and Alterity: A Particular History of the Senses* (New York and London: Routledge, 1993) 34.

50. Thomas, *Mean Streets*, 323.

51. Sánchez González, *Boricua Literature*, 108.

52. Thomas, *Mean Streets*, 323.

53. Ibid., 327.

54. Ibid., 330.

55. Butler, *Theories in Subjection*, 170. "Clearly, the ego does not literally take an object inside itself, as if the ego were a kind of shelter prior to its melancholy. The psychological discourses that presume the topographical stability of an "internal world" and its various "parts" miss the crucial point that melancholy is precisely what interiorizes the psyche, that is, makes it possible to refer to the psyche through such topographical tropes."

56. Junot Díaz, *Drown* (New York: Riverhead Books, 1996) 24.

57. Walter Benjamin, "Surrealism: The Last Snapshot of the European Intelligentsia," in *Reflections: Essays, Aphorisms, Autobiographical Writings*. Peter Demetz, ed., trans. Edmund Jephcott (New York: Schocken Books, 1986, 1978) 182. See also Avery Gordon, *Ghostly Matters: Haunting and the Sociological Imagination* (Minneapolis, London: University of Minnesota Press, 1997) 203–205. Gordon's discussion of the metonymy of profane

illumination in Morrison's *Beloved* (Schoolteacher's hat and all its meanings) is particularly germane.

58. Díaz, *Drown*, 65.
59. Aravind Adiga, Online Review of Junot Díaz's *Drown* in *The Second Circle: A Reader's Guide to Contemporary Fiction* (http://thesecondcircle.com/arv/briefs.html) August 2001.
60. Díaz, *Drown*, 14.
61. Ibid., 6.
62. Ibid., 15.
63. Ibid., 156.
64. Ibid., 154.
65. Ibid., 16.
66. Ibid., 155.
67. Ibid., 157–158.
68. Ibid.
69. Ibid., 19.
70. Ibid., 6.
71. Ibid., 8.
72. Ibid., 6.
73. Ibid., 14.
74. Ibid., 91.
75. Ibid., 101.
76. Ibid., 106–107.
77. Ibid., 107.
78. Ibid., 91.
79. Ibid.
80. Ibid., 104.
81. Bhabha, *Other Question*, 75.
82. Díaz, *Drown*, 104.
83. Ibid., 104.
84. Ibid., 105.
85. Ibid., 105.
86. Junot Díaz, "The Brief Wondrous Life of Oscar Wao," in *The New Yorker* (December 25, 2000; January 1, 2001).
87. Ibid., 106.
88. Ibid., 117.
89. Díaz self-consciously intimates this by alluding to the Martinican surrealist Aimé Césaire's title to his famous poem, "Notebook of a Return to the Native Land" as a subtitle to one of the story's sections.
90. Ibid., 109.
91. Ibid., 112.
92. Ibid., 116.
93. Ibid., 109.
94. Ibid., 113.
95. For a reading on a syncretic Caribbean Identity, which repeats with difference in and beyond the physical parameters of the Caribbean itself.
    See Antonio Benítez Rojo's *The Repeating Island: The Caribbean and the Postmodern Perspective*, trans. James Maraniss (Durham: Duke University Press, 1996).
96. For a discussion of strong women characters in Rodriguez's *Spidertown* see Flores, 180–188.
97. Abraham Rodriguez, *The Buddha Book* (New York: Picador, 2001) 140.
98. The origins of the terms "cholo" and "chola" go back to Mexico in the early 1900s where they were used to refer to "culturally marginal" mestizos. See Mary G. Harris's *Cholas: Latino Girls and Gangs* (New York: AMS Press, 1988).

 99. Yxta Maya Murray, *Locas* (New York: Grove Press, 1997) 147.
100. Ibid., 246.
101. Ibid., 246.
102. Ibid., 39.
103. Ibid., 24.
104. Ibid., 241.
105. Ibid., 25.
106. García, Isela Alexandra García. "Yxta Maya Murray's Locas. A failed vision of Latina cholas." Berkelay, McNair Review 1999–60.
107. Murray *Locas*, 37.
108. Ibid., 9.
109. Ibid., 36.
110. Ibid., 41, 241.
111. Ibid., 41.
112. Ibid., 50.
113. Ibid., 240.
114. Ibid., 41, 240, 241.
115. Gloria Anzaldúa, *Borderlands/La Frontera: The New Mestiza* (San Francisco: Aunt Lute Books, 1987, 1999) 52.
116. Ibid., 60.
117. Murray *Locas*, 246.
118. Ibid., 120.
119. Ibid., 242.
120. Ibid., 246.

WORKS CITED

Adiga, Aravind. Online Review of Junot Díaz's *Drown* in *The Second Circle: a Reader's Guide to Contemporary Fiction* <http://thesecondcircle.com/arv/briefs.html>.

Ahmad, Aijaz. "Jameson's Rhetoric of Otherness and the 'National Allegory.'" *Social Text* 17 (1987): 3–25.

Algarín, Miguel and Holman, Bob. *Aloud: Voices from the Nuyorican Poet's Café*. New York: Henry Holt & Co., 1994.

Álvarez, Julia. *In the Time of the Butterflies*. Chapel Hill, N.C.: Algonquin Books, 1997.

Ambert, Alba. *A Perfect Silence*. Houston: Arte Público Press, 1995.

Anzaldúa, Gloria. *Borderlands/La Frontera: The New Mestiza* (1987). San Francisco: Aunt Lute Books, 1999.

Aparicio, Frances. *Listening to Salsa: Gender, Latin Popular Music, and Puerto Rican Cultures*. Hanover and London: Wesleyan University Press and University Press of New England, 1998.

Arenas, Reinaldo. *Before Night Falls*. New York: Penguin Books, 1993 (1992).

Augenbraum, Harold and Fernández Olmos. *The Latino Reader: An American Literary Tradition from 1542 to the Present*. Boston, N.Y.: Houghton Mifflin Company, 1997.

Bachelard, Gaston. *The Poetics of Space*. Trans. Maria Jolas. Boston: Beacon Press, 1964.

Badt, Karin Luisa. "The Roots of the Body in Toni Morrison: A Matter of 'Ancient Properties.'" *African American Review* 29 (Winter 1995): 583.

Bauzá, Juan López. "Rosario Ferré: el debate del idioma, los escritores de ayer y hoy." San Juan, P.R. *Palique* (February 19, 1999).

Benítez Rojo, Antonio. "Alejo Carpentier: Between Here and Over There." *Caribbean Studies* 27, 3–4 (1994): 183–195.

———. *The Repeating Island: The Caribbean and the Postmodern Perspective*. Trans. James Maraniss. Durham: Duke University Press, 1996.

Benjamin, Walter. *The Origin of German Tragic Drama*. Trans. John Osborne. London: New Left Books, 1977.

———. *Reflections: Essays, Aphorisms, Autobiographical Writings*. Ed. Peter Demetz. Trans. Edmund Jephcott. New York: Schocken Books, 1986, 1978.

Bhabha, Homi K. *The Location of Culture*. London and New York: Routledge, 1994.

Brown, Claude. *Manchild in the Promised Land*. New York: Touchstone, 1999 (1965).

Butler, Judith. *Bodies that Matter: On the Discursive Limits of Sex*. New York: Routledge, 1993.

———. *The Psychic Life of Power: Theories in Subjection*. Stanford: Stanford University Press, 1997.

Cahill, Tim and Russ Ewing. *Buried Dreams*. New York: Bantam Doubleday Dell, 1986.

Caminero-Santangelo, Marta. *The Madwoman Can't Speak: Or Why Insanity is not Subversive*. Ithaca and London: Cornell University Press, 1998.

Cappetti, Carla. "The Beast in the Garden: History and Nature in *Their Eyes Were Watching God*." Unpublished article.

Carpentier, Alejo. *The Kingdom of this World* (1949, 1957). Trans. Harriet de Onís. New York: Farrar, Straus and Giroux, 1989.

―――. "On the Marvelous Real in America." In *Magical Realism: Theory, History, Community*. Eds. Lois Parkinson Zamora and Wendy B. Faris. Durham & London: Duke University Press, 1995.

Césaire, Aimé. *Notebook of a Return to the Native Land*. Eds. Clayton Eshleman and Annette Smith. Middletown: Wesleyan University Press, 2001.

Cheng, Anne Anlin. *The Melancholy of Race: Psychoanalysis, Assimilation and Hidden Grief*. New York and London: Oxford University Press, 2000.

Clifford, James and George Marcus, Eds. *Writing Culture: The Poetics and Politics of Ethnography*. Berkeley and Los Angeles: University of California Press, 1986.

Cofer, Judith Ortiz. *Silent Dancing: A Partial Remembrance of a Puerto Rican Childhood*. Houston: Arte Público, 1990.

Conrad, Joseph. *Heart of Darkness*. London: Oxford University Press, 2003, revised edition.

de Man, Paul. "Pascal's Allegory of Persuasion." In *Allegory and Representation*. Ed. Stephen Greenblatt. Baltimore and London: The Johns Hopkins University Press, 1981.

―――. "The Rhetoric of Temporality," *Blindness and Insight: Essays in the Rhetoric of Contemporary Criticism*. Minneapolis: University of Minnesota Press, 1983.

Deren, Maya. *Divine Horsemen: The Living Gods of Haiti*. New York: McPherson and Company, 1953, 1970.

Díaz, Junot. *Drown*. New York: Riverhead Books, 1996.

―――. "The Brief Wondrous Life of Oscar Wao." In *The New Yorker* (December 25, 2000; January 1, 2001).

Dubois, W.E.B. *The Souls of Black Folk*. Eds. Henry Louis Gates, Jr. and Terri Hume Oliver, New York and London: W.W. Norton & Company, 1999, 1903.

Ellis, Brett Easton. *Less Than Zero*. New York: Vintage, 1998, reprint.

Ellison, Ralph. *Invisible Man*. New York: Vintage, 1990 (1947).

Eng, David and David Kazanjian, Eds. *Loss*. Berkeley, Los Angeles, London: University of California Press, 2003.

Falcón, Rafael. "El tema del negro en el cuento puertorriqueño." *Cuadernos hispanoamericanos: Revista mensual de cultura hispánica* 451–452 (January–February 1988): 97–109.

Fanon, Frantz. *Black Skin, White Masks*. New York: Grove Press, 1967.

―――. *The Wretched of the Earth*. New York: Grove Press, 1968.

Ferré, Rosario. *El acomodador: una lectura fantástica de Felisberto Hernández*. Mexico: Editorial Tierra Firm, 1986.

―――. *La batalla de las vírgenes*. San Juan: Editorial de la universidad de Puerto Rico, 1993.

―――. "The Blessings of Being Ambidextrous." San Juan, P.R.: *The San Juan Star* (January 12, 1997).

―――. *Eccentric Neighborhoods*. New York: Farrar Straus & Giroux, 1998.

―――. *The House on the Lagoon*. New York: Plume, 1995.

―――. *Maldito amor*. Editorial Joaquin Mortiz, S.A. de C.V., Mexico, 1986.

―――. *Memorias de Ponce: autobiografía de Luis A. Ferré*. Narrada por Rosario Ferré. Colombia: Editorial Norma S.A., 1992.

―――. *Sitio a Eros: quince ensayos literarios*. México: Editorial Joaquín Moritz, 1980.

―――. *Sweet Diamond Dust* [1986]. New York: Plume, 1996.

―――. "Writing in Between." *Hopscotch: A Cultural Review* (Preview issue) 49. Duke University Press, 1998.

―――. *The Youngest Doll*, trans. Diana Vélez. Lincoln and London: University of Nebraska Press, 1991.

Fineman, Joel. "The Structure of Allegorical Desire." In *Allegory and Representation*. Ed. Stephen Greenblatt. Baltimore and London: The Johns Hopkins University Press, 1981.

Fitzgerald, F. Scott. *The Great Gatsby*. New York: Scribner, 1995, reprint.

Fletcher, Angus. *Allegory: The Theory of a Symbolic Mode*. Ithaca and London: Cornell University Press, 1964.

Flores, Juan. *From Bomba to Hip Hop: Puerto Rican Culture and Latino Identity*. New York: Columbia University Press, 2000.

———. *Divided Borders: Essays on Puerto Rican Identity*. Houston: Arte Público Press, 1993.

———. "Triple-Consciousness? Afro-Latinos on the Color Line." Unpublished paper presented at the Opening Roundtable of "100 Years of W.E.B. Dubois' *The Souls of Black Folk*" held at Michigan State University, April 2, 2003.

Foucault, Michel. *The Order of Things: An Archaeology of the Human Sciences* [1966]. New York: Vintage Books, 1994.

Friere, Paulo. *Education for Critical Consciousness*. New York and London: Continuum, 1998, 1973.

——— *Pedagogy of the Oppressed*. New York and London: Continuum, 2003, 1970.

Freud Sigmund. *The Freud Reader*. Ed. Gay, Peter. New York and London: W.W. Norton and Company, 1989, 1995.

———. "The 'Uncanny'" [1919]. In *Writings on Art and Literature*. Eds. Werner Hamacher and David E. Wellbery. Palo Alto: Stanford University Press, 1997.

García, Cristina. *Dreaming in Cuban*. New York: Ballantine Books, 1992.

———. *The Agüero Sisters*. New York: Alfred A. Knopf, 1997.

Gelpí, Juan. *Literatura y paternalismo en Puerto Rico*. San Juan: Editorial de la Universidad de Puerto Rico, 1993.

Gilbert, Sandra and Susan Gubar. *The Madwoman in the Attic: The Woman Writer and the Nineteenth Century Literary Imagination*. New Haven: Yale University Press, 1979.

Girard, René. *Deceit, Desire and the Novel*. Baltimore and London: The Johns Hopkins University Press, 1965.

———. *Things Hidden Since the Foundation of the World*. Palo Alto: Stanford University Press, 1987.

Goldman, Francisco. *The Long Night of White Chickens*. New York: Grove Press, 1992.

Goldman, Francisco. *The Ordinary Seaman*. New York: Grove Press, 1997.

Gordon, Avery F. *ghostly matters: Haunting and the Sociological Imagination*. Minneapolis, London: University of Minnesota Press, 1997.

González Echevarría, Roberto. "Sisters in Death." Review of *In the Time of the Butterflies*, by Julia Álvarez. *New York Times Book Review*, December 18, 1994, 28.

González, José Luis. *Puerto Rico: The Four-Storeyed Country and Other Essays*. Trans. Gerald Guinness. Princeton and New York: Markus Wiener Publishing, 1993.

González, Lisa Sanchez. *Boricua Literature: A Literary History of the Puerto Rican Diaspora*. New York and London: New York University Press, 2001.

González-Wippler, Migene. *Santería: The Religion*. St. Paul, Minnesota: Llewellyn Publications, 1999.

Haley, Alex and Malcolm X. *The Autobiography of Malcolm X*. New York: The Ballantine Publishing Group, 1999 (1964).

Harris G. Mary, *Cholas: Latino Girls and Gangs*. New York: AMS Press, 1988.

Hernández, Angela. "How to Gather the Shadows of the Flowers." In *Pleasure in the Word: Erotic Writing by Latin American Women*. Eds. Margarite Fernández Olmos and Lizabeth Paravisini-Gebert. New York: White Pine Press, 1993.

Hijuelos, Oscar. *Our House in the Last World*. New York: Washington Square, 1984.

——. *The Mambo Kings Play Songs of Love*. New York: Farrar, Straus & Giroux, 1989.

Horno-Delgado, Asunción, Eliana Ortega, Nina M. Scott, and Nancy, Saporta Sternbach, Eds. *Breaking Boundaries: Latina Writing and Critical Readings*. Amherst: The University of Massachusetts Press, 1989.

Hurston, Zora Neale. *Their Eyes Were Watching God* [1937]. New York: HarperPerennial, 1990.

Jameson, Frederic. "Third-World Literature in the Era of Multinational Capital." *Social Text* #15 (Fall 1986): 69.

JanMohamed, Abdul R. "The Economy of Manichean Allegory: The Function of Racial Difference in Colonialist Literature." In *"Race," Writing and Difference*. Ed. Henry Louis Jr. Gates. Chicago: Univesity of Chicago Press, 1985.

Johnson, Denis. *Jesus' Son*. New York: Farrar, Straus and Giroux, 1992.

Joyce, James. *Ulysses*. New York: Vintage, 1990, reissue edition.

Keller, Gary D. "The Pioneering Bilingual Persona of Eduardo/Edward Rivera." *Centro Journal*. XIV, no. 1 (Spring 2002): 102–109, 119–123, 127–139.

Laviera, Tato. *Mainstream Ethics/Ética Corriente*. Houston, Texas: Arte Público Press, 1988.

Luis, William. *Dance Between Two Cultures: Latino Caribbean Literature Written in the United States*. Nashville and London: Vanderbilt University Press, 1997.

Lydenberg, Robin. "Freud's Uncanny Narratives." *PMLA*. 112.5 (October 1997): 1073.

Manrique, Jaime. *Latin Moon in Manhattan*. New York: St. Martin's Press, 1992.

Marqués, René. *Los soles truncos*. Río Piedras: Editorial Cultural, 1976.

McCormick, Robert. *Personality Concomitants of the Puerto Rican Syndrome as Reflected in the Minnesota Multiphasic Personality Inventory*. Doctoral thesis, 1986, Department of Psychology, Rutgers University.

McGee, Patrick. "Texts Between Worlds: African Fiction as Political Allegory." In *Decolonizing Tradition: New Views of Twentieth-Century "British" Literary Canons*. Ed. Karen Lawrence. Urbana and Chicago: University of Illinois Press, 1992.

McInerney, Jay. *Bright Lights, Big City*. New York: Vintage, 1984.

Melville, Herman. *Moby Dick*. New York: Penguin USA, 2001, reprint.

Morrison, Toni. *The Bluest Eye* [1970]. New York: Pocket Books, 1972.

——. *Beloved*. New York: Knopf, 1987.

——. *Sula*. New York and London: Penguin, 2002, reprint.

Murray, Yxta Maya. *Locas*. New York: Grove Press, 1997.

Naipaul, V.S. *The Mimic Men* [1967]. London: Penguin Books, 1969.

——. *A House for Mr. Biswas*. New York and London: Penguin 1961, 1969.

Ortiz, Fernando. *Cuban Counterpoint: Tobacco and Sugar*. Trans. Harriet de Onís. Durham and London: Duke University Press, 1995.

Oughourlian, Jean Michel. *The Puppet of Desire: The Psychology of Possession, Hysteria and Hypnosis*. Palo Alto: Stanford University Press, 1991.

Parkinson Zamora, Lois. "Magical Romance/Magical Realism: Ghosts in U.S. and Latin American Fiction." In *Magical Realism: Theory, History and Community*. Eds. Lois Parkinson Zamora and Wendy B. Fairs. Durham and London: Duke University Press, 1995.

Pérez, Loida Maritza. *Geographies of Home*. New York and London: Penguin, 1999.

Preminger, Alex and T.V.F. Brogan, Eds. *The New Princeton Encyclopedia of Poetry and Poetics*. Princeton: Princeton University Press, 1993.

Rank, Otto. *The Double: A Psychoanalytic Study*. Chapel Hill: The University of North Caronlina Press, 1971 [1914].

——. *The Myth of the Birth of the Hero*. New York: Vintage, 1932.

Rodriguez, Richard. *Hunger of Memory: The Education of Richard Rodriguez*. New York: Bantam, 1983, 1982.

Rivera, Edward. *Family Installments: Memories of Growing Up Hispanic*. New York, London: Penguin, 1983.

——. "Segundo's Benefits." In *While Someone Else is Eating: Poets and Novelists on Reaganism*. Ed. Earl Shorris. New York: Doubleday & Co., 1984.

Rivera, Raquel. *New York Ricans from the Hip Hop Zone*. New York: Palgrave Macmillan, 2003.

Rodriguez Jr., Abraham. *The Boy Without a Flag*. Minneapolis: Milkweed Editions, 1992.

——. *Spidertown*. New York: Hyperion, 1993.

——. *The Buddha Book*. New York: Picador, 2001.

Rodríguez, Richard. *Hunger of Memory* [1982]. New York: Bantam Books, 1983.

Rogers, Robert. *A Psychoanalytic Study of the Double in Literature*. Detroit: Wayne State University Press, 1970.

Ruta, Suzanne. "Blood of the Conquistadors: A Novel about the Rise and Fall of a Puerto Rican Dynasty." *The New York Times*, September 17, 1995.

Saldívar, José David. *The Dialectics of Our America: Genealogy, Cultural Critique, and Literary History*. Durham and London: Duke University Press, 1991.

Sandín, Lyn Di Iorio. "Edward Rivera, the Culture-Conscious Scribe." *Centro Journal* XIV, no. 1 (Spring 2002).

Santiago, Esmeralda. *When I Was Puerto Rican*. New York: Addison-Wesley, 1993.

Scarry, Elaine. *The Body in Pain: The Making and Unmaking of the World*. New York: Oxford University Press, 1985.

Shakespeare, William. *Macbeth*. New York: Viking Press, 1981, reprint.

Shakespeare, William. *Othello*. Ed. Alvin Kernan. New York and London: Penguin, 1986, 1963.

Sharpe, Jenny. *Allegories of Empire: The Figure of Woman in the Colonial Text*. Minneapolis, London: University of Minnesota Press, 1993.

Slotkin, Richard. *Regeneration Through Violence: The Mythology of the American Frontier, 1600–1860*. New York: HarperPerennial, 1996.

Sommer, Doris. *Foundational Fictions: The National Romances of Latin America*. Berkeley and Los Angeles: The University of California Press, 1991.

Soto, Pedro Juan. *spiks*. Río Piedras: Editorial Cultural, 1956.

Spivak, Gayatry Chakravorty. *A Critique of Postcolonial Reason*. Cambridge and London: Harvard University Press, 1999.

Stavans, Ilan. "Swooning in Cuban." *The Nation* 264, no. 19 (1997): 32.

Taussig, Michael. *Mimesis and Alterity: A Particular History of the Senses*. New York and London: Routledge, 1993.

Thomas, Piri. *Down These Mean Streets*. New York: Vintage Books (Random House), 1997, 1967.

Torres-Saillant, Silvio. *Caribbean Poetics*. London: Oxford University Press, 1997.

Vega, Ana Lydia and Carmen Lugo, Filippi. *Vírgenes y mártires*. Río Piedras: Editorial Antillana, 1988.

Vilar, Irene. *The Ladies' Gallery: A Memoir of Family Secrets*. New York: Vintage Books (Random House), 1998.

Villanueva-Collado, Alfredo. "Edward Rivera's Family Installments: An Agonistic Reading." *Centro Journal* XIV, no. 1 (Spring 2002).

INDEX

Printed in the United States
107653LV00002B/36/A